Rogue

Rogue

A Biography of Civil War General Justus McKinstry

John K. Driscoll

McFarland & Company, Inc., Publishers
Jefferson, North Carolina, and London

LIBRARY OF CONGRESS CATALOGUING-IN-PUBLICATION DATA

Driscoll, John K., 1935–
Rogue : a biography of Civil War General Justus McKinstry / John K. Driscoll.
        p.   cm.
Includes bibliographical references and index.

ISBN 0-7864-2385-4 (softcover : 50# alkaline paper) ∞

1. McKinstry, J. (Justus), b. 1814[–1897].
2. Generals — United States — Biography.
3. Quartermasters — United States — Biography.
4. United States. Army — Biography.
5. United States. Army. Quartermaster Corps — Biography.
6. United States — History — Civil War, 1861–1865 — Campaigns.
7. McKinstry, J. (Justus), b. 1814 — Trials, litigation, etc.
8. Trials (Military offenses) — United States.
I. Title.
E467.1.M3742D75   2006   355.0092 — dc22   2005031451

British Library cataloguing data are available

©2006 John K. Driscoll. All rights reserved

No part of this book may be reproduced or transmitted in any form or by any means, electronic or mechanical, including photocopying or recording, or by any information storage and retrieval system, without permission in writing from the publisher.

On the cover: Justus McKinstry *(Library of Congress)*

Manufactured in the United States of America

*McFarland & Company, Inc., Publishers
Box 611, Jefferson, North Carolina 28640
www.mcfarlandpub.com*

Table of Contents

Preface	vii
1. The First Court	1
2. The Michigan Frontier	6
3. Cadet Gray and Army Blue	13
4. Swamps and Hammocks	30
5. The Halls of Montezuma	41
6. The Golden Shore	77
7. Wide Missouri	110
8. The Hundred Days	134
9. The Final Court	166
10. Epitaph	182
Chapter Notes	195
Bibliography	205
Index	213

"…one of the most thoroughgoing rogues
ever to wear a United States uniform."
— Ezra J. Warner, *Generals in Blue*

Preface

Justus McKinstry was the only general officer on either side in the American Civil War to be charged, convicted, and dismissed for fraud. He is better known for his reign of corruption as Chief Quartermaster of the Department of the West under Major General John Charles Frémont while at St. Louis during the summer and fall of 1861. However, Justus McKinstry's career of corruption did not spring into being then and there. He came to the position with a trail of waste, fraud, and abuse stretching behind him for more than a decade and a half, as far back as the conquest of Mexico during the fall of 1847. Justus McKinstry was a thoroughgoing rogue.

McKinstry graduated from the United States Military Academy at West Point in the class of 1838. He was commissioned an infantry officer and was mentioned in reports by his superiors for outstanding performance in the field during the Second Seminole War. McKinstry was awarded a brevet for gallantry during the Mexican War at the battles of Contreras and Churubusco. Later, as an officer in the quartermaster corps, he repeatedly accomplished wonders of supply and logistics in spite of overwhelming odds and paralyzing lack of means. He was a husband, a father, and a descendant of a long line of accomplished forebears. His own father was an early settler on the Michigan frontier who achieved prominence and recognition as a competent and capable man in the territory and later in the state. McKinstry's older brother retired as a commodore after a distinguished career in the United States Navy, and his youngest brother became a justice of the California Supreme Court. Yet Justus McKinstry is best known as a rogue.

This work tells the life story of Justus McKinstry, who he was, where he came from, what he did, and how the many forces within his life worked to shape him into what he became. It tells how an officer of the United States Army became a cruel and dishonest man when others about him did not. It tells of a courageous and capable officer who went bad. It tells of a man who went astray in a system that should have worked to keep him on course. And it tells how a series of exigencies that demanded precipitate action were used by persons in positions of public trust to achieve objectives that were not in the best interests of the public. The events and the times that shaped Justus McKinstry are long gone; the means for persons in positions of public trust to take advantage of exigencies for other than the intended results remain with us to this day.

I was drawn to the life story of Justus McKinstry by two very strong forces. The first was my fascination with the Civil War era. Having studied the Civil War for half a century. I found that era filled with interest and wonder, with glory and shame, with pride and deep sorrow. The war that should not have been fought was the war that could not have been avoided. Justus McKinstry was part of the prelude to the American Civil War, one player among the many who left their names and deeds on the pages of that grand tragedy. Justus McKinstry's legacy was not glory or shame acquired on the field of battle, but fraud and deceit garnered in counting houses and dark rooms among dishonorable men. I was drawn to the story of Justus McKinstry as much by the fact that he was not one of the congregation of heroes and blunderers we have come to know as by the fact that his life was hardly known at all. Other than the period during the summer and fall of 1861 at St. Louis prior to and during the hundred day regime of confusion, conflict, and crime that existed under Frémont, McKinstry had become a virtual unknown. I felt his life story should be told.

The second force was the anger I felt when, at the beginning of my research on McKinstry, I delved into the record that was most readily available to me: the transcript of his 1862 court-martial at St. Louis. McKinstry was charged with neglect and violation of duty to the detriment of good order and military discipline, with 61 specifications drawn to support the charge. Each of these specifications was based on an example of fraud, waste, and abuse of power by a public official acting in the role of a contracting agent and disbursing officer. For my entire professional career, I have been a contracting agent and a disbursing officer, both in private and in public positions. I wanted the record to show McKinstry for what he was: a rogue and not an example of the majority of contracting agents and disbursing officers who have made, do make, and will make up the field of private and public procurement.

The life story of Justus McKinstry cannot be told without telling the story of the United States Army in which he served. From his appointment as a cadet at West Point at the age of 18 in 1832 until his disgrace and dismissal at St. Louis at age 49 in 1863, every day of his life was spent within the United States Army, where he was subject to military law. Throughout his career, McKinstry was brought before a court of inquiry or a court-martial an unprecedented six times, but in only one of these cases was his prosecution initiated within the United States Army. That case was his first court-martial as a cadet at West Point. He was charged with assault of another cadet and was exonerated. In every other military case, and in one civil grand jury indictment, the legal process that brought McKinstry to the bar of military or civil justice was initiated by persons or events outside the United States Army. For me this raised the question of whether events brought to the fore by outsiders should instead have been brought to the fore and acted upon by those officers appointed over McKinstry. This question raised the suggestion that the United States Army accepted McKinstry's excesses and wrongdoings. This suggestion raised the supposition that the United States Army was unwilling or unable to police itself.

In no way does this supposition attempt to excuse McKinstry's misdeeds by trying to transfer the blame to the environment in which he served. It does, however, demand that the finger of blame be pointed at both the culprit and the environment that permitted him for so long to disgrace his oath, his duty, and his position of trust. The United States Army is a dual entity: the institution itself, with its codes, traditions, methods, and means, and the individuals who populate the institution with their strengths, weaknesses, needs, and traits. In the life story of Justus McKinstry, neither of these entities comes out well in the telling.

With the exception of his court-martial at West Point, in every example of wrongdoing for which Justus McKinstry was brought before the bar of military justice, he was serving in the line of duty, performing his assigned role and fulfilling his responsibilities often against incredible odds, usually without adequate resources, and generally on his own. In each of these cases, there was an immediate public demand that had to be satisfied on short notice. Established sources of supply were either nonexistent or inadequate. Delays would have caused significant damage to persons, property, or plans. Those in authority over McKinstry concurred that exceptions had to be made to the rules. Under the very real need to act quickly to resolve pressing problems, but without serious and continuing oversight, conditions were perfect for fraud, waste, and abuse. Justus McKinstry repeatedly was allowed to take advantage of these conditions.

A biographical work is limited by the extent to which original records can be accessed. Although I was able to make contact with some of his family, I was unable to obtain McKinstry's personal papers, his private records, or his diaries. Official records about him abound and there are many official documents in his handwriting or bearing his signature, but it was difficult to get a true grasp of the man without anything that might have recorded his thoughts, his plans, and his frustrations. There is little reference to him in the indexes of contemporary writers. McKinstry served with some 500 individuals who were his classmates during the six years he spent at West Point, many of whom served later in the American Civil War. Several of these wrote their memoirs, yet few mentioned him. Present-day authors seldom refer to McKinstry other than in the context of the short era of crime and corruption at St. Louis during the early months of the American Civil War. Finally, there is no central depository for his records.

I want to acknowledge the tremendous help that has been so readily offered by a long list of persons. The list begins with the constant and valuable participation of Paul D. Shaw of Madison, Wisconsin, with whom this work began over a couple of beers in the back booth of the old 602 Club on University Avenue. Paul has continued to encourage, assist, comment, and advise even though he is very busy in his own writing career. I want to express my thanks for the initial direction and advice given by Professor Emeritus Edward M. Coffman, of the University of Wisconsin-Madison, Department of History, and by Richard H. Zeitlin, Ph. D., Director of the Wisconsin Veterans Museum here in Madison. Both of these gentlemen took time over lunch to set a tyro off on the right track for doing effective research. Staff at the archives of the library at the United States Military Academy at West Point, the National Archives and the Library of Congress at Washington, D. C., the Columbia County Historical Society at Kinderhook, New York, and the Wisconsin State Historical Society at Madison were helpful beyond the call of duty. I want to thank Anne T. McKenna for her editing, an effort directed at making me look much better than I deserve. And, finally, I want to thank the members of my family for their constant support.

There is an overall theme to the life story of Justus McKinstry. This man was repeatedly called upon to take extraordinary measures to relieve exceptional conditions and, while doing so, was able to commit waste, fraud, and abuse of the public trust on a massive scale. There is no doubt that exceptional conditions call for extraordinary measures. The story of Justus McKinstry shows that, without oversight and control, abuse of the public trust can take place even in an environment subject to the strict code of military conduct. This is a theme that is as applicable today as it was in the mid-nineteenth century.

Madison, Wisconsin
2005

1.

The First Court

The winter of 1836–37 was slowly releasing its hard grip on the Hudson River Valley. At West Point, New York, solid granite walls, slate roofs, and thick oak floors of the four structures housing the United States Military Academy retained the chill and damp from the preceding months. In the academic building, coals glowing in a fireplace set into the central wall did little to warm the library. Five army officers sitting at a long table had wrapped themselves in blue overcoats and wore woolen mufflers and leather gloves.[1]

Four courts-martial were scheduled for the morning of Monday, April 3, 1837. Cadets Henry D. Walker and Marcellus S. Stovall both were charged with conduct unbecoming a cadet. Cadet Ripley A. Arnold was charged with being absent from quarters after hours. Cadet Justus McKinstry was charged with assault.[2]

The charges against the first three were quickly resolved. Walker and Stovall were acquitted. Arnold was found guilty and sentenced to four hours of extra guard duty. The officers of the court then took a recess to stand, stretch, and move closer to the meager warmth of the fireplace. The officers were part of West Point's twenty-two member academic staff. All held commissions in the regular army and were on detached duty from their parent regiments. First Lieutenant Robert Anderson, 3rd Artillery, was the academy's professor of artillery. First Lieutenant Albert E. Church, 3rd Artillery, was professor of mathematics. Second Lieutenant Henry L. Kendrick, 2nd Artillery, was assistant professor of chemistry, mineralogy, and geology. First Lieutenant Samuel C. Ridgeley, 4th Artillery, was principal assistant professor of military and civil engineering. First Lieutenant William W. S. Bliss, 4th Infantry, was principal professor of mathematics. One of West Point's five member military staff, Second Lieutenant Henry Swartout, 3rd Infantry, served as the court's judge advocate, directing and recording the proceedings.[3]

The officers of the court reassembled at quarter past eleven o'clock. They were reminded by Swartout they had taken oaths to faithfully carry out the orders under which the court had been assembled. This they acknowledged, taking their seats and arranging bell-crowned shakoes on the table before them and swords at their sides or across their knees.[4]

Cadet McKinstry was called by the judge advocate. He rose from his seat at the rear of the room, marched forward, halted, and faced the long table and the officers who were to try him. Wearing his gray dress uniform, McKinstry stood braced in the exaggerated stance of the cadet at attention, his shako tucked under his left elbow. McKinstry was 22 years old, a handsome man standing 6 feet 2 inches tall. He was built strongly and had thick, black, curly hair, a broad forehead, a full face, and deep, dark eyes. He would be described later in life as "the very ideal of a soldier." McKinstry also had a recent wound, a deep and serious V-shaped slash forward and high on his right cheek.[5]

Judge Advocate Swartout read aloud the single charge and its supporting specification which had been prepared and submitted by Major John Fowle, 3rd Infantry, the academy's commandant of cadets:

> Charge: A violation of Paragraph One Hundred and Sixteen of the Regulations of the U. S. Military Academy.
>
> Specification: In this, that he, Cadet Justus McKinstry, of the U. S. Military Academy, did, at West Point, New York, on or about the Twenty-ninth of March, 1837, assault Cadet Richard H. Weightman, of the U. S. Military Academy, with his fist and did knock him down with the same.

When so directed by Swartout, McKinstry pleaded not guilty to the charge and the specification.[6]

In attendance at the court was Brevet Lieutenant Colonel Rene De Russy, Corps of Engineers, superintendent of the academy. De Russy sat at the rear of the room, watching, observing. He would take no part in the proceeding but, due to his rank and position, would be very much a part of it.[7]

Cadet Jeremiah Scarritt was the first witness called by the prosecution. After being sworn in by the judge advocate, he stated, "I saw Cadet McKinstry strike Cadet Weightman with his fist, but I did not see him knock him down." Under military law, McKinstry could question the prosecution's witness. He asked Scarritt how many blows Weightman had struck against him. Scarritt replied that he did not actually see Weightman strike a blow against McKinstry. In response to another question, Scarritt stated that he did not know whether Weightman's attack was premeditated. McKinstry asked Scarritt if he knew whether Weightman was aware that McKinstry had publicly stated that he would not fight him. Scarritt replied that he did not know whether Weightman possessed that knowledge.[8]

Cadet Zebulon Montgomery Pike Inge was called and sworn. He stated, "I saw Cadet McKinstry strike Cadet Weightman with his fist at the time specified, but I did not see him knock him down." Prompted by McKinstry, Inge described the confrontation, "When I first saw the two parties, they were engaged in conversation. That was the first I saw. After a few words had passed, Cadet McKinstry turned as if he were going to pass round. Cadet Weightman addressed him and said, 'I conceive you to be a damned scoundrel,' or words to that effect. Cadet McKinstry turned round to Cadet Weightman and struck him. Cadet Weightman returned the blow. About this time the parties were separated by Cadet Arnold."[9]

Cadet Ripley A. Arnold was called and sworn, the same Arnold who had been found guilty of being absent from quarters earlier and who now faced four hours of extra guard duty. "On the day specified," Arnold stated, "I saw Cadet McKinstry strike Cadet Weightman with his fist after Cadet Weightman had struck him. I did not see him knock him down. I caught immediately hold of Cadet McKinstry. Cadet Weightman did not strike him after I took hold of him, and when I took hold of him his face was bloody." McKinstry asked whether Arnold had seen a knife in Weightman's hand. Arnold answered he had. McKinstry asked Arnold if he felt that Weightman was driven back by McKinstry's blow so he was not able to reach him with the knife. "I think he was," Arnold testified. McKinstry asked Arnold whether he suspected from Weightman's manner before the fight whether he had any intention of assaulting anyone. "I thought he was going to strike Cadet McKinstry," Arnold answered.[10]

At this point Lieutenant Swartout declared he had no further witnesses to call and closed the prosecution's presentation. McKinstry then took up the process. He continued to question Arnold. "Have I not," he asked, "since the affray between Cadets Green and Weightman, uniformly said that no combination of circumstances would induce me to notice Cadet Weightman but that I would notice any of his friends, and have not you, as well as the rest of my friends, said that I would be wanting in self-respect were I to notice him in any manner?" "I have," Arnold replied.[11]

McKinstry then called his assailant, Cadet Richard H. Weightman. "Have you admitted in conversation since the affray between you and myself that you struck the first blow?" McKinstry asked. "Yes," Weightman said, "and I now testify to it." McKinstry asked, "Did you strike at Cadet McKinstry with a knife before he struck you?" Weightman answered, "I struck Cadet McKinstry only once, and that with a knife, and before I had been struck by Cadet McKinstry, he at this time facing me and looking at me."[12]

McKinstry informed the court this completed his defense. The officers at the table discussed matters briefly without announcing a decision. They adjourned to meet the following morning at eleven o'clock.[13]

Lieutenant Colonel De Russy sat quietly at the rear of the room throughout the questioning and testimony. His primary responsibility as superintendent of the United States Military Academy was to maintain discipline in the corps of cadets. It was his duty to personally address the more serous breaches of decorum and order such as this one involving McKinstry and Weightman. He had investigated the incident immediately after he learned it happened. He weighed the evidence and determined the basis for subsequent action. He ordered Major Fowle to draw up and prefer the charge and specification.[14]

De Russy was himself an academy graduate, class of 1822. He understood the tribulations of cadet life. He knew the discipline and dedication that would be demanded of the cadets after their graduation from the academy and commissioning as officers in the regular army. A mere two months after his own graduation, De Russy had earned his brevet for gallantry at the battle of Plattsburg in the War of 1812 while serving as chief engineer under General Alexander Macomb.[15]

Since its inception in 1802, the United States Military Academy at West Point had operated under the direction of the Corps of Engineers. An officer of that corps always held the position of superintendent. Like many of his predecessors, De Russy found the post filled with what he considered boring administrative detail that brought scant recognition and little satisfaction. He looked forward to the end of his tenure when we would resume his active career in the army. He felt his talents would be better employed in engineering projects, river and harbor work, fortress construction, mapping, and exploring.[16]

During the four years he had held the position, De Russy had witnessed the admission, progress, graduation, and, in some cases, the expulsion of some 400 cadets. "An urbane man of polished manners," De Russy tried to understand the young men committed to his keeping and care, their feelings, their needs, their frustrations. He considered the rigid discipline and inflexible demands imposed upon the cadets by his immediate predecessor, Sylvanus Thayer, to be among the primary causes of cadet resistance and misbehavior. As a result, De Russy was popular with the cadets but his successors would consider his administration to have been lax.[17]

De Russy understood the life of a cadet was hard. These young men in their mid-teens to early twenties came to the isolated location in the Hudson River Valley from all over the nation. Single appointments to the academy were made from each congressional district, two from each state at large, and a dozen or so by the President which included appointments from the territories and the District of Columbia. Seldom would an appointee arrive at West Point knowing anyone there. The young men entered the academy alone, probably for the first time in their lives among strangers, far from the comforts of family, home, and friends. Except for a single furlough after the third academic year, the life of the cadet at West Point consisted of four years of Spartan communal living, study, classroom application and recitation, military discipline, and boring routine.[18]

Disrespect, drinking alcohol, smoking and chewing tobacco, slipping away from quarters after lights were out, and gambling were forbidden by the academy's regulations and regularly resorted to by the cadets. Fighting, which was strictly forbidden, was common. The cadet of the nineteenth century was proud with a sense of honor that was volatile and fragile. An insult brought a challenge and occasionally, as in the case of Weightman and McKinstry, weapons were used.[19]

Among themselves, the cadets formed clans despite the institutionalized hostility already present among the four class levels. When McKinstry questioned Arnold, he made mention of not noticing Weightman. This amounted to outright shunning. The practice was specifically prohibited by academic regulations. Weightman's assault on McKinstry was a case in point. The use of the knife was not only because of McKinstry's greater size and strength but also because of Weightman's strong perception of the injustice. While unacceptable, De Russy understood the attack was to have been expected.[20]

De Russy and McKinstry had arrived at West Point at the same time in July, 1833. McKinstry, however, had attended the academy for several months the preceding year. The superintendent knew the young man from Michigan Territory as well as one in the position of superintendent could know any of his over 200 charges. McKinstry's academic standing was toward the bottom of the class of 1838. His ranking in demerits was high, though not yet close to the level of 200 at which he could face expulsion.[21]

Still sitting at the rear of the library after the officers and cadets left, De Russy considered how McKinstry had conducted his defense during the morning's proceedings. The young man had been formal, forthright, and formidable. There had been no hesitation in his manner, no lack of assurance. McKinstry had been charged with a serious breach of academy regulations and could face dismissal if the court returned a verdict of guilty when it convened the following morning. Yet there had been confidence and control in McKinstry's presentation. De Russy was impressed by the manner in which McKinstry questioned Arnold, causing the witness to testify that McKinstry struck Weightman to drive the smaller cadet back and place himself beyond the reach of Weightman's knife, a classic example of self-defense. McKinstry had also managed to bring into testimony Weightman's previous confrontation with Cadet Green, an incident having no bearing on the current court-martial that should have been disallowed by the judge advocate. McKinstry had been impressive in his questioning of Weightman, drawing forth an admission from the younger cadet that he struck first and used the knife. All this had taken place with McKinstry braced at stiff attention before the officers of the court with the blatant evidence of his innocence, the fresh wound on his face, starkly visible. As he left the library, De Russy wondered what the past had been and what the future would be for the self-assured young man from Michigan Territory.

The court convened the following morning with all members present. Cadet Justus McKinstry was declared not guilty and was acquitted of the charge and the specification. Twenty-five days later, Cadet Richard H. Weightman resigned from the United States Military Academy at West Point and returned to the home of his father in Washington, D. C.[22]

2.

The Michigan Frontier

Justus McKinstry was appointed to the United States Military Academy from Michigan Territory but he was descended from an old and established family living just 60 miles up the Hudson River from West Point at Hudson, New York. The family traced its lineage in this country to Captain John McKinstry who was born in Armagh in the province of Ulster in Ireland in 1712. He married Jane Dickey, a widow, and came to America about 1740. Settling initially near Boston, Captain John served in the British army. He moved to Londonderry, New Hampshire, and then to Hudson, New York, where he died in 1776. His four sons took part in the Revolutionary War. Captain John was the progenitor of a long line of McKinstry descendents who lived in the Hillsdale-Hudson area of Columbia County, New York.[1]

Hudson, the seat of law for Columbia County, was an active and prosperous seaport even though it lay upriver and inland more than 100 miles from Long Island Sound and the Atlantic Ocean. Shortly after the American Revolutionary War, seafaring families from the islands off Massachusetts's Cape Cod, who had been devastated by British naval raids, formed an organization known as the Nantucket Proprietors. The Proprietors dispatched representatives up and down the coastline to find a location that would provide a more secure haven from which they could carry on their livelihoods. They purchased land in what was originally the Dutch community of Claverack Landing on the eastern bank of the Hudson River. Claverack Landing eventually changed its name to Hudson. The town became so successful that by 1786 more ocean-going sailing ships were owned and registered in Hudson than in the city and port of New York. Several large ships were abuilding on the stocks of Hudson's yards at any given time. Records indicate more than 15 sailings from Hudson's wharves on some days. Hudson was designated a port of entry for the collection of federal customs duties on imported goods in 1790. The town's commerce included Hudson's whaling and sealing fleets and a large export trade in beef, pork, shad, herring, staves and headers for barrels, hoop poles, leather, and the produce of the farms and forests of central New York State. Hudson's vessels sailed in trade with the cities of the southern coast of this nation, principally Charleston, Wilmington, and Savannah, with Cuba and the islands of the Caribbean, and the ports of Europe. Based on its successful seagoing commerce, Hudson became home to a flourishing mercantile community. It and its environs provided a comfortable setting for the descendents of Captain John McKinstry.[2]

Charles McKinstry, a son of Captain John, was commissioned a brigadier general in the state militia in 1815. John McKinstry, another son, opened Hudson's first public house, the *King of Prussia*, on Warren Street. Justus McKinstry, a grandson, practiced law with Elisha Williams in 1810 and served as president of the Columbia County Bar Association and as postmaster of Hudson. Robert McKinstry, another grandson, went into the hardware and cutlery business supplying the shipbuilding trades. He served as mayor of Hudson and as a director of the Farmer's Bank. By 1810, Columbia County had a population of more than 5,000. At this time, the McKinstry families in Columbia County, the children and grandchildren of Captain John, numbered more than 40 persons.[3]

David Charles McKinstry was born at Hudson in 1778, the second child and first son of Charles McKinstry and a grandson of Captain John. He married Nancy Backus in 1805. They had four children while residing at Hudson: James Patterson in 1807; Sarah in 1809; Augustus Tremaine in 1811; and Justus on July 6, 1814, who was named after David's brother. Another grandson of Captain John, George McKinstry, was a cousin of David. George's six children were Alexander, Jane, George, Jr., Susan, Charles, and Augustus. They were close in age to the children of David and Nancy. Susan, in fact, was only a month and five days older than her second cousin, baby Justus.[4]

As the War of 1812 came to an end, the future of Hudson and its residents suddenly became uncertain. The prosperity of Hudson depended upon its port and upon the industry, manufacture, and commerce that developed around the port. Yet a seaport located 100 miles inland, upstream from the greatest natural harbor on the continent of North America, was an unnatural phenomenon. With the rise of the city of New York and its harbor at the mouth of the Hudson River, the port of Hudson and its commercial base began to change. Hudson's merchant fleet had suffered losses during the revolutionary period in France and the long continental war in Europe when exorbitant freighting rates drew its vessels into a profitable but risky trade under their neutral American flags. There were further losses during the War of 1812 when the port of New York and the mouth of the Hudson River were closed for a year by a British blockade and by the restrictions that were placed on trade under the embargo and non-intercourse acts of the era. As a result, Hudson's commerce fell into decline. And, as if to sound the knell confirming its end, in 1815 Hudson was discontinued as a port of entry.[5]

David was 37 years of age at this time, a husband and father of four. He was not in line for an inheritance nor had he worked toward developing a profession.

And so in 1815, David, his wife. Nancy, and the four small children traveled as far from Hudson as one could at the time, to the edge of the western frontier. Before the days of railroads or canal boats or steamships on the Great Lakes, David took his family up the Hudson Rive Valley, westward along the Mohawk River Valley and across the foothills of the Allegheny Plateau to the village of Buffalo. From there they sailed by lake schooner to the far end of Lake Erie, to the hamlet of Detroit in Michigan Territory. Justus was a babe of one in his mother's arms.[6]

A mere three years prior to their arrival, American General William Hull, fearing a massacre if he resisted, had surrendered the settlement at Detroit to the British and Indians whose hold on the territory was only recenly broken with their defeat at the Battle of the Thames in October, 1813. When David and the family landed there a little over a year later, Detroit was a squalid place consisting of a cluster of log houses with an army garrison stationed nearby, pigs and dogs roaming the muddy byways, and stumps in the streets. A few years earlier the settlement had been devastated by fire leaving the inhabitants in destitute condition camped in the fields. Detroit was described at the time by a visitor as "a town calculated to make but poor impression upon travelers. It was dirty and, seemingly, an irregular built place, with the streets full of Indians and doubtful looking Frenchmen. Scarcely a person was to be seen except in rough frontier garb. The residences were low, dingy, unpainted buildings, with sharp roofs. The streets were muddy and there were no carriages." The youngest son in the family described the house in which he was born and in which David's family first lived at Detroit as "built of squared logs, with a double roof and dormer windows, these as also those in the lower floor and cellar being crossed with iron bars to prevent the entry of Indians."[7]

When the first census of Detroit was taken in 1782, of the 321 names listed, only 47 were other than French. At the turn of the century in 1800, the entire population of Wayne County, which included most of settled Michigan Territory, numbered barely 5,000 free white souls. With the arrival of David, Nancy, and the four little ones, the population of Detroit rose to around 776.[8]

David immediately became involved in the affairs of the village. He did not have wealth nor a trade but what he did have was great ambition, an amiable personality, and the willingness to pitch in and get things done. He enrolled in the local fire department where "fourteen men of long arms and broad backs manned the hand fire engine" under his direction. A hook and ladder wagon and a battering ram rounded out the equipage of Detroit's primitive fire department. Soon David was appointed deputy inspector of the port of Detroit with an office on Wing's Wharf. He was named by Territorial Governor Lewis Cass as one of the commissioners to lay out the road from Pontiac to Saginaw. When construction of Michigan's territorial capitol began, he was one of three contractors. Upon the completion of the edifice, which cost twice its original budget, contractor McKinstry hosted a banquet for the officials of the territory who had attended the laying of its cornerstone. City government was introduced at Detroit on September 21, 1824, and David was one of four aldermen elected. He was involved in building the railroad from Detroit to Ypsilanti and in completing the land road from Ypsilanti to Ann Arbor. On July 18, 1819, Governor Cass appointed David as one of the commissioners to decide on the designation of a new county within Michigan Territory and to determine where the county seat should be located. The commissioners agreed on designating the new county, naming it St. Clair County, and recommending that its seat be located north of Detroit on the St. Clair River, close to Fort Gratiot, an army post. The land on which Fort Gratiot stood was officially reserved for military purposes when General Alexander Macomb, commanding the United States Army from his home in Detroit, spoke with the superintendent of public land sales. Fort Gratiot was named for Captain Charles Gratiot, the army engineer who had overseen its construction. David and a partner, Thomas Palmer, held mortgages on land near the site.[9]

By this time, David was known at Detroit and in Michigan Territory as a reliable and responsible man. He worked closely with Governor Cass, General Macomb, and other influential people. These men formed a corporation called the Pontiac Company to invest in newly opened public lands in Michigan Territory. In addition, David founded a theater at the corner of Gratiot Avenue and Farrar Street in Detroit and a menagerie and circus on the opposite corner of the intersection. The circus was a large wooden building with a sawdust ring and a tall center pole. Another of his major enterprises was the Michigan Garden. The Garden and its accompanying museum, bounded by Monroe Avenue and Brush, Fort, and Randolph streets, contained "many interesting natural curiosities, Indian weapons and utensils, specimens of the taxidermist's art, etc.," Willis Frederick Dunbar wrote of Detroit at the time, "The town is not without its amenities. Major David C. McKinstry operated a theater, a modest museum, and a summer 'pleasure garden' where ice cream and other refreshments were served and where there was a small zoo." David became known as the amusement king of Detroit. Most of his enterprises burned in a fire on January 1, 1824.[10]

David was elected a supervisor of the township of Detroit in 1818 and again in 1828. He established a horse-powered ferry across the Detroit River from his wharf on the American side to one he owned on the Canadian side and ran stage and freight linesthrough Michigan Territory and into Canada. He was one of the delegates from Wayne County to the convention that petitioned Congress for the change from territorial status to statehood in 1836 and in the presidential election, the first in which citizens of Michigan could participate, in the fall of that year he was the presidential elector, casing his vote for his friend, Martin Van Buren. Prosperity rewarded David's efforts and the family moved into a large home on Jefferson Avenue. A ball at the home was attended by some 200 guests who enjoyed bottles of Madeira and barrels of frozen oysters brought in from the East Coast and served with wild turkey.[11]

A daughter, Ann, was born to David and Nancy in 1817, a son, Charles, in 1819, and another son, Elisha Williams, in 1824. Elisha was named for the law partner of David's brother, Justus, back in Hudson.[12]

In 1826, with the help of his Michigan neighbors, partners, and colleagues, David was able to obtain an appointment for his oldest son, James Patterson, as a midshipman in the United States Navy. Twenty years before the establishment of the United States Naval Academy at Annapolis, Maryland, James reported to New York where he was assigned to duty at sea on the wooden deck of a sailing ship of war. He began a distinguished career and eventually retired from the navy with the rank of commodore in 1873.[13]

Two years later, the same process began on behalf of David's third son, Justus. On December 21, 1828, the lad wrote to the commanding officer of the United States Army, General Alexander Macomb:

> Dear General,
>
> Sir, you will excuse me, I hope, for troubling you with my application — but knowing your character and goodness prompts me to the undertaking. I am fourteen years old last July. I am anxious to get an appointment as early as possible for West Point. If you will assist me with my application by writing to the Secretary of War and others in your acquaintances in Washington, it shall be my unconstant duty to conduct myself in such a way you shall not be mortified in having assisted one whose intention is to be serviceable to his friends and country, and leave me to subscribe myself,
>
> Your obedient servant,
> Justus McKinstry.[14]

There was no need, of course, for the writer to refer to the fact that the general was the Detroit neighbor and investment partner of his father.

Over the following four years, a flow of correspondence began from Detroit to and through the members of Congress to the office of the secretary of war. George Willson, in charge of Detroit's English and Classical School, certified that Justus McKinstry had "pursued arithmetic, English grammar, geography, trigonometry, chemistry, history, algebra, and composition; that his deportment in school, his habits of application, and proficiency in his studies had been such as to give entire satisfaction." John Biddle, former mayor of Detroit and now Michigan Territory's delegate to Congress, in one of his several letters of recommendation to the secretary of war mentioned that, while the son "possesses in an unusual degree the qualifications, mental and physical, for the situation solicited for him," the father was in "narrow circumstances." This was surely a pro-form declaration, common in letters of application and recommendation at the time. David was becoming one of the pillars of Detroit's financial upper strata and was hardly in narrow circumstances. One correspondent, in an un-signed

Lewis Cass: governor, senator, McKinstry's father's business partner and McKinstry's benefactor. (Library of Congress).

note, wrote to the secretary of war that he was certain the candidate would "so acquit himself both at West Point and in future as to do credit to his native Territory & shall never disgrace that profession for which a military education will prepare him." There is an obvious similarity among the letters of recommendation in the files of the adjutant general's office in Washington. The writers were men of power, position, and influence in Michigan Territory. They knew David and they were willing to endorse the application of his son. They wrote in glowing terms of Justus, the lad, yet their efforts clearly reflect respect for and deference toward David, the father.[15]

This all made a strong impression on young Justus. He witnessed his father making use of whatever was available to him to improve his life and the lives of his wife and children. He learned that his father had an innate ability to find and become involved in circumstances for his betterment. David was able to identify and respond to the needs of a given situation and then persuade others to join him in working to achieve a favorable result. He held important positions in the locality and, as his wealth and stature grew, he began to decline accepting further positions in order to become the one appointing other men to them. There is nothing in the records to indicate that David was in any way a dishonest or deceitful man. Confidence and ability were his greatest assets—and the firm belief that he would achieve whatever goal he set. Justus learned and remembered this.

At age 18, McKinstry wrote to his father's neighbor and friend, now serving at Washington in the cabinet of President Andrew Jackson:

> Detroit
> March 23, 1832.
> Hon. Lewis Cass, Sec. of War,
>
> Sir, I have the honor to acknowledge the receipt of your letter (dated March 8th) notifying me that the President of the United States had conditionally appointed me a Cadet in the service of the United States. I accept the appointment with gratitude, and shall endeavor by the strictest attention to study and compliance with the rules and requirements of the institution to evince my appreciation and desert of the patronage, and the personal kindness in your part to which I am indebted for so desirable a position.
>
> > With great respect, I am, sir,
> > Your obedient servant,
> > Justus McKinstry.[16]

McKinstry was admitted to the United States Military Academy at West Point on July 1, 1832. Seven months later, on January 31, 1833, he resigned.[17]

3.

Cadet Gray and Army Blue

McKinstry arrived at the United States Military Academy at West Point on July 1, 1832, entirely on his own. He found himself in an uncomfortable world governed by unfamiliar rules and living among strangers. He had not traveled beyond the environs of Detroit since his arrival as an infant and now he was 600 miles away from family, friends, or familiar surroundings. Even though Principal George Willson had written a glowing recommendation highlighting his scholarly accomplishments while a student in Detroit, McKinstry had difficulties with his studies during his first months at West Point, especially with mathematics. He became so concerned about passing the semi-annual examination scheduled for January, 1833, that sometime late in November or early in December of 1832 he wrote to the army's Corps of Engineers at Washington requesting permission to resign his appointment. Commanding the Corps of Engineers was Brigadier General Charles Gratiot, the officer who had supervised the construction of Fort Gratiot in Michigan Territory in 1814. McKinstry's letter and the general's response have not been found. However, shortly thereafter he took a more confident tone in another letter to Gratiot. McKinstry thanked the general for his permission but stated, "I have concluded to remain and stand the test of my examination. Indeed, my situation has improved so rapidly for the better within a few weeks that I am confident I can pass the examination; if, however, between this and January, I have cause to alter my mind, I shall avail myself of the permission to resign you have so kindly granted." There was more to this exchange between the first year plebe and the commander of the Corps of Engineers than a mere case of pre-examination jitters. If McKinstry failed the examination in January, he thought he could face expulsion from the academy. If he resigned before taking the examination, he thought he might stand a chance, a slim chance, of being reappointed. For the first time in his life, McKinstry was thinking on his own, away from the strong influence of his father. His concerns about the pending examination were valid. In fact, subsequently he would indeed fail the mathematics examination in 1835 but would find in that case that he could avoid disastrous consequences without recourse to resignation. However, in December of 1832, he was determined to take matters into his own hands. This indicated an adolescent rebellion from strong paternal influence but it also demonstrated one of the initial moves in a life-long pattern of making quick decisions with little regard to consequences.[1]

McKinstry did resign and leave the military academy on January 31, 1833. That strong paternal influence became very evident a month and a half later. David had been in hurried communications with General Macomb and Secretary of War Cass, both of whom were neighbors and investment partners at Detroit when not occupying their official positions elsewhere. David had invested significant political capital and influence in obtaining the appointment for his son and he would not let that be squandered on the whim of a worried youth. Forty-five days after submitting his resignation and leaving, McKinstry was reappointed. On March 15, 1833, he wrote, somewhat repetitiously, to Secretary Cass that he had received the letter notifying him that the president had conditionally appointed him a cadet in the service of the United States, that he accepted the appointment, and would "endeavor by attention to the rules and requirements of the institution to merit its patronage."[2]

It is significant that this second letter of acceptance is dated at Hudson, New York. On resigning and leaving the academy, instead of traveling the 600 miles to his family home at Detroit, McKinstry traveled just 60 miles by steamboat up the Hudson River to the home of his father's cousin, George McKinstry, at Hudson. He lived there during the intervening months with George's children, his second cousins. In doing so, McKinstry established his own connections with his father's relations at Hudson. In the years to come, he became closer to the children of George McKinstry than to his own family at Detroit. The children of his Uncle George would have far more influence on his life than most other persons with whom he would come in contact. The relocation to Hudson rather than to Detroit indicated that McKinstry felt confident in achieving his reappointment to the military academy. That father and son were in close communications across the miles between the Hudson River Valley and the hamlet of Detroit during this time is evidenced by a letter dated 15 days after McKinstry's letter of acceptance to Secretary Cass. In that letter, David gave his assent to his son's signing articles binding him to serve the United States for five years unless sooner discharged.[3]

On July 1, 1833, McKinstry returned to the United States Military Academy. The hand-written entry of his readmission in the cadet records at West Point is interlined, having been added between two other names as if it was an afterthought to a listing that had been drawn up previously.[4]

The United States Military Academy was not located at West Point by chance. It was purposely placed there because of a bend in a river and the flow of history.

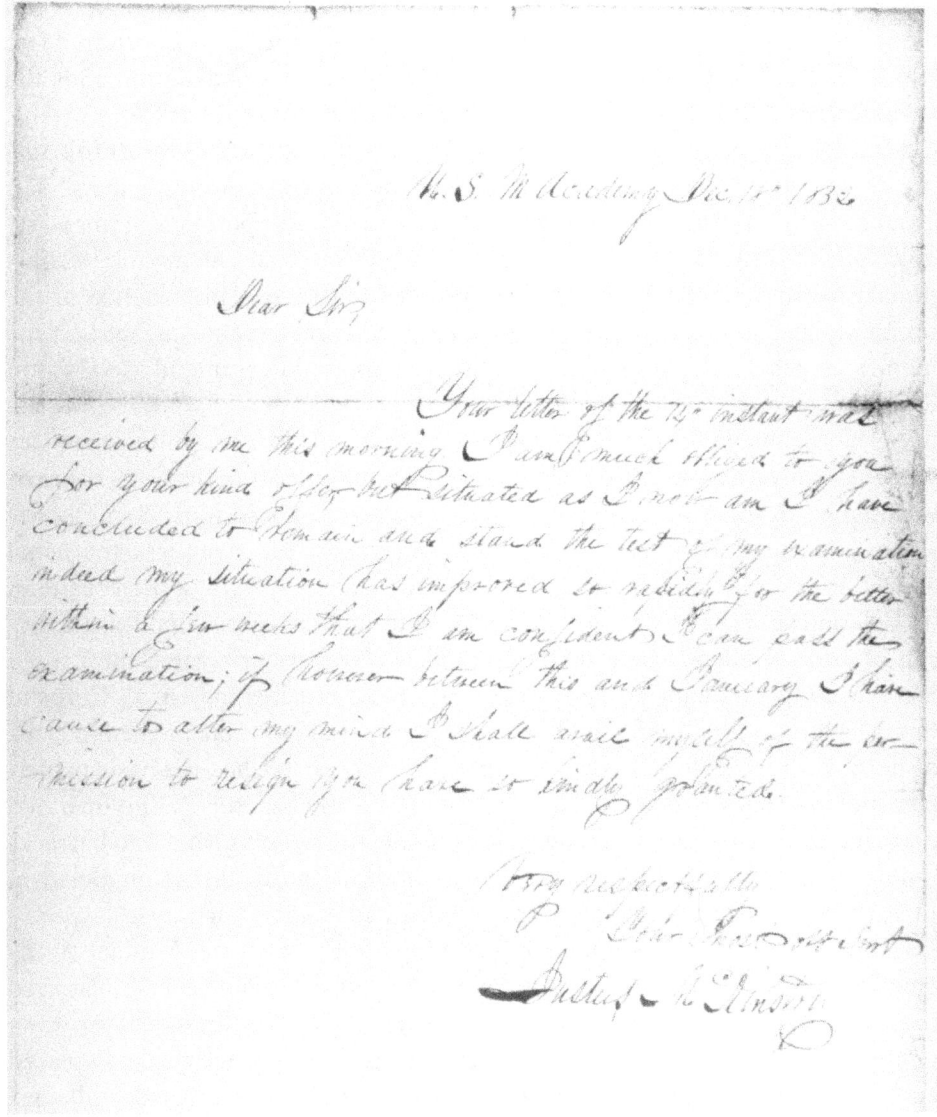

McKinstry's December 18, 1832, letter to Brig. Gen. Charles Gratiot, commanding the Corps of Engineers, expressing McKinstry's confidence in passing the January 1833 examinations at West Point. (National Archives)

The Hudson River, downstream in its course to the ocean, provides the outlet for the watershed of the Adirondack Mountains and the Allegheny Plateau. Upstream, the river provides an ideal invasion route for a hostile force attempting to cut off eastern New York and New England from the Great Lakes basin by penetrating northward from the Atlantic Ocean to the strategically important St Lawrence River. There is a place along this route where the rocks rise and form a gateway through which the Hudson River's current is forced into a narrow gorge that compresses and speeds it along in a sweeping curve south, then east, then sharply south again, around a point of land that stands several hundred feet above the flow. This point of land jutting from the west bank commands the river. A fleet of sailing vessels moving up the Hudson River against the current, hidden deep in the gorge from any helpful winds, would have to resort to hauling, the practice of sending the crews out in rowboats to slowly tow the vessels around the point. British army engineers recognized the importance of this western point of land along the river early in the 18th century. During the Revolutionary War, American engineers agreed on the strategic importance of the promontory then known as West Point. In 1778, Fort Putnam was built on the high ridge behind the point where its heavy guns could command the Hudson River upstream and down.[5]

The advantage of the point in time of war was its inaccessibility; the place was practically unapproachable from the rear. A picket post to the west, the rear, was known to those unfortunate soldiers assigned to guard it as "Stony Lonesome." Because of the mountains and poor roads, the river was the usual approach. In time of peace this inaccessibility made West Point a perfect site in its isolation to serve as a storage depot for guns and ordnance supplies, a garrison of a few soldiers, and a school for cadets. Federal law created the United States Military Academy at West Point in 1802 and directed the army's Corps of Engineers to oversee it. Foundering under poor administration and general lack of purpose or leadership, the law of April 29, 1812, established the basic principles under which the United States Military Academy has existed and operated ever since. Construction of a mess hall, an academic building, and two barracks buildings, one three- and one four-stories high, began in 1814. Completed in 1815, the four granite structures were described as "coldly functional."[6]

The person most instrumental in making the United States Military Academy at West Point into an institution of learning and military leadership arrived there to take the post of superintendent on June 28, 1817. Sylvanus Thayer was a graduate of the academy, class of 1808. Under his direction, the academy placed an emphasis on discipline, order, the study of mathematics, science, and engineering, subjects which would be its focus for more than a century. When McKinstry arrived at the steamboat landing at the base of the high bluff the first week in July, 1833, to begin anew his course of application and study, West Point was an established institution with a faculty drawn from the army and the civilian population and with a corps of cadets numbering some 250 young men divided into four classes. McKinstry was, according to the register in the office of the post adjutant, 18 years and 11 months old.[7]

As generations of arriving cadets had done before and would continue to do, McKinstry carried his luggage from the river steamer moored at the small dock to a horse-drawn cart and followed that up the winding dirt road from the river to the plateau atop the bluff known to the cadets as the Plain. At the office

3. Cadet Gray and Army Blue

West Point, about 1828, showing North and South Barracks for cadets, Administration Building, and Headquarters Building. Cadets are drilling on the Plain. (United States Military Academy Archives)

George Catlin's view of cadets at West Point conducting artillery drills on the Plain. (United States Military Academy Archives)

of the post adjutant, McKinstry identified himself and signed the academy's roster. The post treasurer took from him all his funds; from that moment he would be allowed to have no money in his possession and would be expected to live on his army pay of sixteen dollars a month, which would be kept for him and signed for as expenses occurred. The post quartermaster issued him a pair of blankets, a chair, an arithmetic text and a slate, a wooden pail, a tin dipper, a washbasin, soap, and a meager supply of stationery. Thus equipped, McKinstry moved into the cadet barracks.[8]

His home was a 12 feet by 12 feet vault with stone walls and a plank floor that he would share with four or five other cadets until seniority in his later years would reduce this to just one or two roommates. The quarters were poorly ventilated, hot in summer and cold in winter. There was a small fireplace in each room that burned coal but did little to heat the dank walls or the huddled inhabitants during the cold months of the Hudson River Valley's winter. Beds were not issued to the cadets until the year McKinstry graduated from West Point; he and his roommates slept on mattresses on the floor that had to be rolled and put away every morning before inspection. Illumination was by candles. There were no conveniences in the barracks buildings—no bathrooms for washing, no indoor privies for relief, no water other than what the cadets carried to their rooms in pails from a well in the basement. There were no closets; the very items a cadet could possess were regulated and each had to be in use at the moment or in its assigned place in the crowded rooms.[9]

The gray uniform McKinstry and his fellow cadets wore was, according to one tradition, the uniform worn by American regulars who fought under Brigadier General Winfield Scott at the battles of Chippewa Creek and Lundy's Land in the War of 1812. At some point a touch of blue indigo dye was added to the fabric to give it the distinct cadet-gray coloring. McKinstry's uniform consisted of a single-breasted wool coat with three rows of eight gilt bullet buttons that reached to the waist in front and to the bend of the knee in back. The coat had a stiff, high collar standing to the tip of the ear. The pantaloons were modestly buttoned at the sides in front and were held tight to the legs with understraps. Pantaloons were gray in winter—from the first of October to the thirtieth of April—and white in summer. A top-heavy leather and felt hat called a shako, 7½ inches high with a belled-out crown 11 inches in diameter and festooned with braid, gilt ornaments, and an 8-inch black plume, topped the outfit. The uniform was impressive on parade; in day-to-day living, it was uncomfortable to wear and difficult to keep clean and care for.[10]

Food served to the cadets during McKinstry's time at West Point was the same as the field ration issued to the regular army which consisted of beef—beef boiled, roasted, or baked for dinner, beef cold-sliced or smoked for breakfast, beef boiled in soup twice a week for supper. Boiling was the preferred means of preparation for most foods with "boiled potatoes, boiled meat, boiled pudding, and [boiled] coffee" appearing on the menu day after day.[11]

The purpose of the military academy was to prepare young men such as McKinstry through a four-year course of regimented life and structured study

3. Cadet Gray and Army Blue

THE SOUTH BARRACKS. (Looking Southwest.)
Erected, in 1815; Demolished, in 1849.

South Barracks at West Point in 1832, the year McKinstry arrived at the academy. (United States Military Academy Archives)

to become commissioned officers in the regular army of the United States. Every hour of every day had its place and its purpose under the strict regulations of the academy, even after the departure of Sylvanus Thayer. Reveille sounded at dawn of day with roll call immediately thereafter. Rooms, arms, and accoutrements were policed and inspected 30 minutes after roll call. Breakfast was at 7:00 AM and guard mount was at 7:30. A short recreation interval preceded class parade at 8:00 AM Studies filled the morning until dinner was served from 1:00 until 2:00 PM Classes ran through the afternoon until another recreation interval before dress parade and roll call at sunset, after which supper was served. The cadets were called to quarters 15 minutes after supper from which time they were expected to beat study in their rooms until tattoo was sounded at 9:30 PM Room inspection followed and lights were extinguished at 10:00 PM During the days, the course of instruction for fourth class cadets, boys in their first year at the academy, consisted primarily of the study and recitation of French and mathematics. Third class cadets continued these with the addition of drawing. Second class cadets moved onto the study of natural philosophy, chemistry, landscape drawing, and topography. First class cadets expanded their studies to include engineering and the science of war, rhetoric, moral and political science, mineralogy, and geology.[12]

During July and August, the cadets moved from the barracks buildings into a camp of tents on the Plain. Instruction there was centered on the military side of army life rather than the academic. This was a relief for the young men in gray, a break from the toilsome routine of classes and crowded, uncomfortable quarters. On the Plain, instruction covered the school of the soldier, marching and

West Point cadet uniforms in 1838, the year McKinstry graduated from the Academy. (United States Military Academy Archives)

drilling, artillery, musketry and bayonet practice, living under conditions the cadets would experience in the field with their regiments after graduation. It was during the encampment on the Plain when the most severe hazing of younger cadets took place. Hazing was strictly outlawed by the regulations, tacitly sponsored by the administration, and heartily applied by the upperclassmen.[13]

Each of the academic departments at West Point was under the direction of a professor, usually an army officer, who was expected to carry a full teaching load while also serving as the department's chair. Most chairmen minimized this burdensome requirement by teaching only one section of about twelve cadets, who were generally the brighter and more advanced students, and delegating the instruction of the students in the remaining sections to cadet upperclassmen.

This practice, which was introduced under Colonel Thayer and continued during Lieutenant Colonel De Russy's superintendence, resulted in serious consequences for McKinstry and several of his classmates during the semi-annual examination by the academic board in 1835. McKinstry had been so concerned about passing the examination in the 1833 session that he resigned. He did not take so drastic a step this time, but he still had cause for concern. The academic board, consisting of the superintendent, the various department chairs and the professors, reported to the secretary of war on June 9, 1835, that of the 70 cadets examined in McKinstry's mathematics class, 59 were found proficient and 11 deficient. The high number of deficiencies was blamed on the practice of assigning sections of less-advanced students to the instruction of upperclassmen rather than officers. Five of the cadets who were found deficient — McKinstry, William S. Grandin, William S. Ward, William A. Brown, and Daniel A. Thatcher — asked to be re-examined. They were on September 3, 1835. Grandin was declared proficient and promoted to the next class. McKinstry, Ward, Brown, and Thatcher were again found deficient. McKinstry and Brown elected to be set back to the following class to repeat that year of study. Thatcher resigned and Ward was dismissed later in the year as the result of a court-martial. As a result of this decision on his part to repeat the year of study, McKinstry's term at West Point spanned an unprecedented six years which began in July of 1832, when he registered with the class that would graduate in 1836, his resignation and reappointment to the class of 1837, and his deficiency in mathematics setting him back to the class of 1838.[14]

Academic deficiency was not the only threat to a cadet's continuing existence at West Point. There was also the system of demerits imposed for infractions of the code of conduct. These infractions were spelled out in the regulations and divided into several grades, each with its appropriate number of demerits. An accumulation of 200 demerits during an academic year was cause for the cadet to be declared deficient in conduct and recommended by the academic board to the War Department for dismissal. Though he did receive demerits, McKinstry would hardly have been considered the primary source of bad conduct during his years at West Point. In the seven months for which records exist for the academic year ending in June, 1834, he accumulated 95 demerits. For the following years, each ending in June, his totals were:

1835	110 demerits
1836	117 demerits
1837	137 demerits
1838	187 demerits

There was a disastrous fire at the academy the night of February 19, 1838. Many of the cadet records maintained in the files of the post adjutant were destroyed. As a result, only a portion of the details of McKinstry's demerits are available from the academic year 1837–1838, but they give a profile of the behavior of the cadet from Michigan Territory:

Date	Delinquency	Demerits
Prior to December 31, 1837		112
1838		
January 6	Absent from parade.	3
January 6	In bed in study hours.	2
January 6	Room out of police.	3
January 14	Entering the mess hall of the battery at supper.	2
January 20	Late at breakfast roll call.	1
February 4	Late at breakfast roll call.	1
February 7	Absent from quarters, 6 & 7 PM	2
February 10	Absent from reveille.	1
February 21	Gun lock not sprung.	1
March 5	Late for breakfast roll call.	1
March 7	Floor dirty, 10 & 11 AM	1
March 14	Visiting, 2 & 3 PM	5
March 23	Absent from quarters after taps.	3
March 28	Late for breakfast roll call.	1
April 6	Room not policed 30 minutes after reveille.	3
April 10	Gun lock not sprung.	1
April 14	Bed not rolled and shaped 30 minutes after reveille.	1
April 16	Visiting in study hours.	5
April 20	Late at reveille.	1
May 27	Visiting, 6 & 7 PM	5
June 11	Loitering in front of guard orderly room.[15]	2

This list does not bespeak a hardened delinquent. It does reflect a young man who had a difficult time getting up and getting started in the morning, who was somewhat less than tidy and attentive to details, and who liked to visit. Only one entry, that for March 23, 1838, indicates an absence from quarters late at night. It was apparent that McKinstry was not as prone as many of his brother cadets to slip past the sentries after lights out in order to visit the infamous drinking establishment of Benny Havens, located just off the post in the village of Highland Falls.[16]

McKinstry's years at West Point were spent with young men whose names would become known to history, many of whom he became involved with later in life. His graduating class of 1838 included Pierre G. T. Beauregard, Irvin McDowell, William Hardee, Henry Sibley, and Edward Johnson. In classes ahead of McKinstry were Montgomery Blair, Montgomery C. Meigs, Lloyd Tilghman, Braxton Bragg, Jubal Early, John Sedgwick, John Pemberton, Joseph Hooker, and Arnold Elzey. In classes behind were Henry Halleck, Edward O. C. Ord, Henry Hunt, Edward R. S. Canby, William T. Sherman, George H. Thomas, Richard S. Ewell, Bushrod Johnson, Nathaniel Lyon, John F. Reynolds, Robert Garnett, Don Carlos Buell, Israel Vogdes, and Israel Richardson.[17]

McKinstry contended with the requirements of the course of study, the expectations of the academicians, and the demands of discipline and order. He also competed against his classmates. Final ranking in a cadet's class, which determined placement in the different corps of the army after graduation, were comparative. Under the philosophy in existence at the time, the tabulation of standing in the cadet's class was based on the accumulation of demerits rather than on the accomplishment of positive scores in each course. Thus, the higher a cadet's numbers, the lower his standing. McKinstry's scores in the final examinations of June, 1838, were:

Mathematics	155.3
French	75.5
Natural Philosophy	131.8
Drawing	56.0
Engineering	118.1
Chemistry	112.0
Ethics	109.0
Tactics	56.8
Artillery	61.3
Conduct	166.0
General Merit	1,041.8

McKinstry did well in French, tactics, and artillery, with his best grade in drawing. He did less well in the scientific courses, with mathematics remaining his greatest challenge. Whether this was because of the lack application on his part or the continued use of upperclassmen as instructors is open to conjecture. His grade in ethics stands mid-way between his better and his worse grades.[18]

Under the system installed by Sylvanus Thayer and maintained by Rene De Russy, cadets with higher standings in their classes could hope for an appointment in the more prestigious corps of the army: the engineers, the dragoons, the artillery. Cadets lower in their classes assumed that, after graduation, they would be appointed to the infantry, the largest but least glamorous corps of the line. McKinstry's final standing in the class of 1838 was 40 out of 45. On July 1, 1838, he graduated from the United States Military Academy and was commissioned a second lieutenant in the 2nd Infantry Regiment, taking the position vacated in the regiment by George W. Patten who had been promoted to first lieutenant.[19]

There was a somber side to the activities of the corps of cadets during the final years McKinstry attended West Point. On the morning of December 28, 1835, far to the south in Florida Territory, a column of 117 officers and men of the United States Army under the command of Major Francis L. Dade — Companies C of the 2nd Artillery and B of the 3rd Artillery — marching from Fort Brooke, present day Tampa on the Gulf of Mexico, to Fort King, 125 miles inland near present day Ocala, was ambushed by a force of Seminole Indians and their Negro allies. Dade's column was wiped out except for one man. The sole survivor, Private Ransome Clarke, managed to elude the attackers and stumble back to Fort Brooke to report the massacre despite being severely wounded. The struggle in Florida had been raging ever since. As the members of McKinstry's class of 1838 accepted their commissions in the United States Army, more than 4,000 regular and volunteer troops were conducting a ruthless and frustrating war against an equally ruthless and desperate enemy in the swamps and hammocks of the distant Florida peninsula.[20]

No information has been found regarding correspondence during the five and a half years between when McKinstry resigned from the military academy and lived for several months with the family of his uncle George at Hudson, and his graduation and commissioning as an officer in the regular army. However, it is clear that some communication between the two branches of the McKinstry family, 60 miles up river and down from each other, did take place during this time because, on the day of his graduation, 2nd Lieutenant Justus McKinstry married his second cousin, Susan McKinstry, the daughter of Uncle George.[21]

The United States Army that McKinstry entered in 1838 was small. Its total strength was a little more than 9,000 officers and men and half of those were campaigning against the Seminoles in Florida. The remainder were scattered at forts and stations on the Atlantic seaboard, along the troubled Canadian border, and across the northwestern Indian frontier. With the exception of the troops in Florida, the largest force the United States Army could muster on a regular basis anywhere on the continent at the time was the evening parade of the corps of cadets at West Point. The 250 cadets there outnumbered most units of the army by three of four to one. The United States Army was also relatively new. The Continental Army that had defeated the British and won the nation's independence under George Washington had been disbanded and sent home in 1784, leaving 55 men at West Point and 25 men at Pittsburgh to guard ordnance and military supplies. There were attempts to reconstruct the army over the next five years with little success. This was due to several reasons including disinterest on the part of the states, the lack of any clear and present danger in the eyes of the public, discord amongst Congress, and more important issues on the national agenda. The new United States Army did not come into being until 1789 and that was only after many starts, restarts, questions, challenges, and mis-directions. The several disastrous failures and the few glorious successes of the War of 1812 changed the United States Army dramatically and brought about the forging for it of a new role and structure.[22]

Congress and the people came to realize and accept that the defense of the nation depended upon a core of regular officers and soldiers instead of the citizen militia — the Minute Men. As a result, during the year 1814 alone, enough young generals were appointed to replace the fossilized leadership that cluttered the higher levels of army command to reduce the average age of the incumbents holding that rank from 60 years of age to 36. At the same time the staff departments were organized to provide support and logistical services to the army's line commands. The structure of these departments remained substantially in place for the rest of the 19th century.[23]

Yet in spite of the advances following the War of 1812 and the improvements instituted under the strong and determined hand of Secretary of War John C. Calhoun during the administration of President James Monroe, the army that McKinstry joined was troubled. Officer positions were strictly limited by law to a specific number in each regiment, company, battery of the line, or department of the staff. There were no supernumerary positions—an officer detached from his regiment for professorial duty at West Point, or for recruiting duty, or because of sickness, was not replaced. The detached officer left a void that had to be filled by those officers remaining behind. As a result, junior officers often filled positions of responsibility far beyond their rank and compensation. Additional functions such as those of regimental acting assistant quartermaster or regimental acting assistant commissary of subsistence were usually performed by junior line officers assuming these responsibilities in addition to their regular duties.[24]

There was no retirement system through which aged or incapable officers could be induced to leave the army. Promotion was based entirely on seniority, leaving the next senior lower ranking officer to wait until a position within a regiment became available. The process did not reward ability and dedication and did nothing to negate incompetence. In the years to come, the three line promotions in the 2nd Infantry that became available to McKinstry were the result of the promotion, transfer, or death of the incumbent directly above him. McKinstry was fortunate that there was an opening at all upon his graduation from West Point. It was not uncommon for a cadet to serve a year or more as a brevet second lieutenant temporarily attached to a company, squadron, or battery while waiting for an opening of an authorized position to occur. Promotion therefore was painfully slow; the adjutant general of the army at the time conjectured that it would take a second lieutenant about 58 years to work his way up to the rank of colonel. When McKinstry entered the officer corps of the army in 1838, no West Point graduate had ever been promoted to the rank of general in the regular army. That would not happen until 1860.[25]

An officer's pay was low. It was fixed by law, and often late. The rank of second lieutenant, McKinstry's rank upon graduation, paid $25.00 a month and four rations, or the cash equivalent thereof. This compensation had been in place since March 2, 1827. A West Point graduate's future was bleak, at best. Choosing a military career meant opting for a life of slow promotion, frequent separation from home, hardship to the point of physical suffering, a routine governed by inflexible regulations, and the potential for danger. In return, the graduate received an income far below the norm of his society and no pension or retirement program. Further, assignment to an infantry company stationed at a post on the frontier meant living at the edge of civilization with all the discomforts and dangers that entailed. An infantry company at full strength consisted of a captain, a first lieutenant, a second lieutenant, and perhaps 90 men, though few were at their authorized strength; more often the command would consist of one or two officers and some 40 men.[26]

The enlisted men of the United States Army were a sorry lot, recruited from the lowest strata of American society and the emigrants from Great Britain and the continent of Europe. Those who came in contact with the enlisted men of the American army were struck by the fact that the army was hardly American at all but was primarily Irish, English, or German. Those native Americans who did enlist seemed to be the dregs of the populations of the older states. A future commander of McKinstry's regiment, the 2nd Infantry, wrote of the difficulty encountered in encouraging men to join the army: "To get recruits ... a bounty of six dollars for each recruit ... was provided. Recruiting officers were also given two dollars for each recruit secured. This vicious practice resulted in a personnel, in considerable part, of low or degraded characters. They were largely old men and youths, and 'purchased from prisons, wheelbarrows, and brothels.'" Visitors to army garrisons observed and commented on the low intelligence of the enlisted men and their constant drunkenness. William Addleman Ganoe described the role of officers in command of such soldiery: "The down-and-outer, the foreigner, and the adventurer made up to a great degree the rank and file. The consequence was that the personnel of a company had to be controlled with an iron hand. Ignorant men could not be restrained from mutiny by fear alone ... Cruelty naturally sprang up in a wilderness where one's existence depended upon the obedience of men who could neither read not write, nor understand the reason for discipline."[27]

The United States Army of the 1830s had been designed to fight European forces. The nation had already beaten British armies in two wars. The cadets at West Point studied in detail the campaigns of European commanders such as Napoleon Bonaparte, the master of the grand battle of maneuver and strategic development. Yet in the 1830s the real mission of the United States Army had little to do with fighting set-piece battles against ranks of European regulars. The United States Army was more an internal constabulary than a classic military establishment. It was a peacetime force responsible for moving forward the frontier and keeping order within the territories.[28]

The United States Army that McKinstry joined in 1838 was a dichotomy. Its officer corps was drawn from the better classes of society and consisted of men who were disciplined and educated in languages, philosophy, and the sciences. Its enlisted men were, in the main, illiterate, surly, drunken, and prone to mutiny and desertion. The two groups could not have been more opposite. Yet substantial evidence suggests that the ranks of the American regular army showed considerable capacity for bravery and hard work. The nation exists today as a testament to those attributes.[29]

On the morning of July 11, 1838, 2nd Lieutenant Justus McKinstry reported to Captain Joseph R. Smith, commanding Company B, 2nd Infantry, at Madison Barracks, Sackets Harbor, New York. The barracks was located at the eastern tip of Lake Ontario where the Great Lakes watershed flows into the St. Lawrence River on its way to the Atlantic Ocean. Smith, according to the regimental returns, was present, but sick. Company B's other officer, 1st Lieutenant John M. Clendennin, was absent, serving at regimental headquarters as adjutant. Company B consisted of these three officers, one sergeant, four corporals, and 43 privates, three of whom were carried on the regimental rolls as deserters.[30]

McKinstry called upon his commanding officer wearing his brand new dress uniform which consisted of a dark blue coat cut to the waist in front and the bend of the knee in back, white jean trousers, a crimson sash knotted at the left of his waist under his sword belt, and the recently-adopted cylindrical leather and felt shako that had taken the place of the top-heavy bell-crowned headgear of previous design. Atop McKinstry's shako was the white pompon of the infantry.[31]

Madison Barracks had been home to different companies of the 2nd Infantry since 1815. When the regiment returned from service in the Black Hawk War in October, 1832, regimental headquarters—which consisted of the colonel commanding, the lieutenant colonel, the major, the adjutant, and the band—had located there where it remained when McKinstry reported. Colonel Hugh Brady commanded the 2nd Infantry, as he had since 1815. Brady subsequently moved his personal headquarters to Detroit and, except for a time while serving as commandant of cadets at West Point, continued to command the 2nd Infantry and the left wing of the United States Army from his home in Detroit until his death in a carriage accident in 1851. The published history of the 2nd Infantry claims that Brady's "thirty-six years as colonel of the Second Infantry made him the senior colonel, probably of the world, certainly of our army, past, present, and future." Brady was a neighbor of David McKinstry and one of the important men in the city of Detroit. Colonel Brady's son, Samuel P. Brady, was a boyhood friend of Justus McKinstry prior to West Point. Nothing in the records indicates that collusion took place between David McKinstry and Colonel Hugh Brady regarding the assignment of Justus McKinstry to the open position in the 2nd Infantry upon his graduation from West Point. However, there is the distinct probability that there was some agreement. McKinstry took the position vacated when 2nd Lieutenant George W. Paten was promoted to first lieutenant within the regiment. This promotion and the vacancy it created happened on February 13, 1837, almost 18 months before McKinstry's graduation and commissioning. A year and a half was an inordinately long time for a vacancy to exist in an army that was desperate for junior officers due to death, sickness, and resignation stemming from the war in Florida. The nimble hand of Charles certainly was at play urging his Detroit neighbor to hold the position open for his son.[32]

Colonel Hugh Brady had not been in the field at the head of his regiment since 1822. The responsibility for command over its ten companies therefore fell to the regiment's lieutenant colonel who was, at the time McKinstry reported for duty, Alexander Cummings, and after 1839, Bennett Riley. Though he did not physically fulfill his role as regimental commander, Brady was still able to occupy the colonelcy and prevent younger officers from succeeding to the position. Colonel Hugh Brady is a prime example of the negative implications of a command structure that had no voluntary or involuntary retirement process built into its personnel system.[33]

Susan accompanied her husband from her home in Hudson to his first posting at Madison Barracks. The journey by river steamer, canal barge, and stagecoach was an idyllic honeymoon for the newlyweds. They found Madison Barracks to be an established army post, close to major towns, with spacious quarters for married officers. The quarters probably seemed primitive to the young bride who had been raised in the luxury of her father's home on Prospect Hill in Hudson, but Susan worked to make them warm and comfortable.[34]

Every second lieutenant recently commissioned and newly assigned to a regiment dreaded the possibility of being detailed as the regiment's acting assistant quartermaster which would be in addition to his regular line responsibilities. The acting assistant quartermaster was the regiment's supply officer, responsible for quarters, transportation, clothing, animals, fodder, and equipment. At the time, Congress had authorized only 19 officers to hold the staff rank of quartermaster and assistant quartermaster in the entire army. As a result, junior line officers were required to fill in at the regimental level and perform this important but additional task. A young officer such as McKinstry received no training or instruction for this role, which would require him to spend extra hours struggling with regulations, requisitions and forms, adding columns of figures, and compiling reams of accounts. This was all in an effort to prove to future auditors that he had not misplaced a single horseshoe nor authorized the issue of an extra blanket. The assignment did not involve a transfer to the quartermaster's department, yet it did involve a reporting relationship to the quartermaster general and his assistants without any additional compensation or authority. If there was a discrepancy or shortage in the returns, the value thereof would be deducted from the young officer's pay which was paltry enough. This was exactly the fate that befell McKinstry at Madison Barracks. Within days of reporting, the new regimental acting assistant quartermaster was amassing paperwork, calling for reports and receipts from companies of the regiment at distant posts, reading through army regulations, arranging accounts, and organizing and compiling information for his initial return to the office of the quartermaster general at Washington on the first day of October, 1838.[35]

McKinstry had little time to help Susan get settled into their quarters at Madison Barracks. Thirty days after he reported, headquarters of the 2nd Infantry and Company B were ordered to relocate westward to Fort Gratiot, Michigan. Captain Smith, now recovered from his illness and back on duty, was detached from Company B and ordered to general recruiting duty at Watertown, New York. 1st Lieutenant Clendennin was still at regimental headquarters serving as adjutant. One month out of West Point, 2nd Lieutenant McKinstry found himself in sole command of Company B and responsible for relocating it and the regimental headquarters 600 miles to the west.[36]

The journey from Sackets Harbor to Fort Gratiot followed almost exactly the route McKinstry's family had taken from Hudson to Detroit 23 years earlier but it is doubtful the young officer commanding Company B remembered that trip. The men and their equipment were moved by steamer from Sackets Harbor westward on Lake Ontario to Fort Niagara, near Youngstown, New York. Here the equipment was loaded into wagons and hauled around Niagara Falls to the village of Buffalo. McKinstry marched the men overland in column behind the wagons. From Buffalo, the command steamed the breadth of Lake Erie to Detroit and then up the Detroit and St. Clair Rivers to Fort Gratiot, near present Port Huron, Michigan, sixty miles northeast of Detroit. David and the rest of the family in Detroit were thrilled to receive the son who had been gone almost six years from their hearth and home and to welcome Susan, his bride and their relative. Upon arriving at Fort Gratiot, McKinstry was named the regimental acting assisting commissary of subsistence, the officer responsible for keeping records of the 2nd Infantry's consumption of, and requirements for, food. This was in addition to his other roles as company commander and regimental acting assistant quartermaster.[37]

During the first month at Fort Gratiot, nine enlisted men deserted from Company B. This was probably because they learned their company commander had received orders from the adjutant general's office at Washington to now concentrate his command with Companies C, E, and I of the regiment at Fort Columbus in New York Harbor for movement by sea to join the army in Florida, in spite of the recent location from Madison Barracks to Fort Gratiot.[38]

The returns of Company B show it still located at Fort Gratiot at the end of October, 1838, with 2nd Lieutenant McKinstry noted as being "present, commanding company," but on October 19, McKinstry wrote to the quartermaster's department at Washington, dating his letter "Fort Columbus, New York harbor." It stands to reason that between the demands of his several roles, his responsibility for arranging transportation would take precedence at this time. He turned command of Company B over to 1st Lieutenant Clendennin, who was still serving as regimental adjutant, and proceeded to Fort Columbus to make arrangements for the move of the four companies to the south. He took time en route to deliver Susan, his bride of 90 days, back to her family at Hudson. There was no further change in the status of Company B during October except that another eight enlisted men deserted.[39]

4.

Swamps and Hammocks

At the end of November, 1838, the regimental returns of Company B were dated "Camp near Ft. Butler, Fla." The entry indicated that Captain Smith was "absent, under orders to join," 1st Lieutenant Clendennin was "absent, serving as regimental adjutant," and 2nd Lieutenant McKinstry was "present, commanding the company." Fort Butler was not otherwise identified, which was not unusual. Almost every encampment of troops in Florida was called a fort. Dragoon Bartholomew M. Lynch wrote in his personal journal at the time that new forts were being established so rapidly that after a while the army had to begin giving them numbers instead of names.[1]

On November 30, McKinstry led Company B into the field from Fort Butler to assist other troops in carving out a road to the Ocklawaha River. Working through December 3, they cut trees, cleared brush, and drained ponds. His command also "flushed a party of Indians and captured one squaw." McKinstry's men constructed a bridge and a blockhouse that was named Fort Fowle after Major John Fowle who, as commandant of cadets, had preferred the charge and specification against McKinstry at his West Point court-martial. On December 29, McKinstry moved his command to Silver Spring, 17 miles northeast of Fort King, arriving on January 4, 1839. Silver Spring was located just east of present Ocala.[2]

Six months earlier, McKinstry had marched to music and applause during his graduation ceremony, passing in review with his classmates before officials and guests on the Plain at West Point. The transition from cadet gray to army blue had taken a quarter of his young life. It was a transition that had carried him to a point well beyond anything he ever expected. He now found himself suddenly and completely on his own without another officer or companion to talk to or rely upon. He was functioning without guidance while following his own intuition, which thus far, had served him well. He was coming to understand that he did not need the presence or judgment of others to guide him. He was maturing and learning to think and act on his own. He must have missed Susan to whom he had been so recently married, and from whom he had been so abruptly separated, but he had little time for pleasant thoughts. He was still the acting assistant regimental quartermaster and the acting assistant regimental commissary of subsistence in addition to being the commanding officer of Company B, and he had records to review and accounts to tally. His next return to the quartermaster's department at Washington was dated from Silver Spring on January 7, 1839.[3]

The four companies of the 2nd Infantry, along with regimental headquarters and the band, had embarked at Fort Columbus and sailed by ocean transport to Charleston, South Carolina. Colonel Hugh Brady continued his distant command from his home at Detroit. Under the direct command of Lieutenant Colonel Bennett Riley, the battalion traveled by steamer along the inland waterway to Jacksonville, Florida. There, the men and their equipment were towed in barges 30 miles up the St. Johns River to Garey's Ferry on Black Creek, a tributary of the St. Johns. Garey's Ferry, near present Middleburg, Florida, was the point of arrival for troops from the north and the army's main depot for supplies. It was here that McKinstry was introduced to the reality of the life of the soldier in the field. Jacob Rhett Mott, an army surgeon, described Garey's Ferry when he arrived there two years before McKinstry as "remarkable for nothing but flies, fleas, and heat." Another visitor at the same time noted that in every one of more than 300 huts he visited, he encountered a seriously sick soldier. Surgeon Mott wrote, "Sickness and disease were, by far, the greatest enemy of the troops in Florida. Dropsy, typhus, inflammation of the bowels, consumption, chronic diarrhea, congestive fever, yellow fever, malaria, and 'disease unknown' cut through the ranks with relentless fervor. The prevailing disease was dysentery, caused by drinking turbid water from stagnant pools, and aggravated by the long continued and unvaried heat."[4]

The war that brought McKinstry and almost half of the regular army of the United States to Florida was the Second Seminole War. The First Seminole War had consisted of a series of incursions by American forces under Andrew Jackson into Spanish Florida that ultimately made Florida a territory of the United States. The Second Seminole War was a blatant effort on the part of the United States government, influenced by settlers and southern plantation owners, to remove the Seminole Indians from Florida, take their land from them, and bring their Negro allies— generally escaped slaves, and sometimes grandchildren of the escapees— back into bondage. Henrietta Buckmaster, in *The Seminole Wars*, explained that the war was based on simple facts: "We wanted this land for our own growth; we wanted Florida before England could seize it; we wanted it in order to protect slavery." She went on to say that the Third Seminole War, in which McKinstry would also be involved, happened "because the second war did not achieve its purpose."[5]

By now all ten companies of the 2nd Infantry were assigned throughout Florida, each serving alone at small forts or posts, or sometimes in the field operating in conjunction with other units for short periods of time. On January 8, McKinstry led Company B into the field with elements of the 3rd Artillery, which was serving as infantry, under its Major Churchill. The combined force scouted from Silver Spring to the mouth of the Ocklawaha River. The operation was uneventful and McKinstry brought his command back to Silver Spring on January 12. The following day he marched the company in the direction of Fort Brooks, on the St. Johns River, and later in the day, on orders from regimental headquarters, he moved the company to nearby Fort Gates. From January 29, his men scouted the Ocklawaha Swamp, returning to Fort Gates on the last day of the month. Company B suffered its first casualties of war in late December: Privates William Osborne and John Keiffer fell, not as the result of enemy action, but to the scourge of disease. Both men died of chronic dysentery.[6]

Early in February, McKinstry marched Company B from Fort Gates across the breadth of the Florida peninsula, arriving at Fort Brooke on Tampa Bay on the 12th. He and the command remained there for almost two months until the end of March. Bartholomew M. Lynch, the dragoon, was one of the few enlisted men in the American army at the time literate enough to leave a written record of his experiences. He described life at Fort Brooke:

> Tampa Bay is too romantic and lovely for one to attempt describing of it ... Florida could be made heaven on earth ... There is first rate quarters here at this post and splendid hospitals, good stables for 300 horses or more, a great many citizens to work in the quartermaster's department ... There is not much to do at this post except being going out as escorts for the officers who go a-hunting or a-whoring ... If the officers in Tampa would be half as mad to fight Buck Indians as they are to buck Indian squaws, they would unquestionably be the bravest and gallantest officers in the world. The way they pitch into the squaws is a sin ... At the theater last night, a crowded house, the aristocracy of Tampa present: dragoons, whores, Indians, darkies, soldiers, marines ... a glorious day here, a fight in every direction. Dragoons, artillery, infantry, wagoneers, teamsters, and laborers all equally drunk."[7]

Under orders from regimental headquarters on March 31, 1839, McKinstry marched Company B from Tampa back across the peninsula to Fort Shannon, another post on the St. Johns River. On April 23, he moved the command to what would be known as Post No. 18. Brigadier General Zachary Taylor had taken command of the army in Florida in July, 1837. He installed a new system for waging war against the Seminoles that replaced the deployment of large columns of soldier floundering through the swamps and hammocks with horses, wagons, and brass bands. The Seminoles had no intention of standing and fighting disciplined American regulars in set-piece battles; the natives' method of making war was by means of raids and ambushes, fading into the swamps when faced with larger American forces. Since Taylor could not get the Seminoles to stand

and fight, he sent his columns after resources that could not flee before his troops—their villages and planting fields. Without their homes and gardens, the Seminoles would be without rest, without food. Taylor drew a grid on a map of Florida, laying out the territory in squares. Within each square the army built a blockhouse or a small fort and settled in a garrison. Wagons roads were cut through the wilderness to link the posts. Taylor's plan called for the company-sized garrisons to patrol their twenty-some square miles of swamps and hammocks and keep the Seminoles on the move, preventing them from planting, harvesting, and settling down. McKinstry's Post No. 18 occupied one of Taylor's squares. It sat close to present Sanderson, Florida, about 40 miles west of Jacksonville. Post No. 18 was typical of more than a hundred forts and posts built by the army throughout Florida Territory during the Second Seminole War. Its palisade was of pine logs cut 18 feet in length and split. Each half log was driven upright into the earth close to its neighbor with the flat side inward. The lots were braced with strips of wood nailed to the interior and the tops of the logs were sharpened. Firing holes were chopped seven or eight feet above the ground and a row of benches was arranged around the interior for the men to stand on while firing through the holes, the muzzles of their muskets high above the grasping hands of an attacking force. Living quarters for the officers were simple pole structures with palmetto roofs. There were a few tents to protect supplies from the elements. The enlisted men made whatever arrangements they could. A spring outside the walls provided a source of water. It was a primitive existence. Other companies of the 2nd Infantry were stationed at similar posts: Company C, Captain John Bradley, at Post No. 16; Company E., Captain Julius Kingsbury, at Post No. 20.[8]

For a few days, McKinstry relinquished command of Company B to 1st Lieutenant James B. Penrose who reported to Post No. 18 on May 21, 1839. However, Penrose was immediately ordered to regimental headquarters to take the position of chief of staff and McKinstry resumed command of Company B which he retained for the next six months. For the remainder of the summer, he led the company in the field conducting patrols, pursuing elusive Seminoles and, more often, rumors of elusive Seminoles, repairing roads and bridges, and performing the many duties that devolved upon his command. On October 27, by orders from regimental headquarters, McKinstry moved Company B to Fort Heilman, back at Garey's Ferry on Black Creek, where the company was stationed for the remainder of the year. During 1839, McKinstry's command suffered no losses from hostile action but did lose two more men to disease: Private Thomas W. Eastman died of chronic dysentery in June; Private Michael McMullen died of fever in October.[9]

Although recruits were arriving continuously to reinforce Company B, 40 men deserted during the year, only eight of whom were apprehended. With the strength of the command remaining just over 40 through that time, the desertion and replacement rates of McKinstry's command were 100 percent, typical of army commands in Florida during the Second Seminole War. There is no information available on individual deserters but Ernest Dupuy refers to their probable fate when he writes that, "in order to cope with the serious problem of desertion in the theater of combat, iron discipline and severe punishments were resorted to. This involved, during the Second Seminole War, hunting down deserters and shooting them out of hand."[10]

Captain Joseph R. Smith finally reported to the regiment in Florida and resumed command of Company B on December 19, 1839. He had been away for more than 21 months. With the exception of the short interval of Lieutenant Penrose's presence, command responsibility for Company B had rested solely on the shoulders of 2nd Lieutenant McKinstry who was still serving in the additional roles of the regiment's acting assistant quartermaster and acting assistant commissary of subsistence. He dated his returns to the quartermaster's department at Washington at various times during the year: July 15, July 20, October 21. On December 18, the day before Captain Smith returned, he reported that he was at Pensacola on quartermaster's business.[11]

McKinstry had last seen his company commander at Sackets Harbor in July of the preceding year. Smith had been on duty at the time, listed as sick. By the end of the following month, he had regained his health sufficiently to be ordered away from the command on general recruiting duty. The continuous desertions of enlisted men had such an impact on the army's strength that it was forced to order a company commander away on recruiting duty, leaving the men in the inexperienced hands of a second lieutenant fresh from the military academy. Deserters outside the theater of combat were infrequently pursued: the nation was simply too wide, too open, and too free for successful pursuit. The army's alternative was to continuously recruit among the flow of immigrants and the nation's native unfortunates. Recruiting required the services of experienced officers, so the command of existing companies often rested on the shoulders of young men such as McKinstry. When he turned command of Company B back to Captain Smith, McKinstry had only recently reached 25 years of age.[12]

Joseph R. Smith had graduated from the military academy 16 years before, standing 22nd among 35 in the class of 1823. He had served in the 2nd Infantry since then and would remain with the regiment until promoted to major and transferred to the 7th Infantry in 1851. Smith had already spent some time in Florida with a battalion of the 2nd Infantry prior to being joined by McKinstry at Sackets Harbor. Like McKinstry, Smith was from Michigan Territory; his wife and two little girls lived at Monroe, south of Detroit. He wrote to his family shortly after rejoining the company that he hoped they would hear something favorable about his command. Company B, with the arrival of even more recruits, now numbered 60 men, "almost all of them fine fellows," Smith wrote. Yet he qualified his description of the men, "You ask me about the old soldiers. I have new ones, whom I trust more than the old ones—and always on scouting have two or three near me."[13]

Shortly thereafter, Smith wrote about single-handedly capturing a Seminole warrior while on a four-day scout with McKinstry and the command. Smith wrote that after questioning the captive, he was able to lead Company B to a position from which it could attack the man's village. Smith's men captured, pillaged, and burned the small settlement. He wrote this was the second village he and his men had found, attacked, and destroyed. He mixed into his letters descriptions of the life he and McKinstry were living while in the field: "Hard marches, in wet and cold and heat, in sand and water—through the hammocks, the cypress ponds, the saw grass, and the pine barrens, eating nothing but hard bread & pork or ham." About this time Smith began to develop a scheme that involved himself and his second in command. "Could I get to Picolata, or some other pleasant station," he wrote to his wife, "I do not think I could live separated from you ... McKinstry says he will send for his wife if I will send for mine, but you would not like the trouble, I am afraid. So I told him before we give the subject a thought, we must see what kind of place we could get to put our wives in." Five days later he wrote, "McKinstry has a prospect of obtaining leave for a month to go get his wife. If you could make a good disposition of our dear little Jo and Pamela—I believe I should say make your arrangements to come out with him, too ... If you could come, you must bring six or eight pounds of tea—fifty of loaf or lump sugar—and such dry goods as you may wish to make up within a year—for everything is so dear here." Something did come of McKinstry's prospect of obtaining leave, official or otherwise, for the monthly returns of Company B for May, 1840, carry the entry, "Second Lieutenant McKinstry—absent without leave since 21st of May."[14]

McKinstry traveled north and brought Susan back with him. Through the early years of their marriage, she was willing to travel great distances and face great dangers to be with her husband. Smith's wife also traveled from Michigan to Florida with Justus and Susan. While there she conceived and bore a child who died. 1st Lieutenant George W. Patten wrote and read a touching eulogy at the burial of the little one. Patten was known as the poet laureate of the 2nd Infantry. Patten's promotion to 1st lieutenant had opened the vacancy in the regiment into which McKinstry had been appointed on his graduation from West Point and his commissioning as a second lieutenant in 1838.[15]

Justus and Susan were the parents of five children: two daughters, Angelica and Susan, and three sons, Charles, James, and Carlisle. The three boys were conceived and born after Justus and Susan returned from Florida and all three lived into adulthood. The genealogy of the McKinstry family lists the names of the two girls without dates of birth or death, other than to state that they died in infancy. Their names are listed in the genealogy ahead of the names of the boys. It is most likely the girls were born and died during the time Susan was with Justus in Florida, and it is highly likely they were twins.[16]

With all ten of its companies in Florida at the end of 1839, the 2nd Infantry mustered 24 officers and 406 enlisted men, although its authorized strength was 35 officers and 900 enlisted men. As was the case with most commands in the United States Army at the time, the 2nd Infantry was at barely half its authorized strength. During the first part of 1840, Company B under Captain Smith and 2nd Lieutenant McKinstry was at or near Fort Fanning on the Suwannee River in central Florida. For the remainder of the year, the command was at Fort Holmes in the vicinity of the St. Johns River. Both locations were sufficiently developed with quarters and population that Susan was able to be with Justus when his duties did not take him to the field.[17]

Campaigning was hard on officers and men alike. William Addleman Ganoe described life in the field in pursuit of the Seminoles:

> It was during the Florida war that the most trying duty that could befall to the lot of the troops was performed by nearly all of the regular army constantly for four long years. Moving from swamp to swamp in search of an enemy that never appeared, dying by battalions with fevers and exposure, never able to bring on a decisive engagement with the elusive natives, never daring to separate into small groups without being exterminated by savages who sprang from the soil, at night disturbed by decoys and alarms, always on the move fighting shadows, starved for supplies burned or plundered by the Indians, hindered by thickets, marshes, tropical forests, morasses and jungles of unknown poisons and mysterious extent, balked by an enemy who was never to be trusted in council and resorted to any ulterior means to gain a scalp....[18]

Captain John Sprague, serving at the time with the 8th Infantry, summed up in a report what his own men were experiencing while in the field: "Tracks seen, fields destroyed, country waded, troops exhausted, Indians gone."[19]

Company B scouted and patrolled extensively throughout north central Florida, operating from Fort Holmes with other companies of the 2nd Infantry. These forces found and destroyed several campsites recently occupied by Seminoles and pursued parties of natives but seldom brought them to battle. For the remainder of 1840, scouting and patrolling kept Smith, McKinstry, and the men occupied. In June, McKinstry was ordered to assume command of the guard at Fort Holmes, leaving Smith as the sole officer with Company B in the field. This would be the longest time Justus and Susan were able to be together since their marriage two years earlier.[20]

It was during this period that McKinstry began to evaluate his military career. For the first time since his graduation and commissioning, he had time to compare the realities of life as an infantry officer with the life of officers in other branches of the army with whom he was now in daily contact. He never considered resigning his commission and leaving the army; he was a soldier, an officer, and he intended to remain one. However, as he approached his late twenties, he began to consider options and alternatives to remaining an infantry officer and he decided to pursue one of the many that were available to him. Early in

1840, McKinstry wrote to Quartermaster General Thomas S. Jesup and requested that he be considered an applicant for a regular commission to the quartermaster's department, giving as testimony the manner in which he had discharged his responsibilities in the role of the 2nd Infantry's regimental acting assistant quartermaster. Having learned the value of positive references from his father, he included a letter from Michigan's Senator John Norvell, conveying the senator's pleasure "in recommending Lieutenant Justus McKinstry, of Michigan, now in the army, to the appointment of assistant quartermaster in the staff." This was the beginning of a continuing correspondence between McKinstry in the field, his family in Detroit, his wife's family in Hudson, and the Michigan and New York congressional delegations at Washington. Competition was fierce, requiring all the assistance an applicant could call upon for consideration for an appointment to one of the seldom available positions among the 37 officers who now made up the whole of the quartermaster's department.[21]

In January, 1841, Smith and McKinstry, now back on field duty, led a column of 60 men individually picked from the five companies of the 2nd Infantry at Fort Holmes into the swamps. The small force crossed the Ocklawaha River and scoured the hammocks down to the St. Johns River as far as Fort Gates, returning to Fort Holmes on the 23rd. The scout was uneventful.[22]

In April, McKinstry was listed on the regimental returns as "absent from Company B, commanding Company A." On April 17, 1st Lieutenant Charles W. Woodruff, commanding Company A, died of acute dysentery. The next day, McKinstry, now the senior second lieutenant in the regiment, was promoted to first lieutenant and assigned to Woodruff's place in command Company A. Captain Thompson Morris held nominal command of Company A but Morris was detached on recruiting duty in the north and never did join his command during its time in Florida. Company A's second lieutenant, Edward R. S. Canby, who had been a cadet at West Point in the class a year behind McKinstry's graduating class, was listed on the rolls as "absent without leave." It is probable that Canby was away in the north bringing his wife back to Florida with him, as McKinstry and many other officers had done. McKinstry had little time to become familiar with the men of his new command as Company A was immediately ordered into the field.[23]

The Second Seminole War had been in progress since the massacre of Major Dade's command during the closing days of 1835. By 1841, the war had become a process of rounding up and bringing Indians to Fort Brooke on Tampa Bay and shipping them, against their will, to lands beyond the Mississippi River — or killing them. On May 31, 1841, Colonel William Jenkins Worth assumed command of the army in Florida. Worth pushed his troops in response to the growing frustration of the government over the rising cost of the war and the protracted efforts required to bring a few dozen remaining bands of Indians to the resettlement camps. Commanders of military districts were ordered to keep

Edward R.S. Canby served with McKinstry in Florida, Mexico, and California. (Massachusetts Commandery Military Order of the Loyal Legion and the United States Army Military History Institute)

40 percent of their force always in the field. "Find the enemy, capture, or exterminate," was the directive under which McKinstry and the other company commanders had to operate. Continuing the strategy begun under Zachary Taylor, Worth told his field commanders to go after the villages and the standing crops without which the natives could not exist. In June of 1841, an expedition of the 2nd Infantry set out from Post No. 12 in the direction of the St. Johns River. The force was officered by 1st Lieutenant James W. Anderson, Company C: 1st Lieutenant Justus McKinstry, Company A; and 1st Lieutenant Delozier Davidson, Company H; and included six men picked from each command. The force moved for two days and nights toward an Indian camp with the assistance of a guide who had offered to lead them. The camp contained 57 members of the band of Halleck Tustenuggee, the leader of one of the most active bands still holding out in the swamps and hammocks. The small force attacked the camp and would have captured Halleck Tustenuggee and many of his men if it weren't for what one of the infantry officers termed "the treachery of the guide." As it was, the three officers were mentioned in orders by Colonel Worth. At the time, this was the equivalent of receiving a personal decoration. From the end of June until the day after Christmas, McKinstry had Company A in the field scouting and patrolling, without results.[24]

The Second Seminole War was to end in 1842, yet few of the officers and men who were carrying on the struggle in the swamps and hammocks in the Florida peninsula were aware of this. None of the remaining Seminoles who were fleeing the ever-enclosing arms of Worth's patrols would believe it. When the year opened, the hostiles roaming free numbered no more than the 300 that Worth mentioned in his report to the adjutant general. When the war began, the population of natives had numbered close to 2,000 persons. Half of the United States Army — more than 4,000 men, with marines, detachments from the United States Navy and the Revenue Cutter Service, and volunteers and militia from the states and territories — was in the field to carry out a decision made by Congress in 1832 to move the Seminoles to lands west of the Mississippi River and to take their Negro allies back into bondage. Over time, some of the natives had given up and come to Fort Brooke. Many had been killed. Those who remained free were the ones most determined not to leave their land, those most determined to fight. Among these was Halleck Tustenuggee. A detachment of the 2nd Infantry, Companies G and K, and McKinstry's former command, Company B, made contact with Halleck's band on January 2, 1842. The natives were camped on a hammock near Dunn's Lake, 25 miles south of St. Augustine. An hour-long battle ensued after which the regulars moved in with their bayonets. The Seminoles, carrying off their wounded and their dead, fled into the swamps. The soldiers captured five prisoners, including one of the leaders known as Short Grass. Private Edward Cames, of Company B, was killed in the fighting. On the following April 19, Worth's scouts again made contact with Halleck's band 20 miles north of Fort

Mellon. Worth quickly sent a force of some 400 infantry and dragoons. After a vicious fight, the natives again fled into the swamps leaving two of their dead on the field and several trails of blood leading off into the bush. American losses were one killed and four wounded. McKinstry was at Fort King when this took place; 2nd Lieutenant Camby led Company A in the action.[25]

Three weeks later, Halleck Tustenuggee and 80 of his band came to Palatka and turned themselves in. Worth reported to the adjutant general that, in his estimation, there remained still free in Florida some 42 Seminoles, 33 Mikasukis, ten Creeks, and ten Tallahassees, a total of 95 warriors. Including women and children, the whole population did not exceed 300. On August 12, Worth announced in general orders that the Florida war had ended and that he was sending most of the army back north. John Sprague, the infantry captain, wrote of the 2nd Infantry's service, "The regiment had served in Florida since June, 1837. Two commissioned officers and one hundred and thirty-six noncommissioned officers and men fell victims to the climate and the rifles of the enemy."[26]

On April 25, McKinstry notified the office of the quartermaster general by mail from Fort King that his address would be Hudson, New York. He was listed on the monthly returns of the 2nd Infantry for the month of April as "absent, on detached service at Palatka, relieved of command of the company as of April 28." He was there arranging for the movement of the regiment to the north. The returns for the month of May were dated "At sea." From the first of May, McKinstry was shown as being on a 60 day leave while taking Susan back to Hudson. Upon its arrival at New York Harbor, Company A was ordered to Fort Niagara, near Youngstown, New York, 20 miles downstream from Niagara Falls. Fort Niagara stands on the point of land where the Niagara River flows into Lake Ontario. McKinstry request and was given a 60 day extension to his leave. He and Susan eventually joined Captain Morris, Lieutenant Canby, and the men of Company A at Fort Niagara on the last day of September, 1842.[27]

The Second Seminole War did not come to a formal end. There was no treaty, no capitulation. The surviving bands of Indians slowly withdrew from contact with the white settlers and moved deep into the swamps and hammocks where their descendents remain to this day. McKinstry had served more than three years in Florida. Most of that time he had been on his own with his command, away from the moderating influences of other officers or civilians in authority. He had been involved in a relentless program of driving men, women, and children from their homes, burning and plundering their villages, possessions, and crops, and killing them or herding them into concentration camps for deportation to the west. These years had their effect on him. The savagery, the brutal day-to-day process involved in living and fighting in the swamps and hammocks, had hardened McKinstry.

5

The Halls of Montezuma

When Justus and Susan joined Morris, Canby, and the men of Company A at Fort Niagara, they settled into rooms on the second floor of the French Castle, a three-story stone structure built by French army engineers beginning in 1726. The castle had housed French, British, and American garrisons over its span of more than a century and was the prime feature of an extensive system of fortifications that guarded the mouth of the Niagara River. The castle contained living quarters for officers, storerooms, a kitchen, a chapel, and even a deep well within the building. The rooms that Justus and Susan occupied were a vast improvement over the palmetto huts and tents that housed the couple in Florida. However, here their windows looked directly out onto the waters of Lake Ontario, which would be whipped by freezing winds and covered with floating ice in winter. Army surgeon Thomas Monroe wrote in his personal journal in the fall of 1838 that all the fireplaces in the building had been altered for stoves but the stoves had been stolen leaving the bricked-up fireplaces useless. 1st Lieutenant Barnabas Conckling managed to purchase a few new stoves for the sleeping rooms, and he requisitioned more from the quartermaster's department, but there were never enough to heat the building adequately during the winter months.[1]

The following years were relatively comfortable for Justus and Susan in spite of the difficulties in heating their quarters during the cold season. Until this time, they had not been able to live a normal life under civilized conditions. In 1843, a year after their arrival at Fort Niagara, they had a son, Charles Frederick. Two years later in 1845, another son, James Hamilton, was born. Living on the shore of Lake Ontario, Susan was only 300 miles from her family in Hudson. That distance was readily traveled by river steamer and stage coach. Susan's unmarried sister Jane visited and spent time with the couple shortly after the birth of their second son. Army surgeon James Hovey Sargent wrote to his wife in 1846, "On the other side or English [Canadian] side [of the Niagara River] where the ladies of this place go shopping — on the first of July Mrs. [Captain Thompson] Morris, Mrs. McKinstry, Miss [Jane] McKinstry, Lieutenant McKinstry, & I went over

The French Castle at Fort Niagara, New York. Justus McKinstry and his wife, Susan, lived in rooms on the second floor during the four years they were stationed here. Their first two sons were born at Fort Niagara. (Author's photograph)

in the afternoon to hear the band of the [English] Rifle Regiment play ... their performance, I must confess, was not very captivating."[2]

Still performing as regimental acting assistant quartermaster, McKinstry became involved in efforts to improve the living quarters of the enlisted men of Company A. Their wooden barracks had been built around the time of the War of 1812 and had deteriorated to the point of ruin when the veterans of the Florida War returned. The men were now quartered in two stone redoubts, structures built forward of the walls and designed to shelter soldiers firing on advancing enemies. They were not intended to house troops permanently when they were built in the 1770s and they were woefully inadequate for that purpose years later. McKinstry wrote to Quartermaster General Jesup on October 5, 1845, stating the redoubts had been erected "for defensive purposes" and that, as barracks, their

Aerial view of Fort Niagara, located at the point where the Niagara River flows into Lake Ontario. The French Castle where Justus and Susan lived is in the upper left of the view. (New York Power Authority)

interior arrangements were "inconvenient and confined." Three years later, 1st Lieutenant Montgomery C. Meigs, eventually to become quartermaster general himself, informed the chief of engineers that "Quarters and Barracks about to be occupied are not fit to be used by Man."[3]

McKinstry's efforts to obtain a permanent appointment to the quartermaster's department continued. On May 23, 1842, political activist and former mayor of Hudson, Elisha Jenkins, probably in response to a personal visit by McKinstry during his return trip from Florida, wrote to Secretary of War John C. Spencer that Justus McKinstry, the nephew of the postmaster at Hudson, was a candidate for an appointment to the quartermaster's department and, if so appointed, would be a credit to the service. Major Joseph Plympton, second in command of the 2nd Infantry, wrote to the quartermaster general from regimental headquarters at Madison Barracks on July 20, 1842, immediately after the return of the regiment to the north, "1st Lieutenant Justus McKinstry, 2nd Infantry, has expressed the desire of becoming a member of your department. Justus McKinstry has served in the same command with me and under my command at posts and in the field as quartermaster in Florida and at times, too, when much active and difficult duty was required. He would always discharge his duties with great efficiency. Should there be an opening in your department, you would find him a satisfactory and efficient member." This letter went round about from upper New York State to Washington via Michigan. It was enclosed with a letter from McKinstry to Quartermaster General Jesup on July 31, 1842, in which McKinstry reported that his address would be Detroit where he and Susan were still enjoying his leave with his parents, brothers, and sisters.[4]

In mid-July of 1844, McKinstry was ordered away from Fort Niagara on general recruiting duty at Albany. Even during the peace that followed the Second Seminole War, the army's consistently high rate of desertion demanded that officers be assigned to recruiting duty. Susan and baby Charles went with Justus and divided their time between the quarters he rented in Albany and her family's home in Hudson, now only 35 miles down the Hudson River. In March, 1845, McKinstry was ordered back to Fort Niagara. Upon his return, he relieved 2nd Lieutenant Canby of the responsibilities of acting assistant quartermaster of the regiment, the role Canby had assumed when McKinstry left the preceding year.[5]

As Justus and Susan resumed their lives at Fort Niagara, far to the south on April 26, 1846, a patrol of 63 American dragoons under the command of Captain Seth B. Thornton were ambushed by Mexican cavalry while on a questionable scout in the state of Mexico known as Texas. Sixteen of the Americans were killed. The remainder were captured.[6]

Texas had seceded from Mexico and declared itself an independent republic in 1836. For a decade, the future of Texas had been uncertain. The Mexican government insisted that Texas was still a state of Mexico. The United States government considered it an independent entity moving toward annexation. Texas eventually became the newest and largest of the United States on July 4, 1845. The government in Mexico City warned the government at Washington that the mere act of annexation would be regarded as a declaration of war without further formality. Following the annexation, an American "army of observation" under Colonel Zachary Taylor entered Texas and proceeded southward as far as Corpus Christi on the Nueces River. By mid-October, this renamed "army of occupation" numbered some 4,000 men, about half the total strength of the regular army. On January 13, 1846, President James Polk, in a move of outright provocation, ordered Taylor to move 150 miles further south to the Rio Grande. By the end of March, Taylor's army sat on that river, its batteries bearing on the little Mexican town of Matamoras on the far bank.[7]

Even before receiving notice from Washington of a formal declaration of war by Congress, Taylor crossed the river and defeated a larger Mexican army, first at Palo Alto on May 8, then at Resaca de la Palma on May 9. On the 19th, Taylor occupied Matamoras and immediately began moving his force 400 miles up

5. The Halls of Montezuma

the winding Rio Grande to the village of Camargo at the confluence of the San Juan River and the Rio Grande where he established his base camp on July 17, 1846.[8]

A little more than a month before Taylor's advance, the companies of the 2nd Infantry posted along the Canadian border from Fort Mackinac in Michigan to Hancock Barracks in Maine received orders from the adjutant general at Washington to begin staging for a move to Mexico. Headquarters of the regiment and Companies D, E, F, and K, the commands at the western posts, gathered at Newport Barracks, Kentucky, on August 12, 1846. This battalion boarded steamboats on September 2 for New Orleans and then sailed on ocean transports for Brazos Santiago. From there they sailed on small steamers up the Rio Grande, reaching Taylor's base at Camargo on September 20. Companies A, B, G, H, and I, the commands at the eastern posts, assembled at Fort Columbus, New York Harbor. On September 3, this battalion embarked on the transports *Uncas* and *Ocean* and arrived at Camargo under the command of Lieutenant Colonel Riley and Major Plympton in mid-October. As had been the case when the regiment deployed in the field in Florida under Riley and Plympton, Colonel Hugh Brady, the regiment's nominal commander, remained at his headquarters and his home in Detroit.[9]

On June 30, McKinstry reported by mail to the quartermaster general's department from Fort Niagara. At this time, Captain Morris was present, commanding the company. 2nd Lieutenant Canby was absent, serving at regimental headquarters as adjutant. On July 11, McKinstry reported from Fort Columbus that he was arranging transportation for the eastern battalion of the regiment. He took advantage of his individual travel orders from Fort Niagara to bring Susan and the two boys with him on his way, leaving them at Hudson with Susan's brother, Augustus, and sister, Jane.[10]

Even amid the turmoil of the regiment's deployment, McKinstry continued his efforts to obtain a permanent staff appointment in the quartermaster's department. Prior to leaving Fort Niagara, he wrote to his father's friend and investment partner, Lewis Cass, now one of Michigan's senators, asking, "Will you do me the honor to confer with the Secretary of War?" An unsigned and undated letter of about the same time, presumably from Cass, read, "A young friend of mine, Lieutenant Justus McKinstry, now at Fort Niagara, has asked me to address you on his behalf for an appointment as an assistant quartermaster. He was educated at West Point and has served in Florida. I think him a meritorious officer." Eleven members of the New York congressional delegation endorsed a request to Secretary of War William March dated August 14, 1846, recommending McKinstry for the position of assistant quartermaster. The day prior to that, McKinstry prevailed upon his company commander, Captain Morris, to write to the quartermaster general from Fort Columbus, even as the command was in the midst of debarkation: "I recommend First Lieutenant Justus McKinstry for the position of assistant quartermaster. I have known him for several years at Fort Niagara while serving in quartermaster duties."[11]

When the eastern battalion of the 2nd Infantry arrived at Camargo, McKinstry was suffering from a severe fever and was carried on the regimental returns as sick. A week later he had recovered sufficiently to forward the regiment's monthly report to the quartermaster's department at Washington. By the end of October, both battalions of the regiment, less Company C which was delayed at Fort Mackinac in Michigan, were united and settled near Camargo at Camp Brady, named for the regiment's absent colonel. For several weeks in November, McKinstry temporarily commanded Company H in place of Captain Carlos A. Waite who had been promoted to major and transferred to the 8th Infantry.[12]

Camargo was, geographically, an ideal jumping off point for Taylor's advance on Monterrey, the capital of the Mexican state of Nuevo Leon, but it was a miserable place for Taylor's army to use as its base. The area had recently been inundated by heavy rains and floods which left the village and its surroundings covered with mud that dried into a fine blowing dust. The location was too far inland to receive cooling sea breezes at night and too near sea level to enjoy the effects of high altitude. It was surrounded by limestone rocks that absorbed and reflected the heat of the sun and sent the thermometer over the 100 degree mark at midday. Few provisions were available locally so that Taylor's army was dependent on supplies that had to be freighted upriver from Point Isabel, a small harbor on the Gulf of Mexico near the mouth of the Rio Grande at Brazos Santiago. Taylor's army was made up of thousands of American regulars and volunteers, brave and willing men who were sadly lacking in any appreciation of camp discipline and sanitation. An appalling number of men at Camargo sickened; in some commands as many as a third of a unit's strength were carried on the sick list at one time. Through the months of the war, more than 1,500 men would die of disease at Camargo. Taylor's men referred to the place as a "yawning grave yard." One writer quoted two newspaper correspondents, one stating that the dead march "was never out of our ears," and the other declaring that the tune had become so common that even the birds learned it. Colonel Ethan Allen Hitchcock, grandson of the Revolutionary War hero Ethan Allen, entered in his diary, "We were at Camargo the principal part of yesterday. It was one of the most miserable places I ever saw; dirty and dilapidated and but little more than a Seminole village."[13]

Taylor was forced to remain at Camargo longer than he intended not for lack of reinforcements but because he was desperately short of supplies and transportation. The army's quartermaster's department was unprepared for the outbreak of hostilities and Congress did not appropriate funds until the war bill was signed into law in May. Without this authorization, the quartermasters were required to operate strictly within the limits of their existing appropriations. The quartermaster general's newspaper is an example of the pre-war parsimony that restricted the department. Only an order from the secretary of war permitted the quartermasters at New Orleans and Philadelphia to subscribe to a single newspaper each. They needed the newspaper to obtain shipping lists and current market prices, information which was essential to the execution of their duties. The quartermaster general was not allowed to subscribe to a newspaper, not even the paper in which the laws were promulgated. Quartermaster General Jesup had to write and ask the quartermaster at Philadelphia to send his paper on to Washington when he had finished with it. Tents that the quartermaster's department furnished Taylor's men at Camargo were old and in such poor condition that Taylor's own supply officers rejected them and ordered new ones. Due to a shortage of heavy cloth, the replacements were of such light and shoddy manufacture as to be worthless. Wagons were in short supply. Quartermaster General Jesup contracted for a limited number of wagons in the spring and summer of 1846 but delivery to Camargo was slow. When further funding became available, Jesup sent agents to scour the nation for more wagons and other supplies such as camp kettles, mess pans, horse and mule collars, mules and draft horses, harness and wagon parts, smith and wheelwright tools, oxen and ox wagons with their chains, bows, and yokes, pack saddles, pontoon equipment, scows and barges—an almost endless list of critically needed items without which Taylor could not move from Camargo. When he did begin his march on Monterrey in September, only 130 of the 265 wagons he needed were available on the Rio Grande. He was also desperately in need of wagon drivers, which was also the responsibility of the quartermaster's department. Taylor blamed the department for his problems. In a letter, he complained, "the Qr. Masters dep. is on crutches." 2nd Lieutenant George B. McClellan, one of Taylor's engineers, wrote, "the Quartermasters Department is most woefully conducted — never trust anything to that Department that you can do for yourself." However, the logistical shortcomings that cost Taylor's army at Camargo such human suffering and life did not rest entirely upon the quartermaster's department. Taylor was notorious for not anticipating his needs and not notifying his staff so they could, in some degree, prepare.[14]

The 2nd Infantry, assigned to the brigade commanded by Brigadier General David E. Twiggs, marched from Camargo with Taylor's advance toward the town of Victoria, reaching it on January 17, 1847. Company A, under Morris and McKinstry, took part in skirmishes with Mexican regulars and guerillas along the way.[15]

There were several theaters of operation in the war with Mexico. Brigadier General Stephen Watts Kearny led a column of the 1st Dragoons from Fort Leavenworth in Kansas Territory to Santa Fe and eventually on to California. There, Commodore Robert F. Stockton commanded a small naval squadron maneuvering up and down the coast. The main American effort, however, was that of Taylor in the northern provinces of Mexico. It soon became apparent to the administration at Washington that the Mexican government would never give in to American forces operating in its distant provinces. The base of power in Mexico was at its national capital, Mexico City. The war would have to be won there at the heart of the nation. In order to achieve this, Taylor's force would have to march and fight its way across more than 500 miles of mountainous terrain, moving far from its base of supply while surrounded by hostile Mexican nationals. There was an alternative to this plan. For some time the administration of President James K. Polk had been considering an amphibious landing at the city and port of Vera Cruz, well down the eastern coast on the Gulf of Mexico, as a prelude to a march on Mexico City. The distance between Vera Cruz and the capital was about 200 miles along a fairly substantial highway. This was the plan the administration settled upon.[16]

Winfield Scott, general-in-chief of the United States Army, had remained at Washington as the various operations got under way. He hurriedly put in place the command structure of a burgeoning war effort for which the nation was unprepared. Scott left Washington on November 21 and arrived at Taylor's base at Camargo to find Taylor had gone inland with his column. Scott ordered Brigadier General William O. Butler, commanding at Camargo in Taylor's absence, to immediately put the regulars of Taylor's force on the road for the mouth of the Rio Grande. Scott wrote to the absent Taylor, outlining the Vera Cruz plan and stating that he was going to strip most of Taylor's army from him. Scott had already begun gathering a fleet of transports that eventually numbered 80 vessels and chose as his anchorage and assembly point the Isle of Lobos, 65 miles southeast of the Mexican port of Tampico.[17]

On January 31, 1847, McKinstry mailed his report to the quartermaster's department at Washington from Camp Watson, near Tampico. On February 25, the 2nd Infantry embarked from there. McKinstry and Company A were aboard the transport *Ellersbee* which arrived off the anchorage on February 28. Also aboard the *Ellersbee*, in command of Company I of the 2nd Infantry, was 1st Lieutenant Nathaniel Lyon who had entered West Point during McKinstry's final year at the academy. McKinstry and Lyon were acquainted, although there is no indication that they ever met or served together during the Second Seminole War in Florida. During the intervening years before the move to Mexico, Lyon had been stationed at Madison Barracks, Sackets Harbor, New York, so it was unlikely that the two men came in personal contact with one another. However, they would have corresponded because of McKinstry's regimental quartermaster and commissary responsibilities. Upon their arrival at Lobos, McKinstry, Lyon, and the regiment became part of the brigade commanded by Colonel William S. Harney, nominally commanding the 2nd Dragoons. From this time forward, McKinstry, Lyon, and Harney would share a relationship that would often be close, but seldom be comfortable.[18]

As part of the appropriation passed to support the war, Congress had authorized an increase in the strength of the quartermaster's department by an additional four quartermasters and ten assistant quartermasters. At about the same time, on January 12, 1847, while on the march to Tampico, Captain Thompson Morris was promoted to major and transferred to the 1st Infantry. McKinstry, now the senior first lieutenant in the 2nd Infantry, was promoted to captain and given command of Company A in Morris's place. But now his years of effort, correspondence, and politicking for an appointment to the quartermaster's department finally bore fruit for, on that same day, McKinstry was notified that he had been appointed as one of the newly authorized assistant quartermasters in the quartermaster's department with the rank of captain which he immediately accepted. From that day forward, his place would no longer be among the veteran officers and men of the 2nd Infantry Regiment where he had served for a decade. He would now serve at army headquarters, reporting to Captain James R. Irwin, Scott's chief quartermaster, and he would work among the civilian employees of the quartermaster's department in the supply train. However, he would continue to cross paths with the officers and men of the 2nd Infantry for years to come.[19]

McKinstry's appointment as an assistant quartermaster could not be confirmed until March 3 due to matters such as the posting of a security bond to ensure his honest and complete fulfillment of his new range of duties. As an assistant quartermaster, McKinstry would be responsible for handling large sums of money. His uncle and namesake in Hudson, Justus McKinstry, and his second cousin, Susan's brother, Augustus, readily pledged their property and wealth as the basis for his bond.[20]

General Scott's invasion plan was bold but it was not his own; the president and the secretary of war had developed the idea of landing an army at the port of Vera Cruz and following the national road westward through the mountains to Mexico City, but even they could not lay claim to the origination of the plan. Hernando Cortez had landed his Spanish *conquistadores* at the same place in 1519 and led them along the same route to what would become Mexico City. Once ashore, Scott would be operating under a real sense of urgency. Vera Cruz, low and coastal, was stricken yearly in the spring and early summer with the dreaded yellow fever. Natives of the region developed some natural resistance to the disease but an American army would be devastated if the men were camped in the coastal regions when the sickness appeared. The cause of the disease was not then known; that would be left for discovery by doctors of another American army in another tropical war.[21]

Vera Cruz was defended by a series of forts, foremost of which was the castle San Juan de Ulua, built on a reef half a mile offshore from the city with its heavy guns covering the approaches and the waterfront. It was out of the question for an army of 10,000 men with supplies, horses, guns, wagons, and the mass of impedimenta that Scott's army would bring with it to think of landing at the docks of Vera Cruz. General Juan Morales and his garrison of 3,000 Mexican regulars would prevent that. However, 2½ miles south of the city along the shore and immediately opposite Sacrificios Island, well out of range of the guns of the Mexican forts, there were wide, open, gently shelving beaches. This would be Scott's landing site.[22]

The immense task of transferring men, guns, and supplies from the transports offshore to the open beaches had been studied and addressed. Ingeniously designed surfboats had been ordered by the quartermaster's department. The wooden boats were flat-bottomed and pointed at both ends so they would not have to turn around coming from or returning to the transports. They were built in three sizes which allowed them to be nested in the holds of the vessels, saving precious cargo space. Each boat was rowed by a navy crew of eight men and was capable of landing 40 or 50 soldiers at a time and later carrying a ton of cargo to the shore. Only half of the 141 surfboats contracted for arrived off Sacrificios Island in time for the landing but those were sufficient to put all of Scott's 10,000 men ashore on the afternoon and evening of March 9, 1847.[23]

George Wilkes Kendall, correspondent for the *New Orleans Picayune*, described for his editors and readers what he saw: "A more stirring spectacle has probably never been witnessed in America. Under the sweeps of the navy crews," he wrote, "each surfboat surged forward in order to be the one that landed its troops first, the line of boats speeding shoreward until, as keels scraped sand, officers with swords in their hands and soldiers with muskets and cartridge boxes held high to prevent soaking, leaped into the waist-deep water and splashed ashore." Immediately after the troops were landed and organized to secure the beaches against Mexican interference, which never developed, supplies began to come ashore under the supervision of Captain Irwin's quartermaster officers who worked continuously through the day and the following night. By dawn, stores, munitions, and supplies sufficient to support Scott's army for several days were staged on the beaches. McKinstry began earning his way as a full-fledged quartermaster officer opposite Sacrificios Island, wading in the surf, shouting orders to navy boat crews, organizing the civilian employees of the quartermaster's department, checking manifests, and directing the placement of the incoming cargo. By the end of the first full day of off-loading, cases, bundles, and crates were stacked along the beach for a mile.[24]

Scott demanded the surrender of the city of Vera Cruz on March 22, which was refused. Choosing bombardment instead of assault, Scott ordered the army to open fire on the city with siege guns and heavy mortars among which was a special land battery furnished and manned by officers and sailors from the navy's ships. On the evening of March 27, General Morales surrendered, having defended his honor adequately. Scott was able to take the city and the harbor that would become his base of operations for his approach to the Mexican capital with fewer than a hundred casualties, 19 of whom were killed. Throughout the siege, McKinstry and the quartermaster officers under Captain Irwin worked incessantly to

Wagner and McGuigan lithograph of the amphibious landing at Vera Cruz on March 9, 1847, during which McKinstry began his service as an officer in the quartermaster's department. (Library of Congress)

maintain the flow of materials from the transports to the shore and across the beaches to the many staging areas established above the high water mark. Every item that Scott's army needed had to come from the holds of the transports offshore during the first days at Vera Cruz. McKinstry made his first return as an official member of the quartermaster's department to the office of the quartermaster general at Washington on April 3, 1847, from Camp Washington, the headquarters of the army on the far right of the siege line that ran around the city from water to water.[25]

Scott allowed his army only a week to rest and recover after the surrender of Vera Cruz because of his deep concern over the onset of yellow fever. He faced a significant lack of transportation for his supplies, the same damaging situation Taylor had experienced in the northern provinces months earlier. Captain Irwin sent foraging parties into the countryside with orders to impress wagons, horses, mules, and oxen with little success. The quartermaster's officers did the best they could against great difficulties yet, when Scott's army began the march from Vera Cruz to the interior, it did so with less than a quarter of the transportation it required. To compensate, the marching columns were stripped of all surplus that could be left behind. Each soldier carried on his person 40 rounds of ammunition, his musket and accouterments, one blanket or overcoat, and a canteen of water. In his haversack he had hard bread for four days and cooked bacon or pork for two days. In his push to escape the coastal plain for the highlands before yellow fever made its appearance, Scott's army moved out with minimal supplies and less than adequate transportation.[26]

The advance began on April 2 when Colonel Harney with a mixed command of dragoons and artillery opened the way by crossing the Rio Antigua near its mouth on the Gulf of Mexico. The American columns marched on a national road that was 300 years old and had once been a great highway, graded and paved by its builders. Scott's first objective was the city of Jalapa. Twenty miles before it lay the narrow pass of Cerro Gordo. The Mexican president and commander-in-chief, Antonio Lopez de Santa Anna, had fortified and garrisoned the pass with 12,000 men. Scott's s advance approached Cerro Gordo on April 17. The following morning Scott sent Twigg's division forward with two brigades, one under the 2nd Infantry's Bennett Riley and the other under Harney of the dragoons. Desperate fighting over two days ended with Mexican troops fleeing in confusion before the assaulting American columns. Santa Anna tried to escape from the field with a small party of officers but Brigadier General James Shield's men cut the road to Jalapa behind the Mexican president. Santa Anna's luxurious carriage was riddled with musket balls, its mules killed. He lost his money chest containing $6,000 in coin which he claimed was intended to be payment for his army. The Mexican president and commander-in-chief fled the field on foot and with great difficulty due to his wooden leg. George Watkins Kendall, the correspondent with the *New Orleans Picayune*, wrote, "Santa Anna's most excellent dinner, with delicious wine and some highly flavored cigars, came as a perfect windfall after a hard day's work, to Captain Justus McKinstry and Captain [Thomas] Williams. To say they did not sit themselves comfortably down on his richly cushioned seats and partake of his sumptuous dinner ... would be departing farther from the truth than I care about doing right now." More important to Scott's army than the capture of Santa Anna's dinner and money chest was the capture of his supply and ordnance trains. Captain Robert Allen, another of the recently authorized quartermaster's officers, took charge of that bounty.[27]

Scott's army reached the city of Jalapa on April 19. From this time forward, the army would face a persistent shortage of hard money with which to purchase supplies and pay the troops. The problem was not due to any fiscal shortage on the part of the United States government but the inadequacy of its arrangements for the transfer to the army of funds in the form of silver coin, the only currency useable in Mexico. Soldiers could be made to wait for their pay; they were used to that, but the quartermasters and commissaries could not keep the army supplied with those items they needed to purchase locally unless they had access to this form of money. Occasionally, silver coin could be secured from foreign merchants in Mexico at high rates of interest in exchange for drafts on the United States treasury. This shortage was not resolved until after the capture of Mexico

SANTA ANNA DECLINING A HASTY PLATE OF SOUP AT CERRO GORDO.

Newspaper cartoon depicting Mexican general Santa Anna fleeing the field at Cerro Gordo, after which McKinstry and Captain Thomas Williams enjoyed dining on his abandoned supper. (Library of Congress)

City. While the army rested at Jalapa, Scott's quartermaster officers were working desperately trying to move forward the supplies that had been left behind at Vera Cruz. A major part of the problem they faced was the lack of teamsters and qualified wagon masters who were civilian employees of the quartermaster's department, not military personnel. Since there were no enlisted quartermaster troops, the officers had to rely on civilians hired on a contract basis to perform these tasks. McKinstry was personally involved in addressing the problem. He met and hired as an interpreter and wagon master William H. Richardson, a civilian from Maryland, who would remain with him for several years. Richardson began working among the teamsters and wagon masters arriving at Vera Cruz and earned McKinstry's gratitude and friendship for the success he was able to achieve among these independent and rather fractious men.[28]

On May 1, the terms of enlistment of 3,000 of the volunteers with Scott's column expired. In spite of appeals, the volunteers marched from Jalapa for Vera Cruz to take ship home. Two weeks later, Scott set his column, consisting now primarily of regulars, on the road for Puebla. Once there, Scott's quartermasters were concerned that Puebla sat almost 200 miles from Vera Cruz up a single highway that was threatened by bandits and guerillas. This highway was the only

Captain Thomas Williams, with whom McKinstry shared Santa Anna's supper after the battle at Cerro Gordo. (Massachusetts Commandery Military Order of the Loyal Legion and the United States Army Military History Institute)

supply line for the men and material arriving to support Scott's army from the States. Some reinforcements and supplies did slowly make their way to Puebla with difficulty. By May 20, the quartermasters had managed to bring two large trains from Vera Cruz consisting of more than 1,000 loaded pack mules and nearly 400 heavily laden wagons. One of the trains brought as its escort Company C of the 2nd Infantry, finally joining the regiment after a long delayed trip from Fort Mackinac in upper Michigan. A second train, one that started out from Vera Cruz on June 2, brought with it 700 recruits, more than 400 loaded pack mules, 700 draft and riding horses, and 128 wagons, ten of which were secretly loaded with wooden chests containing half a million dollars in silver coin. The arrival of the money was timely. Captain Irwin had just written: "[Scott] cannot raise funds to keep the credit of the government. He is in great despondency. The General may have to resort to forced loans — something he dreads."[29]

By July 8, with the arrival of reinforcement and through the relentless efforts of his quartermasters, Scott had built his force and accumulated the minimum number of draft animals and wagons needed to being the advance on Mexico City. On August 7, he ordered the march of his column from Puebla, reporting to the secretary of war at Washington: "I resolved no longer to depend on Vera Cruz or home, but to render my little army a self-sustaining machine." Scott set off with a marching column of 10,738 officers and men of all arms to conquer and capture a city of 200,000, protected by mighty mountains, lakes, and marshes, fortified by hills, and defended by a Mexican army that Scott's staff estimated at three times the size of his own. He left a small garrison of 400 men at Puebla and more than 1,800 sick in the hospitals.[30]

On August 11, 1847, Scott's leading brigade under the 2nd Infantry's Riley approached the rim of the valley of Mexico and began the descent to the capital. Taking the lead on August 18, Worth's division moved through the village of San Augustin toward San Antonio where it ran into heavy artillery fire from strong Mexican positions. Worth's division was brought to an abrupt halt. A direct assault upon the works would be terribly costly yet the position could not be flanked. To the east the waters of Lake Xochimilco blocked any turning movement in that direction. To the west a massive waste of volcanic lava known locally as the *pedregal* presented a formidable barrier that was considered impassible. Worth was unable to move and, when Scott joined him later in the day, both commanders considered their situation very serious. The American troops were ragged, their horses exhausted, their rations growing short, and their brigades strung out in single file for four miles along a barren road. One of Scott's engineers, Captain Robert E. Lee, scouted the *pedregal* several times during the night of the 18th and determined that it would be possible for working parties to hack a road across the lava field wide enough to support a flanking movement to the west which would place the force involved in position to attack the village of Padierna by morning. Once Padierna was taken, the force could move up the western side of the *pedregal* against the village of Churubusco where Santa Anna's main force was formed. The American attack on Padierna began at 3:00 a. m. the following morning with a series of musket volleys followed by a bayonet charge. The Americans drove the Mexicans back into the village of San Angel. Scott claimed enemy casualties of 700 killed and 800 prisoners taken in an assault that lasted less than 17 minutes. This first battle of the day was mistakenly described as being at the village of Contreras by the Americans; in fact, no American forces approached Contreras which lay several miles to the south of the fighting that raged at Padierna, but the name Contreras continued to be used to describe the affair.[31]

The second battle of the day at Churubusco began around noon with several assaults by the Americans. One was at the Churubusco bridge, another at the fortified Convent de San Mateo close to the bridge, and a turning movement toward the village of Portales north of the bridge. Superbly served artillery, deadly musketry, and the traditional American reliance on the bayonet as the decisive weapon overwhelmed the Mexican will to resist. Santa Anna's forces broke and fled. Pursuing American dragoons were unable to envelope and take in all the fugitives because the fighting took place over several causeways, yet more than 3,000 Mexicans were captured. In the combined battles of Contreras and Churubusco, American losses numbered 137 killed, 879 wounded, and 40 missing— about one man in seven. Ninety percent of the loss occurred in the fighting at Churubusco.[32]

On August 14, five days prior to the battles at Contreras and Churubusco, Scott's army acquired an unexpected reinforcement. This was an irregular company of mounted volunteers that, prior to that date, had not existed. The unit was the McKinstry Volunteers, headed by McKinstry and made up of civilian wagon drivers and quartermaster's employees mounted on horses from the supply train, organized through the efforts of McKinstry and his friend, William H. Richardson. McKinstry's after-action report is a classic example of self-aggrandizement:

> Tacubaya, August 24, 1847.
> Sir,
>
> Pursuant to the instructions of Col. Harney, commanding the cavalry brigade, I have the honor to report the operation of the independent company under my command during the recent contact with the enemy before the city of Mexico.
> The motives which actuated the gentlemen comprising my command will be best understood by reference to the preamble of the Muster Roll which is as follows:
>
>> *We, the undersigned, citizens of the Army, feeling the importance of the present crisis and anxious to contribute our mite to the honor of the American arms, and to share the glories of the second conquest of Mexico, hereby enroll ourselves as volunteers under the command of Captain Justus McKinstry, and agree to be subject thereto until the issue of the approaching struggle [is resolved].*

This induced the General-in-Chief to issue the following "Special Orders:"

> Headquarters of the United States Army,
> Inspr. Genl. Department
> Chalco, Mexico,
> August 15, 1847.
>
> Captain Justus McKinstry, of the United States Army, is hereby excused from duty

5. *The Halls of Montezuma* 57

Depiction of the assault on Contreras on August 19, 1847. McKinstry led the McKinstry Volunteers in the action that resulted in his earning his brevet majority. (Library of Congress)

in the Quarter Master's Department, to which he belongs, and, at his own request, is recognized as the commander of a body of Volunteer Civilians—to be known as the McKinstry Volunteers—who, under the influence of a viable patriotism, have enrolled themselves for service with the United States Army, pending the resolution of the approaching conflict before and at the Capital of the Mexican Republic.

By command of Maj. Gen. Winfield Scott.
E. A. Hitchcock, Lt. Col., Insp. Gen.

On the 16th, and on our way to San Augustin, a quantity of arms, consisting of lances, sabers, *escapettes,* and muskets were discovered beneath the floor of a church near the road, and were destroyed.

On the 17th, I was ordered to report to Col. Harney and formed a part of his command during the action of the 19th at Contreras.

On the morning of the 20th, I accompanied the army in pursuit of the enemy until our arrival before his entrenched positions at Churubusco, at which place I acted under the immediate orders of the General-in-Chief. In communicating an order of his to Brig. Gen. Pierce [advancing on the eastern rim of the *pedregal*] to ascertain the progress of the battle, I attempted to turn the enemy's right and came under a heavy crossfire from his musketry which slightly wounded three of my command. After reporting the result of my observations, a part of my command joined the regular cavalry in pursuit of the enemy to the gates of the city where two of my men were severely wounded by a discharge of grape from a battery which commanded the road.

Organized but a few days, for the most part indifferently armed, and with little knowledge of the duty of a cavalry soldier, my men, actuated by the true spirit of Americans, submitted to discipline and comported themselves before the enemy in a manner far exceeding my just expectations; and whilst grateful for, and proud of, the support rendered by all, I cannot omit calling to your attention the conduct of George H. Murray, of Arkansas, Henry N. Clarke and Alfred J. Smith, of New York, William H. Richardson, of Maryland, and James Kellogg, of Georgia, whose services at Churubusco, under a heavy fire from the enemy, are deserving of special notice and commendation.

As those comprising my command were not regularly mustered into the service of the United States [and] are, perhaps, not entitled to the rewards which a beneficial government bestows upon those who suffer in the service of the country, I cannot too strongly commend to the consideration of the General-in-Chief the case of Mr. Dresser who lost his leg in the discharge of his duty.

> Very respectfully, Sir,
> Your Obt. Servant,
> J. McKinstry,
> Capt., USA, Cmdr. Vols.[33]

Harney's own after-action report verifies the presence of the McKinstry Volunteers at Contreras and Churubusco, an excerpt from which reads, "As soon as the road was ascertained to be open and practical for cavalry, I was directed by the Gen'l in chief to proceed with two squadrons of cavalry and Capt. McKinstry's Company of Volunteers to the field of battle and to take charge of the prisoners which had been captured. Capt. McKinstry's company of volunteers joined the Cmdg. Genl. near the field of Churubusco just after the engagement at that place had commenced."[34]

There were now 42 officers holding positions as quartermasters and assistant quartermasters in the staff of the regular army. Of those serving with Taylor along the Rio Grande, with Kearny in California, and with Scott before Mexico City, seven died in service during the hostilities. Of the 35 survivors, 21 earned brevets for gallantry, four of these at the battles of Contreras and Churubusco. Promotion within the army was based strictly on seniority and no other means existed to reward or acknowledge merit. The brevet system was developed so that a distinguished officer could be recognized and given a temporary promotion to the next grade but without the corresponding increase in compensation. McKinstry received his brevet to the temporary rank of major for gallant and meritorious conduct at Contreras and Churubusco on August 20, 1847, the basis for which was his after-action report of the adventures of the McKinstry Volunteers.[35]

The steady advance of Scott's army continued. On August 21, the command was at Coyoacan preparing for the final assault on the city of Mexico. On the following day, Scott sent his commissioner, Nicolas Trist, to meet with Santa Anna in an attempt to negotiate the surrender of the city. During these meetings, a truce was established. Scott was criticized within the army and at home for not taking the city by storm at that time but the general-in-chef had sound reasons for agreeing to the respite. His men had suffered severe losses. They were tired, ragged, and many were shoeless. Scott did not feel they were ready for the demands the final assault on the fortified city would require of them. It was his hope that Trist could arrange a surrender that would preclude a bloody assault. Meanwhile, McKinstry wrote his after-action report on the role he and the McKinstry Volunteers had played in the battles of Contreras and Churubusco while at Tacubaya, resting during the truce with the wagon drivers of the supply train. In a strange turn, Scott was able to contact the United States government's financial agent in the city of Mexico and arrange for the delivery of $151,000 in silver coin through the lines to his army. A few days later, $175,000 more came out along with a hundred pack mules loaded with provisions. This unusual flow of money and supplies between the besieged and the besiegers continued for several more days. On September 6, Lieutenant Colonel Hitchcock wrote, "Our money agent, who has brought out $450,000, had yet another $300,000 ready to come out but the Mexican authorities have ... prevented its leaving." Hitchcock added, "We have less than 8,000 men." By September 7, it became apparent to Scott that Trist was making no progress in arriving at a surrender of the city and, in violation of the terms of the truce, that Santa Anna was fortifying the city and receiving reinforcements for his army. Scott ordered Trist to inform the Mexican president that he considered the truce broken and that he would move against the fortifications of the city at his convenience. On September 8, the following day, the American army began a series of bloody assaults that culminated on September 13 in the storming and capture of the fortress Chapultapec and, that night, Santa Anna's army evacuated Mexico City. At mid-day on September 14, Scott rode in triumph into the city's grand plaza to the thundering cheers of what remained of his ragged, worn, tough little army.[36]

During the fighting at Churubusco, 72 men who had deserted from the United States Army to fight with the Mexicans were captured. Mainly Irish immigrants, the men were referred to as *San Patricios*. Tried by a court-martial, 70 of them were sentenced to hang. Five were subsequently pardoned by General Scott and 15 had their sentences reduced to 50 lashes and branding with a letter D. Twenty of the condemned men were hanged on September 10 and 11. On September 13, Colonel Harney received orders from headquarters to hang the remaining 30. Harney ordered up a number of teams, wagons, and drivers from the supply train and had the condemned men seated on boards stretched across the wagon boxes. McKinstry's classmate, William A. Austine, 3rd Artillery, who had previously gone by the name of William A. Brown, described the event in a letter to his cousin dated November 1, 1847. As the assault on Chapultapec went forward, all eyes were on the American flag being carried forward with the troops. When the flag was raised above the tower of the fortress, Harney gave the command and the quartermaster's drivers cracked their whips, moving the teams and wagons forward and leaving 30 men choking and jerking at the end of ropes.

Harney refused to let the local clergy cut the bodies down afterwards, claiming his orders were to hang the deserters; nothing had been said to him about "unhanging" them. McKinstry knew two of the condemned men well: Private John Cutter, who had served under him in Company B of the 2nd Infantry, and Private Richard Hanly, who had served under him in Company A. McKinstry was the quartermaster officer in charge of the teams, wagons, and drivers and took part in the gruesome event.[37]

Scott and his staff had just occupied the national palace when firing broke out from the rooftops and windows of houses and from around the corners of the city's streets. Some 2,000 convicts had been liberated the night before by the Mexican government as it withdrew from the city. They were joined by almost as many Mexican soldiers who had thrown off their uniforms and taken up arms as looters and snipers. Lieutenant Colonel Hitchcock, Scott's inspector general, warned the city council that Scott threatened to destroy the city and give it over to pillage by his own forces if the firing did not cease immediately. Stern measures followed. Orders were given to shoot every man in any of the houses from which there was gunfire and to use artillery against the buildings if necessary. By September 16, the major disturbances had ended, but for several nights there were isolated attacks and killings. The bodies of nine American soldiers were found one morning, all killed with knives. The army of by now scarcely 6,000 able men had to take strong measures in order to bring the captured city with a population of 200,000 under control. It was not until the middle of October that the city was considered pacified.[38]

While army patrols tracked down the last of the snipers and rounded up wandering prisoners, the pathetic condition of the clothing and equipment of the men of Scott's army was addressed. After marching from Vera Cruz stripped of all surplus, the five months of fighting along the road to the Mexican capital had left the men literally in rags. The day after the army entered the city, an ailing Captain Irwin organized his quartermaster's depot at the custom house. Captain Robert Allen was put in charge of the bureau responsible for horses and mules, forage, harness, and all supplies needed by the army's animals. Brevet Major Justus McKinstry was put in charge of the bureau responsible for clothing, blankets, equipment, and shoes.[39]

To obtain funds to refit his army, Scott issued General Order No. 20 which levied a contribution of $150,000 on the city. While he had been reluctant to consider imposing a forced levy while on the march to Mexico City, he had no qualms doing so after fighting his way in and capturing the place. In reality, he had no choice. The funds that had been obtained through the United States government's financial agent had quickly been exhausted in procuring food for the men and forage for their animals. As it turned out, Scott's initial estimate of the amount of money was inadequate to meet his needs.[40]

On September 14, the first day of the American army's presence in Mexico City, with muskets still roaring in the streets and American patrols rushing about, McKinstry met with Clement Perez Garcia, a man McKinstry had come to know earlier while the army was at Puebla. Garcia was there serving as an interpreter on the staff of General Scott in spite of rumors that he was a spy for the Mexican government. At Puebla, McKinstry and Garcia had discussed in general terms the needs the quartermasters would have when the army arrived in the city and the difficulties McKinstry and the other quartermaster officers would encounter being unfamiliar with the language, the resources available, and the local methods of doing business. Immediately after the arrival of the army at the capital, Garcia applied to McKinstry for business as a broker. McKinstry gave Garcia a list of the items he required, foremost being a large quantity of desperately needed blankets and uniforms. That same day Garcia took McKinstry to the commercial house of Carrera & Garay. Lorenzo Carrera, one of the owners, and his overseer, William Frank, met with the quartermaster and the broker. Since Carrera could not speak English, Frank discussed with McKinstry and Garcia the army's requirements for blankets. When he left, McKinstry took with him two sample blankets to submit to Scott's headquarters for approval. One of the samples, priced at $4.00, was considered too heavy for a soldier to carry on his back in the mild climate of Mexico. The other, priced at $3.25, was selected. Within days, McKinstry and Garcia made an agreement with Frank for 6,000 of the lighter blankets. This transaction was oral, Frank understanding that he had a contract with Garcia on behalf of the United States Army. On September 21, the first delivery of blankets was made to the quartermaster's depot at the custom house by Carrera & Garay. Payment was in the form of silver coin from McKinstry through Garcia. That same day Garcia arranged a meeting between McKinstry and Jose Maria de Landa during which they made an agreement for the delivery of what would eventually amount to $45,000 worth of blue army cloth. This agreement also was oral, de Landa understanding that his contract was with Garcia who was acting on behalf of the army as McKinstry's agent. On October 6, McKinstry and Garcia met with Philippe Urriguen to discuss the manufacture of uniforms which would consist of suits of jackets and trousers. The price agreed upon was $3.00 per suit, the quartermaster's department furnishing the cloth which would be supplied by de Landa. This agreement was in writing, Urriguen understanding that his contract was with McKinstry and the army. There were several additional contracts made by McKinstry and Garcia for shoes, caps, and other items which were of significantly less value than the three large contracts for blankets, cloth, and uniforms. As a result of McKinstry's work, just three weeks after the American army stormed into the Mexican capital and began the pacification process, Captain Irwin could write to Quartermaster General Jesup at Washington that he had a thousand people making clothing and that he would be able in a short time to fill every requisition made upon him. The uniform of the United States

Army had just undergone a change for the better, making it more functional for its field rather than its parade role. A soft visored cap replaced the tall shako and officers adopted a thigh-length blue frock coat while enlisted men were issued a shorter jacket. Both ranks wore sky blue trousers with a distinctive outer seam representing the branch of service.[41]

The money to pay for the purchases, in the form of silver coin derived from General Scott's levy on the city, was delivered to McKinstry at the clothing bureau. During the remainder of 1847, McKinstry received significant sums of money from Captain Irwin, initially $4,000 on October 16, followed by $10,000, $15,000, and a series of increments of $10,000 until he had received and signed receipts for a total of $139,000. The money was kept in McKinstry's chest of drawers in his office at the custom house. Disbursements were made from the chest as necessary by Alfred J. Smith, McKinstry's civilian cashier and clerk and one of the men who had ridden with the McKinstry Volunteers at Contreras and Churubusco. Smith usually gave the money to Garcia who paid the contractor upon approved invoices.[42]

In addition to blankets, clothing, and equipment, the quartermaster's department was responsible for furnishing quarters for the officers and men of the army. This consisted of identifying appropriate dwelling places and evicting the owners. Garcia offered to act as McKinstry's emissary in carrying out this difficult and onerous task once he received a proper letter of authority, such as :

> Assistant Quartermaster's Office
> Mexico, December 10, 1847.
>
> Your house is required for the public service, and upon receipt of this, be prepared to turn over the keys.
>
> J. McKinstry,
> Captain, Assistant Quartermaster.
>
> Mrs. Duran,
> No. 10 *calle de Coliseo Viejo,* Mexico.[43]

McKinstry was the officer responsible for selecting and assigning quarters so it can be assumed that the dwelling he shared with Captain John Breckinridge Grayson, General Scott's chief commissary of subsistence, at No. 1 *calle las Damas* was spacious and comfortable.[44]

The closing months of 1847 passed. After bringing Mexico City to a semblance of calm, the army settled into what amounted to garrison duty albeit in the capital of a conquered and still hostile nation. Blankets, blue army cloth, and uniforms were delivered to the quartermaster's depot at the custom house. However, about the middle of December, this somewhat orderly process changed. Garcia became late with payments to Carrera Garay. On December 20, Charles Strebel, the firm's bookkeeper, raised the issue with William Frank, the overseer. The army now owed the firm more than $4,000 for blankets that had been delivered. As a result, Frank ceased making deliveries. When called to the custom house and questioned by McKinstry, Frank explained that he had been informed by Garcia that the army had not paid the invoices he had tendered. Frank told McKinstry that he could not make further deliveries with such a large sum outstanding. McKinstry had Smith open the quartermaster's books to Frank which clearly showed that all payments to Garcia had been made on time. It became obvious that Garcia was holding back payments to Carrera & Garay.[45]

On Christmas Eve, McKinstry learned that Garcia had been forced to sell a valuable necklace of his wife's in order to raise money to fulfill an agreement with Captain Grayson, McKinstry's roommate, having to do with the purchase of a horse. McKinstry divulged the information as well as some additional issues related to the incident and this resulted in strained relations with Garcia. During the final week of the year, Garcia wrote a letter to Captain Irwin containing charges against McKinstry of embezzlement, accepting bribes, spreading false rumors, and several charges of conduct unbecoming an officer. On January 2, 1848, McKinstry wrote the adjutant general of Scott's army demanding a full court of inquiry into Garcia's charges.[46]

At ten o'clock on the morning of January 4, 1848, a court of inquiry met at the palace in Mexico City for the purpose of looking into "such charges against Captain McKinstry as maybe preferred." The order convening the court referred to McKinstry using his permanent rank of captain rather than his brevet rank of major. The officers of the court were Colonel Milledge L. Bonham, 12th Infantry, serving as president of the court; Major P. H. Galt, 2nd Artillery; and Captain R. H. Ross, 7th Infantry. 1st Lieutenant Franklin Gardner, 7th Infantry, was the judge advocate. Garcia's letter to Captain Irwin detailing the charges and their supporting specifications has not been found; the letter was read into the court record and was annexed as "Document A," but it is missing from the transcript. Its contents can be reconstructed from the remaining record of the court of inquiry. The first act by the court was to note in the record that it was sitting go and find Garcia, the accuser, who was not in attendance. While Garcia was being sought, McKinstry's letter to Captain Irwin was read into the record. In the letter, McKinstry stated that "C. P. Garcia, a broker in my office, has accused me of having received from him certain bribes as inducements to furnish him with contracts emanating from your office, and my own."[47]

Garcia was found and brought to the palace. He made his opening statement to the officers of the court with McKinstry present. "I applied to Captain McKinstry on or about the 14th of September, immediately after our arrival in Mexico," he began. He said he and McKinstry had a private conversation during which McKinstry reminded him of a discussion they had back at Puebla. They had talked about how Garcia knew the language and the markets in Mexico City, and that he might be able to make a great deal of money for himself. "In substance," Garcia said, "he told me that he had a friendship for me, and that he would give me all the business he could." McKinstry had told Garcia that he was a married man and wished to save up some money to take home. "I, also, was married," Garcia told the court, "and sympathized with him." After their conversation, Garcia said it was agreed "we should divide the profits on all purchases made by the army through myself." He had gone with McKinstry to the commercial house of Carrera & Garay with the contract for 6,000 blankets at $3.25 each, all of which had been delivered by this time to the custom house. Garcia had been paid $3.75 for each blanket by the government, "the profits of these having been equally divided between Captain McKinstry and myself." Further, Garcia told the court, a few days after McKinstry had been made agent for houses that were to be occupied by American forces, McKinstry informed him that an unnamed person had been offered $15,000 by the bishop and clergy of Mexico City in order for the army to not take over certain convents. McKinstry told Garcia to look into the matter. "He reminded me that it was dangerous business, and in case it was divulged or found out, he would throw the blame on me." Nothing came of this matter, Garcia testified, but later a wealthy merchant offered him $600 if Garcia would save his home from occupation. "Captain McKinstry gave me a paper which saved that man's house," Garcia said. McKinstry did not share in the proceeds of this transaction, he told the court, but did receive "a splendid shawl."[48]

At the end of Garcia's statement, McKinstry asked why he had preferred the charges against him. Garcia answered that it was because they were true and he had been informed by his friends that it was his duty to do so. McKinstry asked Garcia if he had admitted to him before the court convened that he had been drunk when he made the charges. "I did not state that I was drunk when I made the charges," Garcia told the court, "but I said that I would state so to the court to save Captain McKinstry's honor." Garcia added that he "did not wish to ruin him," and would deny the charges if McKinstry would withdraw statements he had made and continue do to business with him. Garcia admitted that his problems with McKinstry began when he heard rumors that McKinstry told others Garcia had taken a diamond necklace from his wife's neck to pawn in order to settle a debt. He admitted he had written the letter to Captain Irwin containing the charges of profiteering on the purchases of blankets and accepting bribes for not occupying certain houses while in a fit of anger. Referring to himself in the third person, McKinstry asked Garcia, "At your interview with Captain McKinstry, did he not jump from his chair and state in the most emphatic terms that he would not enter into any conditions with you?" Garcia allowed that this had taken place. The court wanted to know if McKinstry had directed Garcia to extract from the owners of houses money so that their homes would not be occupied. "Pinch them hard, Garcia," were the words McKinstry used, Garcia answered. The court went on to examine other witnesses it had called before it. William Frank, the overseer at Carrera & Garay, testified that when he tried to discuss matters with McKinstry, he was told by the quartermaster to deal through Garcia. "He is my agent, address yourself to him," he had been told. Frank also testified that Garcia was being paid a brokerage by his firm of one percent on sales to the United States Army, a fact that McKinstry did not know.[49]

The court of inquiry did not meet on Friday, January 7, 1848, in order for the members to attend the funeral of Captain James R. Irwin, Scott's chief quartermaster and McKinstry's immediate superior. Irwin had been ailing since the army's arrival at Mexico City. His long exposure on the march from Vera Cruz and the demands of his duties after the occupation of the city were too much for the frail officer. Irwin died of an unspecified cause on January 5.[50]

On the following Tuesday, Albert J. Smith was called by the court. "How long did you know that the blankets were being bought from the contractors for $3.25 and sold to the army for $3.75?" the judge advocate asked. Smith replied that he found a paper lying on the desk about two months ago that showed Garcia was buying the blankets for $3.25. "I gave it to Mr. Garcia, saying that he was showing his profits." Did Garcia tell Smith that the amount of $149.50 Smith had kept back from the total given to Garcia on December 20 was McKinstry's share of the profits on 598 blankets delivered to the custom house that day? Smith responded to the judge advocate, "I told Garcia I supposed it had been left for the purpose of meeting a draft that Captain McKinstry would draw on me, at which time Garcia used the following words, 'Smith, you are such a damned fool as not to know what it is for.'" The court asked Smith if Garcia had a large share of the business transacted for the American army through Captain McKinstry's office. "I should think that he has had a large share of it," Smith responded. Ignacio Amesarri, a clothing contractor in Mexico City, was called. He testified that he had offered in writing to make 8,000 uniforms at $2.50 each from cloth to be furnished by the quartermaster's department. He had handed his proposal to McKinstry personally who passed it to Garcia in Amesarri's presence. Amesarri testified that he had never received a response to the proposal which was lower by $.50 a suit than the bid that was accepted. Philippe Urriguen, the merchant who held the clothing contract, testified that he gave Garcia $.25 from the $3.00 he received for each set of uniforms. Urriguen added that Garcia had forbidden him from telling McKinstry about this. The court wanted to know why Urriguen gave $.25 to Garcia, when he could have saved the money by dealing directly with McKinstry. "I was not related in business to Captain McKinstry," Urriguen answered, "and not knowing the English language, I was obliged to go through Mr. Garcia. The amount was demanded by Mr. Garcia, not offered by me." Joseph Ignacio, who often counted money at the custom house for Garcia, testified that he had observed that one payment to Urriguen for uniforms seemed to be $1,000 short. When he mentioned this to Garcia, he was told "that amount was to remain at the office because it belonged to Captain McKinstry as due him as part of the profits on this present transaction, and for others previous, which had not been paid to Captain McKinstry." The court asked if Ignacio knew whether Urriguen gave Garcia, over and above the $.25 for each suit, any additional money to get the clothing contract. "The contract cost Mr. Urriguen $1,000," Ignacio answered. At this point, the prosecution rested its case.[51]

McKinstry began his defense, acting as his own council. His opening address was long, filling ten pages of small print in the official record printed by the government in 1862. He described the details of his relationship with Garcia from their meeting when the army was at Puebla until its arrival at the Mexican capital. He mentioned the rumors then current that Garcia was a Mexican spy, yet he admitted to arranging contracts with him once the army was at Mexico City. He contended he understood Garcia had a recommendation from General Scott urging the quartermasters to give him contracts "in case he would do business as cheap and as well." McKinstry brought his opening statement to an end with the following, "Such, gentlemen, is a brief narrative of Mr. Garcia's connection with our army, commencing *in falsehood* and ending *in open villany!*" McKinstry led the court through the same series of events that had been presented earlier, ignoring all mention of splitting profits or accepting bribes. He contended the events that brought the court of inquiry into being were based on Garcia seeking revenge for reports that had been circulated, and that Garcia was "urged on by persons who hoped to profit by *my ruin!*" McKinstry launched a personal attack on Garcia, on the evidence Garcia had presented, and on the witnesses Garcia had summoned. He challenged whether a contract for blankets had ever been made by the quartermaster's department with Carrera & Garay, claiming that the contracting party had been Garcia himself. McKinstry showed inconsistencies in Garcia's background, that he claimed to have been born in New York City when witnesses testified he had been born in Havana or on a ship between those two places; that Garcia claimed to be a Protestant, but had married in the Catholic church; that he claimed he had been driven from the city of Mexico by the forces of Santa Anna, yet he had willingly joined the American column at Puebla in the role of a Mexican spy. McKinstry demanded that if he could prove willful perjury on Garcia's part in any one instance of these matters, the court must throw out all of Garcia's other testimony "in accordance with the laws of reason and the well-established rules of evidence." McKinstry moved into his peroration with cutting sarcasm. "To establish his character, he introduced three gentlemen, the likenesses of either of which would serve admirably as the frontispiece for the next edition of *Celebrated Criminal Trials*." Finally, McKinstry reminded the court of Garcia's willingness to withdraw the charges he had made in return for certain conditions. He also ridiculed the person of Joseph Ignacio and his testimony regarding shortages of money, stating, "whose evidence may go for what it is worth; we would only call the collective recollection of the court to his appearance and conduct while on the stand."[52]

McKinstry called as his first witness Jose Maria de Landa. He questioned him about selling blue army cloth to the quartermaster's department. De Landa denied paying a premium to McKinstry as part of the transaction. He did admit to paying William H. Richardson, McKinstry's interpreter and one of the McKinstry Volunteers at Contreras and Churubusco, 25 percent of the profits of the business. McKinstry had been unaware of this prior to de Landa's testimony. The court asked de Landa if he had presented McKinstry "with a beautiful blanket, or did your brother?" McKinstry interrupted to state he had been informed by mail that his wife Susan in Hudson had received a shawl from the brother of Mr. de Landa.[53]

On February 8, 1848, the 29th day of hearings, Garcia returned to court in the morning with a large portfolio of documents. When asked by the judge advocate what the folder contained, Garcia said that he had brought original bills of purchase and statements of money paid by him to McKinstry. The list contained items running from bed sheets for the hospitals to brass regimental insignia plates and infantry caps. The list showed a total of $12,543 paid to McKinstry by Garcia. Among the more significant items listed were:

> His share of 6,000 blankets. $1,500
> His share of 8,000 blankets. $2,000
> His share of 4,000 yards of cloth. $7,000

The judge advocate asked Garcia for the total amount of business he had done with McKinstry's office. Garcia said it amounted to about $140,000. The questioning continued with the judge advocate asking whether or not one of the persons who had induced Garcia to prefer the charges had not said, "This McKinstry is a troublesome fellow and must be got rid of." Garcia confirmed the statement. The court asked for the identity of the parties who had urged him to press the charges. Garcia identified three army officers, 1st Lieutenant Pierre G. T. Beauregard, a West Point classmate of McKinstry: Captain John B. Grayson, McKinstry's roommate in the house on *calle las Damas*; a 1st Lieutenant Hamilton, not otherwise identified; and Richard H. Crawford, Grayson's civilian clerk. Later Garcia added the names of two officers from the regiment of mounted rifles, 1st Lieutenant Gordon Granger and a 1st Lieutenant Lindsey, not otherwise identified. Finally, on the morning of February 12, 1st Lieutenant George Lay was called and asked by the court whether he had seen Garcia deliver money to McKinstry at any time. Lay testified that one night around Christmas, "in a public house called the Astor House, or the *Grand Sociedad*, I saw a sum of money, several hundred dollars, or a thousand dollars, in doubloons, delivered to Captain McKinstry by Mr. Garcia, the impression left in my mind was that Mr. Garcia and Captain McKinstry were jointly playing monte, Captain McKinstry betting the money." The *Grand Sociedad* in Mexico City was a notorious public house offering American officers drinking on the first floor, high stakes gambling on the second, and a bordello on the third.[54]

Questioning concluded and final statements were taken. The court of inquiry closed and the officers went into secret session, meeting from Wednesday, February 23, until Tuesday, February 29 — 1848 being a leap year — examining the record and discussing the testimony. On Saturday, March 1, the 45th day of its sitting, the court of inquiry met in open session and announced that it had determined the facts of the matter it was ordered to investigate and gave, as its opinion, "that further military proceedings in the case are demanded by the good of the service." The court of inquiry then adjourned.[55]

There was a significant difference between a court of inquiry and a court-martial. A court of inquiry was convened to determine the facts of a matter and to express an opinion whether further action was required. A court-martial was a tribunal convened under military law to determine whether military persons brought before it were guilty or innocent of certain charges. Depending on the level of the court-martial, guilty findings could result in sentences ranging from reduction in rank to confinement for a period of time, even to death. At 11:00 on the same morning that the court of inquiry announced its opinion, General Scott's headquarters ordered a general court-martial to meet at the palace "for the trial of Captain McKinstry, quartermaster's department, and such other persons as may be brought before it." There were nine officers detailed for this court-martial, a signal from army headquarters that the matter was to be taken seriously. The members of the court were Brevet Colonel Dixon S. Miles, 5th Infantry, president of the court; Major S. P. Mooney, quartermaster's department; Major G. Porter, 4th Artillery; Major G. A. Caldwell, *voltigeurs*; Captain Richard C. Gatlin, 7th Infantry; 1st Lieutenant C. H. Humber, 7th Infantry; 1st Lieutenant Israel B. Richardson, 3rd Infantry; 1st Lieutenant Nathaniel Lyon, 2nd Infantry; and 2nd Lieutenant F. S. K. Russell, mounted rifles. 1st Lieutenant Franklin Gardner, 7th Infantry, would again serve as judge advocate for the court-martial as he had served for the court of inquiry. McKinstry knew all the officers on his court and they knew him. The one officer with whom he was most familiar was 1st Lieutenant Nathaniel Lyon of his former command, the 2nd Infantry. Lyon was now 30 years of age, a native of Connecticut, and currently recovering from a wound suffered during the fighting to enter the city of Mexico. Lyon's wound had been minor but infection had set in and the short, wiry officer had been laid up for some time because of it. Lyon was a frail-looking man with bright red hair and known for his often uncontrollable temper.[56]

McKinstry was placed under arrest and relieved of his sword. Standing before the court, he was arraigned on a single charge of bribery and corruption with three specifications: sharing with Garcia in the profits derived from the procurement of blankets; sharing with Garcia in the profits derived from the procurement of uniforms; and receiving as gifts from Garcia wine, cigars, and a pair of gold uniform trousers stripes. McKinstry pleaded not guilty to the charge and the specifications. However, he explained, he had received a pair of gold stripes but did not know, at the time, who had sent them. Garcia was called into court and asked to repeat his testimony given before the court of inquiry. The court was particularly interested in what he meant when he said the amount paid to him for deliveries of blankets was short by the amount of McKinstry's share of the profits. Garcia explained that he would sign a claim against the government for $3.75 per blanket. Smith, McKinstry's cashier, would pay him. After Smith counted out the money, Smith would separate McKinstry's share and hold it for him. When asked about the gifts of wine, cigars, and the gold trousers stripes, Garcia said, "His residence was with Captain Grayson. I took the stripes there myself and left them in his room, and sent the cigars and wine by some boy, I don't know who."[57]

The following day, General-in-Chief Winfield Scott was called to testify. McKinstry questioned him about the selection of the sample blankets that were submitted to his headquarters, and Scott verified that the lighter of the two samples had been selected. Scott stated, "Being no judge of prices myself, I simply gave the caution, often repeated, that great care should be taken that the prices might not be overcharged." McKinstry did not ask the army commander for, nor did Scott offer any information about, McKinstry's earlier claim of a recommendation from headquarters that preference for contracts be given to Garcia. McKinstry called Andrew Harris, an American who had been living in Mexico City for several years, and asked how long he had known Garcia. Harris said, two years. McKinstry asked about Garcia's reputation for honesty. Harris said, "Since I have been acquainted with him, his reputation has been that of a most refined scoundrel." McKinstry's next witness was William H. Richardson, his interpreter, wagon master, and one of the McKinstry Volunteers. McKinstry asked about events that had transpired in McKinstry's quarters the evening of January 4, the first day of the court of inquiry. Richardson described Garcia bursting into tears, claiming to have been drunk when he wrote the charges against McKinstry. Richardson testified that Garcia said that the charges were without foundation, and that he had been led on by three or four American officers who wanted McKinstry's position. The court did not meet on Saturday, March 8, because funeral honors were being paid by all units of the army to the recently deceased sixth president of the United States, John Quincy Adams. On Monday morning, McKinstry called a series of character witnesses who gave their opinions of Garcia. Charles Bedford Young, another American living in Mexico City for several years, stated, "Garcia's general reputation is that of a *calavero,* which means a scapegrace, or a hair-brained fellow, and a notorious gambler." On Wednesday, March 12, McKinstry declined to make a closing statement after the prosecution announced it had no further witnesses to call. The nine officers went into closed session and that same day, after "mature deliberation on the testimony before it, find the accused, Captain Justus McKinstry, assistant quartermaster, United States Army, as follows: not guilty of the first specification; not guilty of the second specification; not guilty of the third specification; not guilty of the charge; and does therefore fully and honorably acquit him."

Brevet Lieutenant General Winfield Scott, general-in-chief of the United States Army and McKinstry's superior throughout most of this military career. (Massachusetts Commandery Military Order of the Loyal Legion and the United States Army Military History Institute)

General Orders No. 38 from army headquarters in Mexico City on March 24, 1848, read, "The proceedings of the foregoing case are approved. Captain McKinstry will resume his sword."[58]

The court of inquiry had taken 45 days to hear witnesses give testimony and a full week of secret deliberations to arrive at the opinion that further military proceedings in the case were demanded for the good of the service. The general court-martial took nine days of hearing witnesses give testimony and only a few hours of deliberation to arrive at the conclusion that McKinstry was not guilty. McKinstry did resume his sword and his role as chief of the quartermaster's clothing bureau at the custom house. He mailed his next regular return to the office of the quartermaster general at Washington on April 2, 1848.[59]

Prior to McKinstry's court-martial, American and Mexican commissioners had been meeting at the shrine of Guadalupe Hidalgo near Mexico City where they drafted a treaty that formally brought hostilities between the two nations to an end. Ratification of the treaty would be delayed since the document had to travel from Mexico City to Washington where it would be considered by the administration and the Senate before it was eventually signed. However, as of the date of the initialing at Guadalupe Hidalgo on February 2, 1848, the war between the United States and Mexico was over.[60]

It may have been that the nine officers sitting on McKinstry's court-martial saw little purpose in pursuing the charge and specifications that were brought against one of their own by a Mexican national, knowing that the war had ended and the army would soon be leaving Mexico for home. Perhaps the rapid acquittal was simply a way to bring the issue to closure. Whatever the reasons, the verdict can only be seen as a blatant whitewash. Taking into account the finding and the recommendation of the court of inquiry, the officers of McKinstry's court-martial could not with any degree of integrity, or in compliance with the oaths they had taken, accept McKinstry's flippant version of what had taken place, rejecting so completely the evidence and the testimony of many others who were involved. Too many witnesses had spoken, too many transactions had taken place, and too much money had improperly changed hands for the matter to be dismissed so easily. Even taking into consideration the time in history, the finding of the court-martial surely must be considered unacceptable.

Corruption did exist in the army as it did in other aspects of American life including politics, commerce, and society in general. McKinstry's actions in Mexico City, while operating from a position of public trust, were an example of that corruption. The officers sitting on his court-martial board were hardened veterans of the vicious combat that had taken place against Mexican forces from the landing at Vera Cruz until the storming and capture of Chapultapec. As a result, perhaps their moral values had changed and they didn't care whether one of their own was pocketing a share of the coinage passing through his hands on the way to the coffers of Mexican firms and contractors. After all, McKinstry had done a remarkable job against seemingly endless difficulties in providing clothing and equipment for their troops in a foreign land. Garcia's testimony that other officers were trying to get McKinstry's position suggests that there may have been interest by some in the army in sharing the profits, not eliminating what was taking place. Yet this type of corruption goes against the nature of an institution that demanded for its very existence honor, discipline, and duty. Although it did exists, corruption was not the norm. Fraud was not acceptable. Given similar circumstances and opportunities, the other bureau at the quartermaster's depot in Mexico City was never tarnished with even a suggestion of corruption under the direction of the capable Captain Robert Allen.

The officers sitting on McKinstry's court-martial were federal officials sworn to uphold the Constitution, army regulations, and the laws of the land which were to be obeyed even on foreign soil. They failed on all counts. No record exists explaining the deliberations or reasoning behind their verdict; members of a court-martial were protected from justifying their reasoning and their individual findings. While the verdict of the McKinstry court-martial stands as a blemish on the honor of the United States Army in Mexico, that verdict confirmed in McKinstry's mind that he was above the law, the rules, and the restraints imposed on the majority. He had openly violated the rules and yet had been publicly vindicated by a court of his peers. He now understood that he could talk himself out of just about anything. He had done so at West Point, and now again at Mexico City. He certainly felt that his rhetorical abilities would serve him well again in the years to come.[61]

It is worth considering how much his attitude of being above the rules had been founded and reinforced during McKinstry's years in the swamps and hammocks of Florida. There he had faced on a daily basis the threat of mortal danger both from enemies in the brush and from his own men at his back. He had no one to teach or advise him there. He had followed his instincts and had survived. However, the theater of conflict in Florida was far removed from the quartermaster's depot in Mexico City. The harshness of the one cannot stand in justification to the outrage of the other. It is also worth considering how much of this attitude of relying on his instincts and natural abilities in taking advantage of opportunities can be traced back to the role model provided by his father. David Charles McKinstry was a man with little more than his natural skills and his capacity to exploit events and personalities who made use of what he had and achieved success in life. Yet there was a major difference between the McKinstrys, father and son. Somewhere in the passage between them, the son seemed to have lost or mismanaged the integrity, reliability, and honesty the father was known for.

The years after McKinstry's return from Florida had been served in closely confined garrison duty at Fort Niagara or on recruiting duty where there had been limited opportunity or temptation to proceed beyond the established limits. It was not until he was on his own at Mexico City that opportunity, greed, and lack of restraint led him to commit acts most officers would not consider. He had little guidance or direction there from superiors due to the illness and subsequent death of his commanding officer, Captain Irwin. He did what his instincts told him to do and he got away with it. His acquittal in the Mexico City court-martial resulted in a major change in his moral character.

The war had been costly for both nations. In all, the American land forces engaged in the war numbered 31,024 regular soldiers, 548 marines, and 75,532 volunteers. Of these, 944 soldiers, nine marines, and 607 volunteers were killed or died of wounds received in battle and 5,281 soldiers, three marines, and 6,408 volunteers died of disease in the filthy camps. About one American death in eight occurred as a result of action with the enemy. The numbers of losses of the Mexican forces involved in the war are difficult to determine.[62]

Although the cost in lives and treasure was high, the tremendous gain on the American side was in square miles. The commissioners at Guadalupe Hidalgo established a new boundary between the two nations that ran from the Gulf of Mexico inland along the Rio Grande to El Paso, Texas, then westward to the mouth of the Gila River and the Gulf of California and from there further westward to the Pacific shore. In return for the acquisition of this land, the United States assumed a $3 million debt that Mexican citizens owed American citizens and paid an additional $15 million to Mexico for the territory ceded. The United States now stretched to the Pacific. Manifest Destiny had been achieved. On May 30, 1848, the treaty of Guadalupe Hidalgo was ratified by the United States Senate at Washington. That same day, plans were made for the movement of the United States Army from Mexico City to Vera Cruz, and then on to home. Two weeks later, Worth's division formed and marched eastward, back on the national road it had fought so desperately and bravely along nine months before.[63]

McKinstry debarked from the transport that carried him from Vera Cruz to the port of New Orleans on June 29, reporting to the quartermaster in charge there, Major D. D. Tomkins. McKinstry was at the office of the quartermaster general at Washington on July 26. Two days later, he submitted a request to proceed to Hudson where his family awaited his return. Nothing in the record indicates that McKinstry brought any large sum of money with him from Mexico. There is the strong possibility that most of the gains derived from his dealings with Garcia were left in Mexico City at the monte tables. He reported to the quartermaster's department by mail from Hudson on August 16. On September 13, he wrote to Quartermaster General Jesup: "Recent intelligence from Detroit represents my aged father's health as very poor, and I am solicited to visit him at once. I am therefore induced to request that I may be permitted to repair to that city. My accounts, with the exception of a clothing return for the last quarter, have all been completed and forwarded to your office. I am only waiting to hear from two officers owing me receipts to complete and send on that return. I

Thomas S. Jesup was quartermaster general of the United States Army until McKinstry returned from the California frontier. A demanding officer, he raised charges against McKinstry. (National Archives)

have not visited my parents in seven years." McKinstry repeated the request on September 30. Apparently, permission was granted, for he reported next from Detroit on October 10, 1848. Susan and the boys traveled to Detroit with him and

5. The Halls of Montezuma

the family of four spent the following two months with his parents, brothers, and sisters. On November 1 and again on November 21, he reported to the quartermaster's department by mail from Ypsilanti, Michigan, a suburb of Detroit where his father and the family had moved. McKinstry was unaware at this time that Companies C, D, H, and I of his former regiment, the 2nd Infantry, were at sea, having marched from Mexico City to Vera Cruz and there embarked for New Orleans. The command steamed up the Mississippi River to Jefferson Barracks, at St. Louis, and traveled overland to Fort Hamilton, in New York Harbor, where it boarded transports for the long voyage to the recently acquired territory of California.[64]

McKinstry, Susan, and the boys were back at Hudson, staying at the home of Augustus and Jane when McKinstry received a letter from Quartermaster General Jesup regarding the matters that had taken place in Mexico. McKinstry responded, "I have the honor to acknowledge receipt of your official communication of the 6th instant in which I am informed that you shall avail yourself of the testimony taken before the Court of Inquiry, of which Colonel Bonham was president, to have pecuniary charges raised against me at the Treasury." McKinstry asked for the most full and rigid scrutiny into all transactions of every nature but argued that the terms of Jesup's letter were so general as to require McKinstry to request a more specific definition of the pecuniary charges the quartermaster general intended to have raised against him. "I am at an utter loss to conceive what they may be," McKinstry contended. He apparently received a response because he wrote back to Jesup on December 29, referring to the testimony of General Scott, "It will be perceived that the general selected the blankets from the samples submitted ... and that I was *ordered* to make the contract with C. P. Garcia. I received the order from the late Captain Irwin, at that time the chief quartermaster." McKinstry wrote further, insisting that every cent of the contract price was paid to Garcia and that this could be verified by referring to the testimony of Alfred J. Smith who had been his cashier at the time. There was no further correspondence on the matter and McKinstry continued in the service of the quartermaster's department. However, Thomas S. Jesup had a long memory and a remarkable set of files. Jesup was a strict guardian of the principles that had governed his own performance in the 30 years he had been quartermaster general and he insisted on no less from the officers serving under him. Upon assuming the post in 1818, he established three prime objectives for his department which were to ensure ample and efficient systems of supply to the units of the army, to facilitate and effect the movements and operations of its units in the field, and to enforce a strict accountability on the part of those officers and agents handling monies and property of the government under his direction. Jesup jealously protected the reputation of his department and its officers. He would not forget the cloud formed by the performance of the officer in charge of the clothing bureau in Mexico City even though a court-martial had exonerated him from the allegations raised by the court of inquiry.[65]

The new boundary established between the United States and Mexico was readily apparent along much of its distance, following the winding valley of the Rio Grande from the Gulf of Mexico, at Brazos Santiago, to the northwest as far as El Paso. From there westward, it was merely a line drawn on paper and an indefinite line at that. Major William S. Emory, 1st Cavalry, was ordered by the secretary of war at the request of the secretary of the interior to organize and conduct a survey of the new boundary west from El Paso. Emory was familiar with the region; during the war with Mexico, he had been the chief topographical engineer with the column of Brigadier General Stephen Watts Kearny that marched from Fort Leavenworth to Santa Fe and then on to California. Emory requested a military escort for the party of surveyors, engineers, scouts, and teamsters who would make up the American contingent of the joint commission; the Mexican contingent would provide its own escort. Apache and Yuma Indians were restless and unsettled along the route the commission would traverse, and Emory wanted protection. Company A, 1st Dragoons, commanded by 1st Lieutenant Cave Johnson Couts, and Company H, 2nd Infantry, commanded by Captain Julius Hayden, were on the sand waiting for Emory's party when it disembarked from the merchant vessel and waded through the surf of the open beach at the tiny settlement of San Diego, California, on June 1, 1849. Wading ashore with the commissioners was Brevet Major Justus McKinstry, assigned as the quartermaster to the commission's military escort.[66]

6.

The Golden Shore

When he waded through the surf at San Diego, McKinstry was accompanied by his brother, Elisha, age 24, who was 11 years younger than he. Their father had not had to seek a position in the navy or army for Elisha as he had for the two older sons. Due to the developing prosperity of the family while he was coming of age in Detroit, Elisha was able to attend Kenyon College, at Gambier, Ohio. He graduated in 1843 and went on to Columbia Law School at New York, completing his studies in 1846. Elisha was admitted to the New York state bar in 1847 and entered the practice of law at New York City. When the formation of the commission to survey the new boundary between the United States and Mexico was announced, Elisha applied for the position of clerk to his brother.[1]

Justus and Elisha were not the first of the McKinstry clan to set foot on the soil of California. Their second cousin, Susan's older brother, George McKinstry, Jr., came west traveling across the continent with an emigrant wagon train and arrived some time in July, 1846. George lived for a while at John Sutter's fort at New Helvetia, near present Sacramento. Almost immediately upon arriving from the east, George was appointed sheriff of sparsely-populated northern California. On October 15, 1847, the district court sitting at Sacramento directed George to summon a jury for a trial. His arrival in California was timely. On January 24, 1846, James Marshall, working for Sutter erecting a millrace on the southern fork of the American River, had found gold. While living in California, George maintained an irregular correspondence with his younger brother, Augustus, and his older sister, Jane, both of whom were still living at the family home on Prospect Hill in Hudson. On September 6, 1847, Augustus wrote to George, "Justus, I suppose, is now in the Halls of Montezuma, the last we heard from him he was at Puebla. He is in Twiggs' division, he holds the rank of Capt., and I believe he belongs to the staff. He was at the battles of Vera Cruz and Corrogordo [sic] and dined in Santa Anna's carriage and partook of his fine wines and cigars. Sue is staying with us with her two boys. Fine fellows." On March 19, 1849, Augustus wrote to George that Justus had received orders to proceed to San Diego and

George McKinstry, Jr., McKinstry's brother-in-law and second cousin. The two were business partners in California until their falling out, after which George tried unsuccessfully to have Justus cashiered from the army. (San Diego Historical Society)

would be carrying family letters out with him. Augustus expressed the hope that George would meet Justus and proposed, "Should there be an opportunity for him to secure a fortune after his service is over, I take it for granted you will direct his energies that way. The life he now leads is anything but desirable especially to his wife. Susan is now at the Hudson House and will remain there until Justus returns." Jane had written to George five days earlier, mentioning that Susan and the boys were living at the hotel because Susan did not want to bother her brother and sister with the two little ones. Jane added that McKinstry had written to Susan that he would try to exchange his position with another officer in the hope that he might be stationed somewhere the family could be together, although nothing came of this. Jane ended her letter, "Sue is feeling badly."[2]

McKinstry had corresponded with Major Emory before leaving Hudson. He received a reply dated February 26, 1849, informing him that the military escort for the commission would consist of one company of infantry and one company of dragoons, and that the commission planned to run its survey continuously from San Diego eastward. The party, Emory wrote to McKinstry, would require sufficient wagons to transport its baggage and six months provisions for the escort and the five officers and civilians making up the commission itself. In addition, Emory wanted two ambulances with mule teams to transport the fragile surveying instruments and an additional 50 mules with pack saddles to allow detachments to be made on those parts of the journey where wagons could not roll. Emory surmised in his letter that "wagons sufficient are already in the country or on the way to it." McKinstry disagreed. He recalled the problems the quartermaster's officers faced in Mexico when they tried to organize transportation through local resources or to rely on promised support from home. He submitted a requisition to draw what he anticipated the commission's needs would be from the quartermaster's depot in New York, intending to carry the items with him. Major Henry Whiting, chief quartermaster at the port of New York, objected to this. Whiting wrote to the quartermaster general that McKinstry had asked him to provide 125 four-mule wagons, three ambulances, and animals and harness for both types of vehicles. Whiting suggested that instead of furnishing McKinstry's request from the New York depot, they be obtained "from suppliers of that kind who probably have them on hand at some southern depot." Whiting's interference caused McKinstry to sail without the transport he requested and he was unable to obtain any of it along the way. When the boundary commission waded through the surf at San Diego, Emory reported: "There was not sufficient means of transportation on hand to provide for the escort; it was necessary to assemble these means under very great disadvantage. There were assembled by Major McKinstry with energy and ability."[3]

McKinstry, Elisha, and the commissioners sailed from New York on the steamer *Falcon* on March 8, 1849, for Panama. At the tiny port of Chagres on the Atlantic coast, the passengers disembarked into native canoes and, with their baggage and precious instruments, were paddled upriver to the village of Gorgina. From there they traveled on mule-back across the mountainous spine of the isthmus to Panama City on the Pacific coast. The party arrived on March 30 and McKinstry was immediately incapacitated with a severe fever. He remained ill for the entire month of April. It was not until May 1 that he was well enough to report to mail to the quartermaster's department at Washington, apologizing that indisposition was the cause of his reporting late. His illness alone, however, did not delay the progress of the commission; during McKinstry's sickness and recovery, Major Emory tried unsuccessfully to engage passage on any ship steaming from Panama. These were the days of the California gold rush; captains and crews were sailing their vessels into San Francisco harbor and abandoning them there to rush off to the gold fields. As a result, there was a severe shortage of shipping all along the Pacific coast. The delay at Panama City was long, but eventually a vessel did arrive and Emery booked passage. When the commission finally landed on the open beach at San Diego, the population there was said to consist of "247 whites, three Sandwich Islanders, three blacks, 438 'tame' Indians, and 1,550 'wild' Indians."[4]

The Mexican commissioners and their escort did not arrive for a month. Three days after they did, the leaders of both commissions met to select the place from which to commence running the boundary eastward. They chose a spot one marine league south of the southernmost point of the bay of San Diego. Two years later a monument was erected and dedicated at that place.[5]

McKinstry was acquainted with one of the escort commanders waiting on the beach. Captain Julius Hayden was not a graduate of West Point but had been appointed a second lieutenant in the 2nd Infantry directly from civilian life from Florida on June 16, 1839, almost a year after McKinstry graduated from the military academy. McKinstry and Hayden had served together in Florida, along the Niagara frontier, and in Mexico. Hayden was seriously wounded in the fighting at Churubusco where he earned his brevet for gallantry. The officers of Company A, 1st Dragoons—the company commander, 1st Lieutenant Couts and his second in command, 1st Lieutenant George F. Evans—were strangers to McKinstry. Couts and Evans had only recently arrived in California after marching their command overland 1,600 miles from Monterrey, in Mexico, to Los Angeles, California, and then down the coast to San Diego. This was a grueling and dangerous ride across the mountains and deserts of northern Mexico and southern California that took six months. Couts was a native of Tennessee. His uncle and namesake had served as postmaster general in the cabinet of President James K. Polk. Appointed to the military academy from his home state, Couts arrived at West Point on June 2, 1838, less than a month before McKinstry graduated. There is nothing in the record to indicate the arriving plebe and the matriculating first classman ever came in contact during the four weeks they shared at the academy. Couts did not see combat during the Mexican war. Graduating from West Point in 1843, he was appointed a brevet second lieutenant in the regiment of mounted rifles where he served while waiting for an opening in the officer's ranks of a regiment of the line into which he could move on a permanent basis. After garri-

Cave Johnson Couts, dragoon and rancher, was McKinstry's nemesis during the years they served together in California. (The Huntington Library, San Marino, CA; photDAG 047)

son duty in Louisiana and the Indian Territory, Couts was appointed a permanent second lieutenant in the 2nd Dragoons and then a first lieutenant in the 1st Dragoons. After the fighting in Mexico came to an end, Couts was transferred to Monterrey, Mexico, where he assumed command of the regiment's Company A which was performing occupation duty there.[6]

The reliable Robert Allen served with McKinstry at the quartermaster's depot in Mexico City and on the California frontier. After the dismissal of Frémont and McKinstry's expulsion, Allen was brought in to bring order to the chaos at St. Louis. (National Archives)

Cave Couts was 27 years old, standing well over six feet in height and weighing a solid 165 pounds. After the trek from Monterrey, Couts rested his command at Los Angeles, a tiny settlement at the time, where he was charged with conduct unbecoming an officer for receiving profits from a gambling operation run by two other men, probably members of his command. Couts was ordered to consider himself under arrest but to continue on duty until the short-handed occupation force was augmented by enough officers to form a court-martial to try him.[7]

Couts's second in command, Evans, graduated from West Point with the class of 1846. In February, 1847, Evans earned his brevet first lieutenancy for gallantry at the battle of Buena Vista. He first met Couts when the Tennessean was assigned to Monterrey. On the long ride to Los Angeles, Couts and Evans became close friends, even tenting together.[8]

Once ashore at San Diego, McKinstry immersed himself in the duties of his office. On June 11, he wrote to Major David H. Vinton, chief quartermaster of the newly established Department of the Pacific, headquartered in Monterey, California, asking for $25,000. This amount was in addition to the $30,000 of quartermaster funds he brought with him from the east and also in addition to about $25,000 that he received from Captain Nathaniel Lyon, 2nd Infantry, serving at San Diego in McKinstry's former role of regimental acting assistant quartermaster. A little more than a year before, Lyon had sat on McKinstry's court-martial in Mexico, and the righteous Lyon had not forgotten the charges that had been preferred and the testimony given against McKinstry. Both Lyon's and Hayden's companies of the 2nd Infantry had recently arrived in San Diego from the east. McKinstry now had to face the consequences of Major Whiting's refusal of his requisitions back in New York in March. In sparsely settled California, McKinstry found himself desperately trying to bring together animals, wagons, harness, and drivers to provide transportation for the members of the boundary survey commission and its military escort as the joint American-Mexican party prepared to move eastward toward the mouth of the Gila River. On July 6, McKinstry wrote to Lyon, whose office was just across the small plaza at San Diego, asking for the horses in the corrals of the 2nd Infantry. "I have to provide for 61 Dragoon horses and 200 mules ... on the eve of a severe campaign. The Mexican commissioners are now here and my instructions inform me that not a moment is to be lost." On July 11, he wrote to Major Robert Allen, with whom he had served in the quartermaster's depot at the custom house in Mexico City, "Herewith a requisition to meet the demands of the escort of the boundary commission. The party designated to appear at the mouth of the Gila intends leaving here by the first *proximo*." Allen was now assistant quartermaster for the Pacific Division and stationed at headquarters at Monterey. On the same day, McKinstry wrote to Major E. R. S. Canby, his former second lieutenant while in Florida and at Fort Niagara, now departmental assistant adjutant general, "I have directed W. H. Richardson, as an agent of the Dept., to proceed to Monterey, to purchase 200 mules required by my train." Richardson, of the McKinstry Volunteers in Mexico, had joined his former chief.[9]

San Diego was a tiny settlement, built around the old Spanish mission. McKinstry was working there under primitive conditions with few resources available to him other than money which was often without value when there was little to purchase. Except for Hayden's and Lyon's companies recently from the east, and Couts's Company A of the 1st Dragoons, the rest of the United States Army that had arrived in California was stationed some 500 miles north of San Diego at Monterey. Major Emory was still determined to set off for the mouth of the Gila on the first day of August. Due to McKinstry's "energy and ability," he wrote that he was planning on keeping to that schedule. A month later, seven additional companies of the 2nd Infantry arrived from the east at Monterey. Five of these were ordered to San Diego, two setting up their tents in the groves of the old mission and three moving 50 miles up the coast and camping at Mission San Luis Rey. Both contingents of the regiment were commanded by McKinstry's friend, Major Samuel P. Heintzelman.[10]

On the evening of June 18, 1849, less than three weeks after arriving at San Diego, McKinstry joined Couts and several other men in Couts's room for a game of brag. Others there included Captain Hayden; 1st Lieutenant James E. Slaughter, 2nd Infantry; Captain E. L. Hardcastle, topographical engineers; 1st Lieutenant Samuel D. Curtis, 1st Dragoons; and a civilian, George F. Hooper, assistant surveyor with the boundary commission. In the course of the evening, Major Emory visited the room and watched the game for a time. Testimony later established that the game came about at the suggestion of McKinstry and that it ran all night. During the game, McKinstry, losing heavily, asked Couts whether the dragoon had any money he could lend. Couts said that he had some. McKinstry borrowed in increments an amount eventually reaching $700, promising Couts he would repay the loan in the morning. He failed to pay it back the next day and during nine days that followed. Couts confronted McKinstry on June 28 on the street in San Diego and demanded payment. He followed the quartermaster to McKinstry's room where McKinstry took gold coins from a bag in his trunk. He paid Couts $400, claiming that was as much as he could conveniently pay at that time, but that he had plenty of pay coming and he would make up the difference when army paymasters arrived at San Diego.[11]

The debt was not the only issue between McKinstry and Couts. Don Juan Bandini had been justice of the peace at San Diego under Mexican rule. He was the head of one of southern California's distinguished families and a major landowner. Couts boarded at the Bandini home and the game of brag took place in the dragoon's room in the Bandini house. Couts and Bandini had become close and were about to go into business together raising and selling horses. Bandini's daughter, Ysidora, was an accomplished woman in her own right; she and Couts eventually married on April 5, 1851. However, some time during June, 1849, according to Couts, McKinstry "slandered a young lady who would not permit the free use of his vulgar tongue in her presence." Whether the lady was Ysidora Bandini has not been established; in the mid-19th century, a woman's name would not have been included in this type of record, but the vehemence of Couts's accusation and his continuing challenges to McKinstry indicate that it was. Judge H. H. Robinson, a resident of San Diego, commented on the animosity that developed between the quartermaster and the dragoon, saying, "It had arisen through Lieutenant Couts charging him with having slandered the character of a lady, which charge he repelled in a written notice, in which he charged dishonor and cowardice upon Couts." The issue was not allowed to rest. An exchange of notes between McKinstry and Couts began. McKinstry wrote Couts on the evening of August 5, apparently referring to Couts's accusation. Evans, Couts's second in command and friend, wrote back on Couts's behalf, arguing McKinstry's version of statements made by several other people. Couts wrote a note that McKinstry took to be a challenge to a duel; he discussed it with his associates and decided not to accept it as such. Evans, now completely involved in the controversy on behalf of his commanding officer, wrote to McKinstry on August 24: "I shall proclaim you (as Lieutenant Couts has already done) a liar and a coward, and that shall be your standing and reputation in San Diego, and wherever you may hereafter go, if truth will have influence with honorable men." Couts later told Richard Rust, a citizen of San Diego, that he had sent a further note to McKinstry and expected McKinstry to attack him once he received it. Couts told Rust that, after allowing a reasonable time for McKinstry to receive and read the note, he walked out onto the plaza and, had McKinstry approached, Couts would have shot him. On the morning of August 31, Evans left the quarters he rented in a home of one of the citizens of San Diego and headed for the mess tent for breakfast. He approached McKinstry who was standing at the edge of the plaza reading some official-looking documents held in his left hand. McKinstry stopped Evans. Witnesses heard only a few words of the exchange which included McKinstry shouting "God damn you!" McKinstry hit Evans several times in the face with his right fist before Evans could clutch and grab McKinstry's arms. The two fell to the ground with McKinstry, by far the larger and stronger, on top of Evans, striking him repeatedly with both fists. McKinstry demanded, "Do you beg?" Evans, struggling to cover his face and head, nodded. McKinstry let the dragoon up. Evans walked to several of his friends who had gathered as the fight took place and said something to them. McKinstry came bounding at him, shoving him, and demanding, "Did you not beg?" When Evans admitted he had begged, McKinstry let him go. Evans's friends led him away and helped him wash dirt and blood from his face and head.[12]

Late in August, army paymasters visited San Diego. McKinstry had not drawn any of his pay since leaving New York the previous March, so he had at least five months pay coming. He made no effort to pay Couts the outstanding balance from the game of brag that he still owed the dragoon. The amount was $300, less some draws by Couts which had been covered by Elisha McKinstry on his brother's behalf. The animosity between McKinstry and Couts had by now developed to such an extent that Major Emory felt he had to interpose. As the senior officer at San Diego, he was responsible for both staff and line commands. After the fight between McKinstry and Evans, he asked several persons who had witnessed the affray for particulars. As much as he wanted to proceed with running the boundary survey, he could not permit his officers to slug it out with each other in plain sight of the populace and the troops without taking appropriate action. What Emory decided was tempered as much by his need to maintain discipline and order in his command as his need to retain the services of those officers who were critical to the success of his mission. Evans was directed to consider himself under arrest and was ordered to report to the office of the adjutant general of the army at Washington, a continent away. Couts was ordered to prepare his command for the immediate departure from San Diego for the mouth of the Gila River. McKinstry was relieved of his duties as quartermaster to the military escort and ordered to report to division headquarters in Monterey. McKinstry turned over his quartermaster's responsibilities to Captain Hayden who, on September 10, 1849, gave McKinstry a receipt for his stores, supplies, animals, and $11,404 in cash.[13]

On the morning he was to depart for the mouth of the Gila, Couts wrote a long letter to Quartermaster General Jesup at Washington. He described the events that had taken place during the game of brag and the loans of money, stating that although McKinstry was at the time unknown to him, "he being an officer in the army was sufficient to me." Couts wrote that McKinstry repaid $400 under demand and promised the balance when paymasters visited San Diego but had refused to make good the difference since then. Couts added that McKinstry built a home in San Diego and furnished it "more elegantly than officers generally can afford." He concluded with, "I make this statement to the Quartermaster General not with any view or expectation of having money refunded, but to show the character of an officer we have in the army, which I consider it the duty of every officer to keep purified." Jesup carefully considered Couts's letter before forwarding it up the chain of command. Jesup was most demanding that the officers of his department be discreet and act completely within the limitations of army regulations. He had in his files the transcript of McKinstry's court of inquiry and court-martial in Mexico City. His written endorsement on Couts's letter reads, "Respectfully referred to the Secretary of War. It is important to the interests of the public service that this case be investigated, and if it be found that Brevet Major McKinstry, a disbursing officer of the army, had violated paragraph 857 of the Army Regulations, I deem it my duty to urge that the penalty imposed by that regulation be enforced by the removal of Major McKinstry from his office on the staff." An additional endorsement reads, "A court-martial will be detailed by the commander of the Pacific Division for the trial of the officer within named on charges which have been preferred. (signed) G. Crawford, Secretary of War."[14]

Sometime between September 14 and 18, 1849, McKinstry left San Diego and traveled north by coastal steamer. Reporting at headquarters at Monterey, he was assigned to a post even further north. On October 10, he mailed his return for the month of September from Camp Far West, California, some 30 miles north of Sacramento on Bear Creek, near present Maryville. Camp Far West guarded the routes between San Francisco and the gold fields on the western slopes of the Sierra Madre. Camp Far West, incidentally, was considered one of the most unhealthy places in the Sacramento River valley.[15]

McKinstry made contact with his second cousin, Susan's brother George, soon after arriving at San Diego. He wrote to George at New Helvetia, about 35 miles from Camp Far West, on November 1, 1849, opening his letter, "Dear Mac," and writing that he was sending an army express rider down in the morning and would use the opportunity to thank George for his recent letter containing newspaper clippings. McKinstry wrote, "We had a council of administration yesterday and appointed [William H.] Richardson sutler to the post — he will go down in the course of a week or ten days for goods." McKinstry advised that he would have little use for his supply wagons during the coming winter months and was sending them down. He offered to arrange matters so that George could use them for freighting until spring in return for feeding the teams and paying the hire of the teamsters. He commented, "I am of the opinion that a store here this winter will do very good business provided the right kind of assortment is kept — of this you be the judge." McKinstry closed asking a favor, "When I left Sacramento, I loaned an acquaintance one hundred dollars and just as I left, I gave Mr. Diggs an order for the money. If he is fortunate enough to collect it, please retain it until we meet. Remember me to Elisha."[16]

McKinstry was kept as busy with quartermaster duties at Camp Far West as he had been at San Diego. On November 16, he wrote to the proprietors of a ferry over one of the forks of the American River asking that they let army express riders cross without collecting tolls and then bill the quartermaster's department for the passage on a monthly basis. The proprietors were to send their invoices not to McKinstry at Camp Far West but to the firm of Smith, Bensky & Co., Sacramento, who would make payment from quartermaster's funds on deposit with them. McKinstry's November quartermaster's return was mailed from Camp Far West on December 1. On January 4, 1850, he wrote to his former comrade in the 2nd Infantry, Captain George C. Wescott, informing the officer he had paid $60 reward money for the apprehension of "Privates Paris and Grider, deserters from your company." Three days after that, he wrote to Captain Hannibal Day, "I have this day paid on the certification of an officer $90 for the apprehension of Privates Coglan, Finison, and Ryan, deserters from your company." Apparently, the attraction of the nearby gold fields was reaching deep into the veteran ranks of the 2nd Infantry. The same month McKinstry corresponded with Smith, Bensky & Co., drawing on them for $375 payable to the order of George McKinstry, Jr. In February, Smith, Bensky & Co. billed J. B. Hyatt $41.49 for hams, cheese, tea, boot blacking, and brushes with payment being made by a draft on

McKinstry. McKinstry's idea of store near Camp Far West was coming to fruition. McKinstry himself added to its inventory on February 10 with a consignment of sardines and saleratus in the value of $11. The store was located at Nicolaus, about mid-way between Camp Far West and Sacramento. J. B. Hyatt was hired to manage the enterprise, Justus and George McKinstry were the financial partners, and William H. Richardson was an employee. Nicolaus was a typical gold rush boom town. Justus and George purchased several town lots and put up a kitchen and boarding house on one of them, entering into business with Alfred Wheeler and his wife, "a capital cook." On April 14, 1850, McKinstry wrote to George to inquire whether they should go into the auction and commission business. "My commercial friends here advise that business and regard the present as a very favorable opening. You are aware, of course, that everything depends upon your *ipse dixit* and I shall await your reply. Should that be unfavorable, I shall, upon the return of General [Persifor F.] Smith, apply for orders to the States and return there." McKinstry later sold his interest in the Nicolaus businesses to Wheeler who, on June 25, wrote to George asking to purchase his share for the same amount paid to Justus, $1,500. McKinstry's personal enterprises in and around Sacramento suddenly came to an abrupt halt with the receipt of General Order No. 6 from division headquarters directing a court-martial to meet in San Diego on September 10, "for the trial of Brevet Major Justus McKinstry, assistant quartermaster, and such prisoners as may be brought before it." Cave Couts's letter to Quartermaster General Jesup, written exactly a year before, had worked its way east and the long army of military justice had worked its way back west. The dragoon was about to have his day in court.[17]

Nine officers were detailed for the general court-martial: Brevet Lieutenant Colonel Silas Casey, 2nd Infantry; Major R. B. Lee, commissary of subsistence; Major A. S. Miller, 2nd Infantry; Brevet Major Henry Wessels, 2nd Infantry; Brevet Major E. H. Fitzgerald, 2nd Dragoons; Brevet Major Samuel P. Heintzelman, 2nd Infantry; Captain Hannibal Day, 2nd Infantry; Captain Henry S. Burton, 3rd Artillery; and Captain Christopher S. Lovell, 2nd Infantry. Captain George C. Wescott, 2nd Infantry, was would serve as judge advocate. Six of the nine officers and the judge advocate were from McKinstry's former command, the 2nd Infantry, and were well acquainted with him and his history. Captain Lovell had been the officer appointed to the command of Company A when McKinstry accepted the appointment to the quartermaster's department. They were familiar with the court of inquiry and the court-martial in Mexico a little more than two years in the past and they were aware of McKinstry's general rep-

Opposite: Samuel P. Heintzelman served with McKinstry in the 2nd Infantry in Mexico and on the California frontier. Together, they operated a gambling house in San Diego. (Massachusetts Commandery Military Order of the Loyal Legion and the United States Army Military History Institute)

utation in the army. Major Lee was a disbursing officer himself and knew well the regulations that governed the conduct of an officer in such a position. It would not be fair to consider the court biased but it would be fair to consider that McKinstry would receive a demanding and detailed hearing.[18]

Immediately upon the court's sitting, Major Heintzelman presented a note to the judge advocate making the case that he should be excused from serving because an article in the *Alta California*, a local newspaper, had stated that McKinstry had a strong friend on the court. When questioned, the editor of the newspaper identified Heintzelman as that friend. This caused the court to go into closed session during which the members questioned Heintzelman about his relationship with McKinstry prior to California and after the arrival of Heintzelman's battalion at San Diego the preceding year. The complete article from the *Alta California* was read into the record. It contained the allegation that McKinstry and Heintzelman had operated a "little house," a gambling operation, at San Diego. The officers of the court decided that the article and its allegations did not afford sufficient grounds for Heintzelman to be excused. As it was, detailing ten officers for the court from the recently-arrived garrisons in California had already stretched the limited resources of the Pacific Division.[19]

The charges on which the court convened were read into the record. The first was a violation of paragraph 857 of the General Regulations of the United States Army, promulgated in 1847, the paragraph that Jesup had referenced in his note to the secretary of war. The specification to support the charge stated that McKinstry, while serving as a disbursing officer, had gambled with cards for money. The second charge was that of conduct unbecoming an officer and a gentleman. This referred to the money McKinstry borrowed from Couts which he promised to pay back, but had failed to although the means were there and demands were made. At the last moment, just as the court was preparing to hear testimony, two additional charges and specifications were introduced. The first of these was for un-officerlike conduct. It stated that McKinstry "Did violently abuse and maltreat the aforesaid Lieutenant Evans by beating him with his fists, this is the public square of San Diego, in the presence of a number of persons collected there." The second was for conduct subversive to good order and military discipline which was based on the same specification as the first. The court went into closed session to consider these additional matters. The officers decided to strike the first additional charge, determining that the offense stated in the second additional charge covered both offenses. The revised charge and specification were read into the record and McKinstry was asked by the judge advocate, "What say you? Guilty, or not guilty?" Instead of pleading, McKinstry addressed the court, reading into the record a long statement. Before he would plead, he deemed it proper, he insisted, "to call the attention of the court to matters that, in a court of civil law, would induce a jury to carefully receive, if not exclude, testimony of an individual resorting to such means to effect his object: namely, the extraordinary efforts of Cave Couts, the prosecuting witness, to influence in anticipation of this court, public opinion by the circulation of written and printed slanders having a direct bearing on the questions the court would be called upon to decide." The judge advocate interrupted McKinstry and told him he must first plead to the charges before he could be allowed to finish his opening statement. McKinstry pleaded not guilty. "Every man," he told the court, continuing his statement, "is presumed innocent of crime until proven guilty. But, in this case, circulation of charges founded on *ex parte* testimony, often made under excitement by persons smarting under real or imagined wrongs, may cause the judgment of conviction to be passed long before the day of the trial had arrived." When that happened, he argued, the role was reversed and the presumption of guilt was substituted for the presumption of innocence. The continuation of Couts's slanders through the columns of the public press should induce the court "to weigh well his statements and exercise unusual care in endeavoring to find the grain of truth presented in the bushel of chaff." As had been his style in Mexico City, instead of forming his defense on hard evidence to refute the charges, McKinstry attacked the credibility of the witnesses who would be called to testify against him and, in his opening statement, tried to discredit any and all evidence even before it was brought into court. The prosecution, having patiently listened to his diatribe, began to call a series of witnesses who confirmed that the game of brag had taken place, that McKinstry borrowed money from Couts in the course of the game, he promised to repay the loans the following morning, and that he failed to do so for some time even though the paymasters had visited San Diego and paid the officers and the men of the garrison. Witnesses established that there had been a fight between McKinstry and Evans on the plaza, that McKinstry instigated the fight, and that Evans had been severely injured in the struggle. No evidence was introduced regarding the "little house" that the editor of the *Alta California* alleged McKinstry and Heintzelman had operated.[20]

McKinstry interrupted the proceedings on the third day of testimony, September 13, 1850. He told the members of the court that he had just been informed that the prosecuting witness, Cave Couts, had offered a sum of money for his assassination. He insisted that the prosecution's witnesses be examined to determine whether they were aware of this threat. The prosecution revised its list of witnesses and called Robert D. Israel, a citizen of San Diego, who was asked if he knew anything about an attempt Couts had made to induce two soldiers, recently discharged from his Company A, 1st Dragoons, to kill McKinstry. Israel testified that he had heard a former soldier, known as "Bunty" Owens, say that Couts had attempted to bribe him and another former soldier, John Decker, to kill McKinstry. Israel said that Owens claimed to have held a cocked pistol pointed at the head of man in San Diego whom he though was someone connected to McKinstry but found out before he fired that he was mistaken. Another witness, William Curley, testified he had heard "Bunty" Owens say that Couts had bribed him and a man called Decker to kill McKinstry. Hugh "Bunty" Owens was found and brought before the court. He was asked if he knew of a proposition by Couts, or anyone representing Couts, to take the life of McKinstry or anyone connected with him. Owens answered that he did not. The judge advocate asked if he ever stated to anyone that Couts had offered to bribe him to kill McKinstry. Owens answered that he did not. He was asked if he ever mentioned killing McKinstry in his conversations with Israel or Curley. "Not that I took notice of," he answered. When asked if he ever stated to anyone that he held a cocked pistol aimed at the head of a man he believed connected to McKinstry. Owens answered that he had not.[21]

This brought the prosecution's presentation to a close. McKinstry requested that he be allowed until the following Monday morning, September 15, to prepare his defense. When the court convened after the weekend, one of the members, Major Fitzgerald, was ill. The court moved to his quarters, its members, the judge advocate, and the accused all crowding into Fitzgerald's sickroom. McKinstry made his closing statement standing at the side of Fitzgerald's bed. After deliberation, the court found: of the specification of the 1st charge: guilty; of the first charge: guilty; of the specification of the 2nd charge: the court found for the facts as set forth in the specification of the 2nd charge: not guilty; of the specification of the additional charge: the court found for the facts as set forth in the specification of the additional charge: not guilty.[22]

Based on the finding of guilty on the one charge and specification, the court sentenced McKinstry to be suspended from rank, emoluments, and pay for a period of three months and to be reprimanded in orders by the general commanding the Pacific Division. Brigadier General Persifor F. Smith, on reviewing the transcript and findings of the court, raised objections that McKinstry had been allowed to read into the record his opening statement attacking the witnesses and the evidence that might be presented against him before the witnesses had been heard or the evidence examined. Still, Smith confirmed the verdict and the sentence of the court, and ended his reprimand with the statement, "In inflicting the censure awarded by the court, nothing can be added to the pain Brevet Major McKinstry must already feel, knowing that the testimony recorded in these pages is to remain henceforward in the archives of the army."[23]

McKinstry forwarded his monthly return for September, 1850, to the quartermaster's department at Washington from San Diego on October 2. Then, without post or position, suspended and on his own for the first time since he entered West Point almost 20 years in the past, he traveled northward by coastal steamer and arrived at San Francisco on October 23. Throughout his life, Justus McKinstry did not develop lasting relationships with others. There is no evidence in the archives and files stating that his classmates at the military academy claimed him as one of their own. Likewise, there is no evidence of McKinstry claiming such a relationship with any of them. His commanders and fellow officers mentioned him in their correspondence only in passing. Those of his superiors who wrote letters of recommendation for him did so out of duty as they would for any subordinate seeking promotion or transfer. Sometime in 1850, his brother, Elisha, left his position as McKinstry's clerk and his law practice in San Diego to relocate to Napa; thereafter, there were few contacts between Justus and Elisha, not even through members of their families. Elisha prospered after leaving the shadow of his older brother. In 1852, he was elected to a six year term as judge of California's Seventh District Court, and in 1873, he was appointed a justice of the California Supreme Court. In his reminiscences, written late in life at age 75, Elisha makes no mention of Justus by name, merely writing that his brother entered West Point as a cadet and "afterwards served in California." William H. Richardson had followed McKinstry from Mexico to California but that relationship was based more on the prospect of mutual gain than on affection or respect. Samuel Heintzelman befriended McKinstry prior to and during their time in California but afterwards their paths veered away from each other. Of his own family in Ypsilanti, no record of correspondence has been found other than in the case of this father's ill health. McKinstry did spend time between assignments with his family there but there is no evidence of any attempt at maintaining contact. Of Susan's family in Hudson, her brother, Augustus, openly despised the man. Susan's brother, George, with whom McKinstry engaged in business in California, eventually tried to have him dismissed from the army. Other than the loyal and trusting Susan, there was no one in McKinstry's life for any extent of time from whom he could seek help or support. McKinstry led a lonely life, not having anyone to whom he could turn for counsel or guidance and not really indicating a need for anyone. When he suddenly found himself suspended and on his own at San Francisco in the fall of 1850, the only person he knew well enough to approach was his fellow quartermaster, Major Robert Allen. Allen had been appointed to the military academy from Indiana in 1832. He and McKinstry entered West Point as plebes in the same class. However, McKinstry had resigned and been appointed to the following class upon his reinstatement. He and Allen were fellow cadets during the remaining three years until Allen graduated and was commissioned a second lieutenant in the 2nd Artillery in 1836. Allen served in Florida and Mexico where he earned his brevet majority for gallantry at the battle of Cerro Gordo. Allen was appointed to the expanded quartermaster's department in 1847 and, alongside McKinstry, served with the supply train during the advance on the Mexican capital and in the quartermaster's depot in Mexico City under the ailing Captain Irwin. After Irwin's death, Allen was put in charge of the depot and became McKinstry's commanding officer for a time. When McKinstry arrived in San Francisco, Allen was chief quartermaster of the Pacific Division. On October 24, McKinstry wrote to Allen at headquarters at Benicia, near San Francisco. He had not yet learned of the confirmation of the

McKinstry's younger brother, Elisha McKinstry, accompanied the quartermaster to California as his clerk, but the two parted and there was little contact between the brothers or their families. Subsequently, Elisha became a California Supreme Court Justice. (Columbia County Historical Society, Kinderhook, NY)

sentence of his court-martial and he asked Allen to look into the issue for him. There was no indication of remorse or even a hint of culpability in the letter, only regret at events that had befallen him, and his version of the affair with Couts.

> I arrived here night before last from San Diego and am desirous of learning the result of my court-martial. Your position is such to afford an unusual facility toward forming a correct opinion as to the result, even if it is not to be promulgated for some time.
>
> I think I mentioned to you that Colonel Donnelly, Barton, and myself were working one hundred Mexicans in the mines on Amador Creek and when I left there I

was led to believe that new prospects of success were exceedingly good and I flattered myself that a "good time was coming." The roof has fallen in. Almost the first man I met on landing was the Colonel. Three weeks after my departure the concern blew up and I am minus my little all, and in debt. I left at Bensky & Co. a note written by Wheeler (the purchaser of our property in Nicolaus) to George McK. and myself and due on the 30th Sept. I had the assurance of Dr. Nicolaus's agent that the money would be paid when due but I find that, instead of the money, I must foreclose the mortgage and again I am deceived and betrayed on all sides. I am almost as pretty a wreck as can be found. I can now form no idea as to what I shall do or — if compelled to leave the service, can I look to you for some type of employment? I believe I am able, and I know I am willing, to work at any honest employment.

In regard to the court, or rather, my trial, I will simply remark that not one of the allegations contained in Mr. Couts's letter — except the playing him [which] passed on if public opinion is any criteria — I would not now have to face a dismissal. I would call your attention to my defense in order that you may see the difficulties under which I labored. My sense of propriety interdicted any steps on my part that would introduce a lady's name. Consequently, the actions that actuate Couts would only be made manifest. I have learned a lesson in its inferences and effects. Couts's and Evans's brothers have some terrible business and wore their revolvers constantly. They had many opportunities of making good their threats but I am satisfied that they came to the conclusion that a demonstration on their part might prove fatal: discretion, you know, is often times the better part of valor. I am not well nor happy. My wife is ill [in Hudson] and I shall have to go to Sacramento to foreclose the contracts I hold on the property I mortgaged — but should wait here the decision of the court unless the proceedings have gone to Washington, which I think not.[24]

The suspended quartermaster quickly got over feeling sorry for himself. A month and a half later he wrote to his brother-in-law from San Francisco on December 12, 1850, sending George $700 and blaming his delay in departing the city before the coming Monday on the municipal surveyor. A property Justus and George owned on Vine Street was in the process of being subdivided into 14 building lots and McKinstry reported he had found purchasers for three or four of them. "There are immense quantities of real estate now in the market," he wrote, "and owners seem determined to realize at about any price."[25]

In the final month of 1850 an issue other than land speculation rose to occupy McKinstry's attention. The 1848 charge against Cave Couts of conduct unbecoming an officer had worked its way to the top of the army's list of priorities. Couts had been ordered to remain on active duty after allegations of receiving profits from a Los Angeles gambling operation were made against him, awaiting the arrival from the east of sufficient officers to form a court to try him. He was notified on December 27 to consider himself under arrest and to prepare to stand before a general court-martial that would convene at San Francisco on January 27, 1851. Similar to what had taken place during McKinstry's San Diego court-martial, a last minute additional charge was entered against Couts of conduct prejudicial to good order and military discipline. The prosecuting witness entering the charge was McKinstry himself, specifying that Couts had written the article published in the *Alta California* during his own court-martial stating that McKinstry had a friend on the court, Major Heintzelman, and that the two of them had operated a "little house" in San Diego. On February 1, 1851, the general court-martial found Couts not guilty of all the charges and specifications including the additional charge and specification entered by McKinstry. The president of the court, Major John B. Magruder, berated McKinstry in the court's official record for having brought forward the charge and specification without sufficient evidence to substantiate it.[26]

McKinstry's imposed period of suspension ended in February, 1851. He returned to duty and resumed his quartermaster's functions. He wrote on March 29 from Stockton to Lieutenant J. S. Windrum, assistant quartermaster at Camp Frémont, questioning a requisition for dragoon saddles and bridles. On April 5, he wrote to Major Allen at Benicia, forwarding duplicates and receipts and, on April 14, he mailed his quarterly return to the quartermaster's department at Washington from Stockton. On May 8, McKinstry acted on behalf of the government of the United States when he, with Captain Henry Burton, accepted the surrender and parole of William Walker and his small force of filibusters who were accused of violating the neutrality act by organizing the invasion of Baja California. McKinstry and Burton held Walker's force until they could ship it off from Rancho La Punhã, near San Diego, to headquarters at San Francisco. In June, McKinstry was in the field with troops operating against Indians. His returns through the summer and early fall are dated "Camp in the Mountains," "Upper Sacramento," "Camp on Cache Creek," and, on October 9, "Benicia." Less than a month later, McKinstry was back in San Diego. On November 3, he relieved Captain Nathaniel Lyon of the temporary duties at the quartermaster's depot that Lyon had assumed with McKinstry took to the field with the troops.[27]

On April 5, 1851, Cave Couts and Ysidora Bandini were married. Couts had been boarding at the family home since his arrival at San Diego. The wedding gift to the couple from Ysidora Bandini's father's friend, Able Stearns, who was reputed to be the wealthiest rancher in southern California, was a 2,219 acre spread close to the old Spanish mission of San Luis Rey. Six months later, Couts resigned his commission in the dragoons and began to develop his lands, eventually bring his holdings to 20,000 acres.[28]

There was unrest among the local natives during the final months of 1851. Early on the morning of November 21, a party of about a hundred Indians surrounded the ranch of Juan Jose Warner, three miles from the spring at Agua Caliente. Defending his homestead with the help of two ranch hands, Warner opened fire as the Indians approached. One of Warner's hands was killed in the exchange of gunfire and at least four of the attackers were shot. When they ran low on ammunition, Warner and the remaining hand fled on horseback leaving the ranch and its stock to pillage and fire. At about the same time, four white men were murdered by renegades close to Agua Caliente. A total of nine white men died in the uprising. Two columns of civilians formed and set out from San Diego on November 27. Cave Couts, now a civilian, rode with the column led by Major G. B. Fitzgerald. On December 2, Fitzgerald's column destroyed the Indian villages near Agua Caliente and rode on to the Warner Ranch which they found burned and totally desolate. The second column, under Colonel Augustin Haraszthy, captured and brought in the renegade known as Bill Marshall who was thought to be responsible for the murders at Agua Caliente and who was suspected of instigating the uprising. At the same time, local Indians brought in Juan Verdugo, one of the outlaw chiefs. Marshall and Vergugo stood trial in San Diego on December 9. Colonel Haraszthy sat as president of the court, Judge H. H. Robinson prosecuted on behalf of the people, and McKinstry volunteered his services as attorney for the defense. At 2:00 p. m. on the afternoon of Saturday, December 13, 1851, Marshall and Verdugo were hanged from a scaffold in the plaza at San Diego. Soon afterwards, Antonio Garra, the chief of the band of Indians residing in the vicinity of Warner's Ranch, was taken and brought before the same court that had tried and condemned Marshall and Verdugo. McKinstry again volunteered his services and conducted the defense. On January 10, 1852, Garra was shot by a firing squad furnished by the local garrison, a company of the 2nd Infantry.[29]

Some time during the month of February, 1852, McKinstry signed a quitclaim contract with Jose Joaquin Ortega and his son-in-law, Edward Stokes, for the purchase option on the Rancho Santa Ysabel located 53 miles northeast of San Diego. Rancho Santa Ysabel consisted of four square leagues of San Diego County, some 17,708 acres of land, the title to which had been granted by the Mexican government to Ortega and Stokes in 1844. McKinstry's contract was conditional on Ortega and Stokes having the Mexican land grant patented and confirmed under United States law. W. C. Ferrell, the attorney representing Ortega and Stokes in the transaction, said the terms of the agreement were $4,000 down and $4,000 to be paid when the original owners were able to provide a clear title to the land. Ferrell added that it was his understanding that McKinstry bought the land on behalf of his wife whose money he had out in California to invest. This is highly unlikely since Susan's well-being depended almost entirely on McKinstry's army salary and some small assistance from her brother, Augustus, in Hudson. Later in her life, Susan would claim that none of her own funds had gone into the purchase of Santa Ysabel.[30]

The story of Rancho Santa Ysabel began in the 18th century when Spanish Franciscan fathers at Mission San Diego grazed large herds of cattle and sheep in its lush valleys during the summer months when grass and grain were scarce along the coast. In 1818, the fathers began construction of buildings at Santa Ysabel which included an adobe chapel, a granary, several houses, and a cemetery. In 1834, the Mexican government forced the Catholic church to give up its extensive mission holdings and for the next decade Santa Ysabel — Saint Elizabeth, in English — was without ownership until it was conveyed by the land grant from the Mexican government to Ortega and Stokes.[31]

The special significance of Santa Ysabel lay in its location in the mountains northeast of San Diego, and its water, grain, and grass. The United States Army was operating against the western Indians out of Fort Yuma, in Arizona Territory, where the Gila River flowed into the Colorado River, the same point from which Major Emory and the boundary survey commission had jumped off on the way eastward. Major Heintzelman had established the post in 1851. Supply of the troops at Fort Yuma was accomplished through the quartermaster's depot at San Diego which was the closest American port into which American flag vessels could carry troops and military supplies. Fort Yuma lay more then 200 tortuous miles inland over mountains, deserts, and barren landscape. The horses and mules of the supply trains from San Diego would exhaust the forage and water they carried with them by the time they reached the vicinity of Santa Ysabel and they still faced ten or eleven days of harsh travel before they arrived at the mouth of the Gila. McKinstry began grazing government herds at Santa Ysabel as soon as he took temporary title to the place. H. W. G. Clements, McKinstry's clerk after the departure of his brother, Elisha, testified to the beneficial effects of Santa Ysabel on the government's horses and mules. He said there were grass and water at all seasons of the year and the trains coming and going in each direction were able to exchange animals at Santa Ysabel. He said the animals improved materially in a very short time. When asked whether Santa Ysabel was superior to other localities on the route from San Diego to Fort Yuma for herding and grazing animals, Clements replied, "I have traveled it, I think, five or six times, backwards and forwards, from San Diego to Fort Yuma. I don't know of any place so convenient for the government purposes. There may be little valleys which would keep the herds for a month or two, but the year through, there is no such place as Santa Ysabel." McKinstry's enterprise won praise from Major Osborn Cross, Robert Allen's replacement as chief quartermaster of the Pacific Division, who wrote on August 31, 1852, that the depot at San Diego was the most expensive one in California other then the main depot at Benicia, because of the need to keep up the wagon trains to supply Fort Yuma, but he was "pleased to find that under the admirable system now adopted by Major McKinstry, the depot quartermaster, much public property is saved, and particularly, public animals, compared to the loss heretofore at that station, previously to his taking it." On the last day of February, McKinstry was on duty at the depot at San Diego, corresponding with 2nd Lieutenant Francis E. Patterson, currently the regimental acting assistant quartermaster of the 2nd Infantry's garrison there. On April 15, McKinstry mailed his quarterly return to the quartermaster's department at Washington from San Diego.[32]

In May of the following year, there began a complicated and questionable series of transactions involving purchases of hay and grass by the quartermaster's depot at San Diego for the forage of animals on the route to and from the Gila. Men were hired to cut hay which they were told to bring to Santa Ysabel. Indians were told to cut grass in the valleys close to the rancho and carry it to the wagon road where army officers would give them receipts for what their commands consumed in passing. Farmers were instructed to cut hay and grass and bring it to the San Diego depot. In the testimony of several merchants who regularly dealt in hay and grass, more tons of forage were paid for by the quartermaster's department at the San Diego depot in 1852 under these arrangements than ever could have been grown and harvested locally during the entire season. Francis R. Maretowsky, a recent immigrant from the states in the east, told people in and around San Diego that he had the contract for cutting and delivering hay and grass to the quartermaster's depot. The men who actually cut and delivered the forage testified later they never saw Maretowsky when the work was being done. When the Indians who cut and hauled grass to the wagon road, numbering some one hundred, came to the San Diego depot for payment, McKinstry told them he could not accept the receipts they offered, stating that he did not think the quartermaster's department nor the treasury would accept the receipt of an Indian as the basis for reimbursing him for his disbursement of government funds. Instead, McKinstry had citizens who were present, including Frank Maretowsky, take up the Indians' receipts on the premise of settling with them later. The citizens signed the receipts and McKinstry paid them. Arrangements must have been made to settle with the Indians because they departed, apparently satisfied. On May 20, Maretowsky signed a voucher and receipt drawn on the quartermaster's department in the amount of $7,500 for 250 tons of hay delivered at various locations between February 20 and May 5, 1852. The court of inquiry that later investigated this matter never could determine whether 250 tons of hay had been delivered to the depot by Maretowsky, by the ranchers, by the Indians, or by others. Maretowsky had a reputation as a gambler and a dishonest man. Louis A. Franklin, a citizen of San Diego, would later testify as to whether he knew if McKinstry gave money or other consideration to Maretowsky to get him to sign a false voucher: "I have heard Frank Maretowsky so state, and subsequently deny it." Lorenzo Soto, Maretowsky's partner in several business transactions, when asked whether he knew if McKinstry gave money or other consideration to anyone to sign a false voucher, said Maretowsky had come to him to sign a paper in the amount of $5,000 against the United States. Soto testified that he refused, but Frank Maretowsky told him he would sign it himself and Major McKinstry would give him $500 and a wagon for doing so. During the haying season at San Diego, carts, wagons, and pack mules bearing hay and grass were sent in many directions on behalf of the quartermaster's department. Watching and recording all of this was Cave Couts. The bad blood between McKinstry and Couts had not settled. Couts's life had taken a new direction after his resignation from the army and his becoming a major landholder through the generous gift of a friend of his wife's family but the former dragoon was not one to forgive what he considered a wrong.[33]

Samuel Heintzelman wrote to McKinstry from Fort Yuma on September 23, a letter opening with a statement that he was glad McKinstry had returned from exile in the north. Heintzelman was commanding companies of the 2nd Infantry operating from Fort Yuma. His letter brought McKinstry up to date on army matters and gossip and some speculations having to do with promotions. It closed with the postscript, "[Couts and his friends] talk plain. He doesn't think much of the General's opinion and talks of asking for [another] court-martial. You know how little he values your reprimand."[34]

On October 8, 1852, the citizens of San Diego County convened to make their nominations for the November elections, the second since statehood had been achieved two years earlier. Among the candidates was Cave Couts standing on the democratic ticket for state senator. After dark, three government wagons drawn by teams of government mules arrived at the polling site with about 30 employees of the quartermaster's depot aboard. The late arrivals, according to several witnesses, started fights and broke up the convention, driving away most of the candidates and their supporters. The interlopers then put forward the names of three of their number, all employees of the quartermaster's depot: William Conroy, the wagon master, for sheriff; D. B. Kurtz, a carpenter, for state senator; and Thomas H. Tilghman, a clerk, for the state house of representatives. In the primary election that followed, Couts was defeated. Conroy, the wagon master, later testified that he took the wagons and mules from the depot without McKinstry's knowledge or consent, stating that he told the men with him they would wait until dark and, when McKinstry went to his house, they would hitch up and drive away. In the general election a month later, Conroy, Kurtz, and Tilghman were elected. Kurtz's seat was confirmed. Tilghman's nomination and election were contested and investigated by the legislature but further action was tabled. All three men took their offices and served their terms. During the election, the two companies of the 2nd Infantry stationed at San Diego were commanded by Captains Henry E. Burton and John B. Magruder. Captain Charles P. Stone, ordnance department, testified later that both officers told him most of the men in their commands had voted in the election but, to the best of the knowledge of either officer, there had been no undue influence by McKinstry to effect their choices. Burton and Magruder each gave McKinstry written statements to this effect. Stone later testified that, on the day of the election and for ten days thereafter, he and McKinstry were traveling to Fort Yuma and serving on a court-martial there, McKinstry as the judge advocate and Stone as a member of the court.[35]

George McKinstry was now living at Santa Ysabel, managing the government herds and operating a small store selling to the teamsters and army express riders passing on the road between San Diego and Fort Yuma. George began grazing horses and cattle belonging to private parties along with the government's animals, charging the private parties a fee. Captain Magruder corresponded with George in May, 1853, on what would be the proper cost for keeping cattle belonging to Magruder's wife. An arbitrator, D. W. Sandequito, established the price at one and a half cents per head per day, or $45 per hundred head per month, the keeper being responsible for the loss of any stock.[36]

What was taking place at Santa Ysabel became the basis of rumor and speculation among the people of San Diego County. The fact that the officer responsible for the maintenance and feeding of government animals was also the owner of record of the ranch on which most of the government's stock was herded and fed did not pass without comment. In question was the source of the funds for the down payment of the purchase price of the ranch. Was this money that McKinstry's wife sent to California for investment, as he claimed, or had it come from the quartermaster's money chest in exchange for vouchers fraudulently signed by Frank Maretowsky shortly after the purchase had been arranged? For more than six months, toward the latter part of 1852 and the early part of 1853, George McKinstry, while managing the private affairs of Santa Ysabel and herding stock for private parties for pay, was carried on the books of the quartermaster's depot at San Diego as a government employee as were others working for George at Santa Ysabel. This was known and discussed openly and there was speculation among the people of San Diego County regarding what was happening at Santa Ysabel.[37]

A major disagreement developed between the brothers-in-law involving the animals at Santa Ysabel. Justus insisted that the government not be charged for herding and grazing public animals there. George claimed that the government should pay its fair cost since the amount involved would have run into thousands of dollars. 1st Lieutenant Asher R. Eddy, 1st Artillery, then acting assistant quartermaster with the San Diego garrison, later testified that George told him he never received money from the government for the use of the ranch. Eddy suggested that George take the matter up with Major Cross, chief quartermaster of the Pacific Division, but George did not do this. Justus was now being extremely careful regarding what took place at Santa Ysabel. J. N. King, a quartermaster's employee at the ranch, testified that his instructions from McKinstry were that no public property should be used improperly. "He gave as his reason," King said, "that a scoundrel by the name of Mr. Couts was spying all his movements, and he wished his agents' as well as his own hands to be clean."[38]

Couts persisted. On May 2, 1853, he again wrote Quartermaster General Jesup. He gave details of the quartermaster's employees breaking up and taking over the political convention at San Diego and accused McKinstry of hiring potential candidates at high salaries to either run against Couts or refrain from supporting him. "The county of San Diego has a very sparse population," the former dragoon wrote, "and with such a quartermaster, these employees are bound to control our local elections." Couts went into detail about how McKinstry's penchant for gambling should disqualify him from a position as a government disbursing officer. Couts declared that McKinstry had been involved in a heavy game of brag at his quarters at San Diego, "and a day or two afterwards was in this town 'tapping the monte banks' in public bar rooms." Couts brought up the issue of the Mexico City court-martial and mistakenly inferred that McKinstry had been found guilty there. He wrote that McKinstry "gave one Frank Maretowsky a large sum of money and a wagon to sign him a receipt against the government for five thousand dollars, the receipt purporting to be for grain, or hay, or both." Couts repeated the talk of the town that McKinstry maintained Santa Ysabel at the expense of the quartermaster's department. He closed his letter writing, "Having but recently resigned from the army, to which I have so much respect and admiration, and located probably for life in San Diego, my object evidently being his removal from this place." Handwritten on the back of Couts's letter in the archives is the notation, "The charges against Major McKinstry are of so serious a nature that I consider it due him, as well as to the character of the public service, to ask that the matters be made the subject of a military inquiry. Major McKinstry would, no doubt, ask for an inquiry were he acquainted with the charges. I respectfully ask that a court be ordered, by the authority of the President, to investigate the charges preferred. (signed) Thomas. S. Jesup, Quartermaster General." Couts published his letter to Jesup in the San Diego newspaper. McKinstry immediately began calling on his own resources to negate the letter's possible effect. The late governor of California, J. D. McDougal, wrote to Secretary of War Jefferson Davis on McKinstry's behalf, blaming politics for the problems that had risen between the two men. "The people of our state," he wrote, "will feel much regret at his removal, and I trust, as he had just gotten his family out here, that he will be permitted to remain." As the governor stated, Susan and the boys had recently arrived in California. On May 9, 1853, Heintzelman wrote to George McKinstry in San Diego from Fort Yuma: "Mrs. McKinstry and her children had a narrow escape. It was too bad, after running the gauntlet of yellow fever [crossing Panama] to be carried by and shipwrecked here."[39]

Special Orders No. 61, Headquarters, Pacific Division, by direction of the secretary of war, called for a court of inquiry to assemble at San Diego on December 1, 1853, "to examine into certain accusations made against Brevet Major McKinstry by C. J. Couts. The court will report the facts and an opinion." The members of the court of inquiry were Brevet Major Amos B. Eaton, commissary of subsistence; Brevet Major Henry W. Wessels, 2nd Infantry, who had sat on McKinstry's court-martial three years earlier; and Brevet Captain Charles P. Stone, ordnance, who was also the recorder. The court did not meet as scheduled, but later in the month, and then it met for 12 days, taking Christmas Day off. The court investigated the charges against McKinstry: exercising undue interference at the San Diego convention in 1852; gambling in his own quarters and at public gaming tables; bribing Frank Maretowsky to sign a fraudulent voucher against the United States; maintaining Santa Ysabel at the expense of the quartermaster's department; paying some employees at the depot less money than they had signed vouchers for; and transporting private goods in government wagons. The court of inquiry's final report was anything but concise and specific. The court found that government wagons carrying government employees had been driven to the democratic convention at San Diego in October, 1852, but that, in the opinion of the members of the court, this had been done without the sanction or knowledge of McKinstry. It found no evidence to support the charge that McKinstry had gambled in his own quarters or at public gaming tables. It found no evidence to support the charge of bribery. It did find that during the second quarter of 1852, Frank Maretowsky had signed two vouchers against the United States—one for 250 *fanegas* of barley at $8 per *fanega,* and one for 250 tons of hay at $30 per ton. It reported that Maretowsky had furnished a portion of the barley while the remainder was probably furnished by Indians who were paid by having their claims introduced into Maretowsky's voucher. The court found no evidence of a third transaction involving 210 tons of hay other than vouchers for the labor of the men involved in bringing it in. The court gave as its opinion that these several transactions involved unnecessary departures from the system subscribed in army regulations. The court opined that Santa Ysabel was the property of Mrs. McKinstry, that the ranch had been used as a sub-depot for the feeding and grazing of public animals, and that McKinstry had not been paid for its use or for the grass consumed by the public animals. The court also found no evidence that the ranch had been improperly maintained at the expense of the quartermaster's department. However, in the opinion of the court, there had been unnecessary mingling of public and private interests in the management of its affairs. The court found no evidence of an employee of the quartermaster's department being paid less that the vouchers he signed. Finally, the court found that public wagons had transported private goods from San Diego to George McKinstry's store at Santa Ysabel, but that Major McKinstry had not interest in the goods nor did he receive any pay for their transport, and there had been no effort on his part to conceal the actions from his superiors. The court commented that at the special request of Major McKinstry, it made a thorough examination of his accounts and papers and placed in the appendix copies of all documents that might reveal information on the subjects investigated. The court complained that it had been greatly inconvenienced by the fact that so much time had elapsed between the occurrence and the investigation and that much of the evidence had been, on the most part, conflicting and unsatisfactory.[40]

Brigadier General Ethan Allen Hitchcock commanded the Pacific Division

Ethan Allen Hitchcock knew McKinstry throughout his military career. Hitchcock wrote the order authorizing the McKinstry Volunteers in Mexico, and reviewed the San Diego court of inquiry, ordering McKinstry to northern California instead of to a court-martial. (Library of Congress)

of the army at this time. He reviewed the findings of the court of inquiry and its opinion. Normal procedure would have been for Hitchcock to order a court-martial to convene and take further action. Hitchcock, who knew McKinstry from as far back as his cadet days at West Point through his time in Florida and in Mexico, decided on an unusual course of action. Realizing that hard evidence to support the allegations probably would not be readily available after the passage of so much time, he thoughtfully and carefully issued his determination. He wrote that he had examined the testimony and opinion of the court of inquiry. He approved of the proceedings of the court and concurred with its opinion. However, it appeared to him "that Brevet Major McKinstry has been instrumental in creating embarrassments in the execution of his public duties at San Diego. Therefore, McKinstry was relieved of duty at the San Diego depot and his place would be filled by Lieutenant Eddy. McKinstry was ordered without unnecessary delay to depart for Fort Redding and to report to the commanding officer there. This change of station, Hitchcock noted, had been rendered necessary by the condition of things brought about by McKinstry himself, first by making contracts with Frank Maretowsky, and second, by the purchase of a ranch so situated as to make it difficult, if not impossible, to discharge his public duties without the hazard of mingling private with public interests. In giving these orders, Hitchcock cautiously wrote, he did not assume that any actual pecuniary loss had been sustained by the United States in the payment of Maretowsky's vouchers, nor did he deny the right of an officer to purchase in his own name, or in his wife's name, property on the market for sale. "But it is not just," he wrote, "either to the officer, to the quartermaster's department, or to the army that an officer should be required to remain at a post where he cannot discharge his public duties without incurring suspicion, to the prejudice of his own and the public interest, and when, as in the present case, the embarrassments have been created chiefly by the agency of the officer himself, it becomes more imperatively necessary to change his station." As ordered, McKinstry turned over his responsibilities to Lieutenant Eddy and reported to Fort Redding, 150 miles north of Sacramento, near present Reading, California. He did not remain there long.[41]

Cave Couts was still determined to see the last of McKinstry and he was furious at what took place after McKinstry arrived at Fort Redding. Couts wrote again to Jesup on June 4, 1854, "Ask you carefully to review the proceedings of the late Court of Inquiry at San Diego, examining the testimony of Justus McKinstry. The opinion of the court I have not seen and only know that it resulted in his immediate removal from this place by General Hitchcock. After his arrival at San Francisco, after having been relieved from this depot, it appears he met with General Wool and ingratiated himself so much as to get the promise of being ordered back to San Diego as soon as General Hitchcock left the country. One steamer leaves with General Hitchcock for the Atlantic states, and the next brings Major McKinstry back to San Diego."[42]

McKinstry re-established himself at San Diego in his house off the plaza with Susan and the boys, resuming command of the quartermaster's depot while, at the same time, buying and selling and transacting business involving the private operations at Santa Ysabel. Couts was determined to drive the quartermaster from the land. At his urging, a civil grand jury sitting in the court of sessions for San Diego County in December, 1854, entered a bill of indictment — "The state of California vs. Justus McKinstry"—that laid out in detail the transactions involving Maretowsky and the contracts for hay and grass, and concluded with, "The Grand Jury find Justus McKinstry guilty of the crime of embezzling money from the United States." McKinstry's civilian lawyer had the bill of indictment quashed on the grounds of jurisdiction: matters taking place within the military establishment were not the concern of the citizens of San Diego County.[43]

Shortly after the turn of the year, McKinstry received orders to return to the east. He traveled north from San Diego during the early months of 1855, winding up his personal affairs. He wrote on February 11 from San Francisco to H. W. G. Clements, his clerk at San Diego, that he would "thank you to send from my chest my 'Lawyer's Assistant.' You will also, I think, find a bundle of bills which I want as I do not remember the cost of my household property. Mr. Keene has one of our horses—do you have receipts?" He mailed returns to the quartermaster's department at Washington from San Diego on March 10 and March 15. On April 12, 1855, he was at Washington, writing to the quartermaster general regarding the suspension of several vouchers he had issued while in California.[44]

This brought to a close a significant period in McKinstry's life. He was now 41 years old with 17 years in the army. He was married to a loving and supportive wife and the couple had two sons, 12 and ten years of age. The future of the little family should have been secure as it looked forward to its return to the east, yet McKinstry had brought himself and his family close to disruption and destitution through the corrupt and even careless antics he perpetrated while in California. There was a long interval of time and a great distance between what had taken place in Mexico earlier and his subsequent dealings in California. McKinstry could have left the Mexican incidents behind and made a fresh start but instead he lost no time getting back into the pattern of corruption, theft, and disregard for the rules that had become his nature as soon as he landed at San Diego.

In the middle of the 19th century, corruption and fraud ran rampant in American society, especially in the far west. In California, men wore revolvers on their belts for a purpose; indeed, claim jumping was a rewarding profession, if successful. Yet, society had not lost its basic understanding of what was right and wrong. Successful thieves were still thieves in the eyes of most of the public. The United States Army was a reflection of American society and a corrupt army officer using his position and power for personal gain was still seen by the majority of those in the officer corps as a corrupt officer. There were some flagrant cases of waste, fraud, and abuse of power in the army. The *New York Evening Post*, for example, reported the commander of Fort Riley, Kansas, shifting military property to the public domain, buying it himself, and building and selling town lots on the land. He was court-martialed, of course, yet he stands as an example along with McKinstry of corruption in the army and in society.[45]

By this time McKinstry had earned the reputation throughout the United

States Army of a corrupt officer. He was a rogue who operated outside the ranks and rules of the officer corps. He never had another officer as a close accomplice in Mexico or in California. He acted alone, either because he would not permit another officer to share in his gains, or because he could not find another officer willing to join him in his dangerous and only minimally rewarding enterprises. In Mexico, his endeavors were known to his fellow officers, but much of what he and Garcia were doing was out of sight of other eyes. However, in California, McKinstry made no attempt to hide what he was about. Santa Ysabel consisted of more than 17,000 acres of land lying directly across the main route from the quartermaster's depot at San Diego to the forces operating in the field out of Fort Yuma. Citizens and soldiers alike were not able to overlook the existence of Santa Ysabel and the questionable events surrounding its acquisition, ownership, and operation. The blatantly visible transactions that McKinstry conducted with Maretowsky were common knowledge among the citizenry of San Diego County. McKinstry's affairs eventually reached the point where the local citizenry through the grand jury tried to bring him to account when the army was unable or unwilling to do so. It is unbelievable that the army did not take effective measures to stop the embarrassing disregard of the basic elements of its code of conduct and discipline. In California, the only person willing to act was Cave Couts and his motives were based on revenge more than indignation. In Mexico, it had been the falling out with Garcia that resulted in the army ordering the court of inquiry. The office of the inspector general — the senior officer in the army charged with finding and eliminating waste, fraud, and abuse — initiated no action in either case. The quartermaster general took action only after being confronted by Couts's letters several years after making empty threats of action based on the records from Mexico. This was the United States Army of the mid-19th century. This army had its own morals and methods, its own means for investigating and determining action when called upon to do so but, apparently, only after it was found to be unavoidable. In California, McKinstry was charged with offenses, tried by a court-martial, found guilty, and suspended for three months. Justice had, in army terms, been done. Once again, he was charged, investigated by a court of inquiry, and, although not tried and convicted, he was denounced and transferred by his departmental commander. Again, in army terms, justice had been done. The army had satisfied itself in its own fashion. This was the army's way. This was the army's officers corps way.

What is ironic is that it was also Justus McKinstry's way. He did what he wanted to do, gained what he wanted to gain, and came through unscathed, unharmed, unchanged, and unrepentant.

When he was transferred to the east, he still held claim to the title of Santa Ysabel yet there is no indication that he brought any significant amount of money with him. He did bring a blemished record, although one that did not bar him from further assignments in the army's quartermaster corps.

After Justus, Susan, and the boys left for the east, George McKinstry continued to manage affairs at Santa Ysabel while residing in San Diego. He wrote on December 11, 1855, to Francis Ames, a commission agent, with instructions to pay Frank Maretowsky $50 on behalf of the ranch. Prior to that, he had obtained a receipt from San Diego County for $120, the total of the state and local taxes on the 17,000 acre spread, which was valued for that year at $4,400. The original quitclaim for the purchase of Santa Ysabel called for a second final payment of $4,000 to Ortega and Stokes when they could provide a clear title to the land under California and United States laws; this did not happen until May 21, 1866. By then, George had lost interest in the ranch with his sister and brother-in-law off in the east. Ortega and Stokes eventually sold the ranch to other parties. George took up the practice of medicine and began using, and being addressed by, the title "doctor." He was appointed collector of customs for the port of San Diego while continuing his medical practice from the front parlor of the family home of John and Seraphina Minter with whom he boarded. He never married. He did maintain a correspondence with his brother, Augustus, and sister, Jane, in Hudson until his death in 1890. He carried for the rest of his life an abiding hatred for his second cousin and brother-in-law.[46]

Cave Couts continued to develop his lands. He was appointed by the governor to the judgeship of San Diego County in 1854. During the same year he was indicted twice for attempted manslaughter, in both cases for whipping Indian servants with a leather *riata*. In the first case, the charge was dropped. In the second, Couts was released on a technicality: it was learned that one of the men on the jury was not an American citizen. Later, in 1863, an epidemic of smallpox swept San Diego County. Couts, then serving as justice of the peace, sent his brother and two servants armed with shotguns to stop a burial Couts suspected was being done improperly. Firing broke out at the burial site; one of the mourners was shot dead and two others were injured. Couts and his brother were charged with murder. When the case came to trial two years later, the matter had to be dropped because the district attorney had failed to post the bond required for his term of office. Couts's penchant for violence did not abate. On February 6, 1865, Juan Mendoza, a "revolutionary" and former hand at the Couts ranch, rode into the plaza of Old San Diego. Couts, who was standing on the plaza, mentioned to a bystander that Mendoza once had threatened his life. When Mendoza approached him, Couts fired twice with his shotgun, killing Mendoza. A year and a half later when Couts's trial was held, he was found not guilty of murder. It became known that several men serving as jurors at his trial had put up the money for his bond while the trial was pending. There was another incident that took place at Couts's ranch on May 7, 1870, when a tutor, Waldemar Müller, opened the door to Couts's bedroom one night, possibly thinking he was opening the door to a daughter's room. Couts fired his shotgun, seriously wounding Müller in the arm and side. Müller did not press charges, so the matter never came to court. The former dragoon suffered serious reversals later in life. His massive ranch and his herds of cattle came up against what was known as California's "no fence law." Owners of range were required to fence their land or suffer the legal consequences of their animals straying onto the property of others. Fencing a spread of some 20,000 acres was more than Couts could handle. He was forced to sell land and stock at ruinous prices. Cave Couts died at the Horton House Hotel in San Diego on June 10, 1874, of an aneurysm that had troubled him for years. His son, Cave Couts, Jr., later divided the ranch into town lots that eventually became the city of Oceanside, California.[47]

Justus McKinstry outlived his California nemesis by more than two decades.

7

Wide Missouri

Back in the east, McKinstry was assigned to duty in the office of the quartermaster general at Washington for six months. On October 9, 1855, he submitted a request that he be returned to duty in California which was denied. He then requested leave and within weeks he, Susan, and the boys were spending the early autumn of the year with his family at Ypsilanti. This, however, did not last. On November 20, McKinstry received orders by mail to report to Fort Brooke, at Tampa, Florida, where he was to assume the duties of chief quartermaster of the Department of Florida. Susan, who was pregnant again, and the boys would live with Augustus and Jane at Hudson during McKinstry's absence. He stopped briefly at Washington at the quartermaster's department on December 9. On December 22, he reported by mail from Fort Brooke.[1]

Trouble had continued between settlers and the remaining Seminoles on the Florida peninsula after the final skirmishes of the Second Seminole War. Raids and sporadic killings on both sides became a regular pattern until the War Department ordered 2,200 regulars to Florida, reinforced by several regiments of volunteers, to serve under Brigadier General William S. Harney. The force was to be supported and supplied by McKinstry's quartermaster depot at Tampa where Harney established his headquarters. Using the same tactics Zachary Taylor developed during the second war, Harney sent his men into the swamps and hammocks on forays against the natives, their villages, and their planting grounds. Harney was relieved on April 25, 1857, when problems in troubled Kansas Territory caused the Buchanan administration to send him there. Command in Florida passed to Colonel Gustavus Loomis under whom McKinstry continued to serve. Loomis declared the Third Seminole War at an end on May 8, 1858. A month later the War Department transferred all but one company of regulars out of the state. During the 30 months he served in Florida this time, McKinstry operated under the immediate observation of departmental commanders in an atmosphere that was closely controlled. He had no opportunity to broaden his endeavors anywhere close to what they had been in Mexico and California.[2]

On August 17, 1856, a third son, Carlisle P. McKinstry, to be known as "Cy," was born to Susan and Justus at Hudson. McKinstry managed to be in New York City from where he reported to the quartermaster's department by mail on October 7. On October 12, he was at Hudson attending the christening of his youngest son. McKinstry's father, David, had died a month earlier at Ypsilanti at the age of 78. There is nothing in the record to indicate whether Justus was able to visit Ypsilanti to be with his mother, his brothers and sisters, for their father's burial. McKinstry returned to Fort Brooke where, the following year on June 7 and again on September 24, he signed contracts with the Southern Steamship Line for the transport of troops and supplies from Tampa to New Orleans.[3]

After McKinstry returned to Florida and while Susan and the two boys were still living at Hudson with him, Augustus wrote to Quartermaster General Jesup on November 27, 1857, "You have a bond made by Brevet Major McKinstry, Assistant Quartermaster, United States Army, dated some time in March, 1849, and signed by Justus McKinstry, Esq., and myself. The major is, I suppose, in readiness to substitute other names." The elder Justus McKinstry, the major's namesake, passed away on May 24, 1849, thus leaving Augustus the sole person standing with his property and wealth pledged as the basis for McKinstry's performance bond. By this time, Augustus was well aware of McKinstry's reputation in the army. He had heard from his brother, George, in considerable detail about McKinstry's manipulations and transgressions while in California. Augustus was understandably anxious to protect himself from the detrimental effect of his brother-in-law's actions. There is no indication that Augustus sent McKinstry a copy of his letter to the quartermaster general.[4]

On May 12, 1858, four days after Colonel Loomis declared an end to the war in Florida, McKinstry reported himself sick at Fort Brooke, suffering from what he described as "fishita," a skin condition. He wrote to the quartermaster general that the illness incapacitated him from field duty and requested he be permitted to "repair to a northern post to seek treatment." He mailed his return from Fort Brooke on September 5, and on September 27, he was at the quartermaster's department at Washington where he remained through September 30 after which he reported from New York City on October 9. For the remainder of 1858 and most of 1859, McKinstry was on leave, awaiting further orders. He reported to the quartermaster's department during this time from both Hudson and New York City, informing the department that his address of record would be 6 State Street, Hudson. On September 1, 1859, in an effort to be remembered at headquarters, he wrote to Quartermaster General Jesup, "My leisure time here has been taken up by the study of books on the British and French *Intendant* and Commissariat departments. I have taken the liberty of forwarding two of them by mail to your address."[5]

While McKinstry was living in the same house with him, Augustus wrote a second time to the quartermaster general on August 25, 1859, and a third time on September 9, repeating his inquiry as to whether McKinstry had made arrangements for other parties to take up his bond. It is curious that Augustus addressed these queries to the quartermaster general instead of to his brother-in-law. Apparently, this final effort succeeded, either through contact with the quartermaster general or directly with McKinstry, for later Augustus would refer to the years during which he was responsible for the bond in the past tense.[6]

After more than a year of inactivity, on December 24, 1859, Special Orders No. 253, adjutant general's department, directed McKinstry to proceed from Hudson to St. Louis, Missouri, where he was to replace Captain Robert E. Clary as chief quartermaster of the Department of the West. McKinstry's responsibilities at St. Louis would involve supervising quartermaster's operations related to supplying army posts and garrisons and overseeing the movement of troops from the Canadian to the Mexican borders and from the Mississippi River to the crests of the Rocky Mountains. While covering a large geographic area, McKinstry's role and responsibilities were quite limited and closely regulated. During peacetime, major contracts were let by the quartermaster's offices in the east. Deliveries of supplies and materials were made to depots for breakdown and distribution to posts and garrisons across the continent. Requisitions were introduced at posts and stations as needs arose and were reviewed, approved, signed, and forwarded upward on established schedules. Departmental quartermasters such as McKinstry had limited discretion over the disbursement of government funds.[7]

On November 1, 1860, Augustus McKinstry at Hudson wrote to George McKinstry at San Diego, "Susan and family are still in St. Louis ... have not had but two letters from her since they left, say some 12 months ... all well when last heard from." But Augustus wrote to George again on December 27, 1860, this time almost in a state of panic, "I have been interrupted in writing by one of Major's clerks who called to have a private talk with me on the subject of your letters to parties in St. Louis, which have been shown to the Major and his wife. He says you got your information from a relative in Hudson, leaving the inference that I am that relative." Augustus wrote that he was not involved in the matter but, having been shown and permitted to read the letters, he felt he had to write regarding their content which contained serious charges and inferences against McKinstry. He continued:

> I would suggest the prospect of your discontinuing the matter on the grounds that should the Major be expelled from the Army, there might be something turn up in his accounts during the period I was on his bond and further, his dismissal may reduce his family to want. I trust you will think of this in all its light. The pecuniary mind of myself [and] the legacy of your sister might restrain any personal feelings you may have against him, for I am fully convinced that if he is dismissed from the army, that will bring disastrous effects on the whole family. You are aware that I have no love nor fear of the man, that induces me to write in this strain. I

will close with the request that you will discontinue your efforts to dismiss the man from the army on my account as well as the peace of your family.

Sister Jane wrote to George the following day expressing her deep regret and sorrow that he had mentioned to others the incident involving McKinstry she had described in a letter to George she had written the previous August. Jane wrote that Augustus had denied to Edward C. Terry, McKinstry's clerk who had called upon him, that he had ever written about the matter involved, "consequently I shall be the one censured," Jane wrote. "I regret very much that you repeated what I had written. I intended it as strictly confidential. I am asking you to burn my letters wherein it was said anything about that person, not that I have the loathing for him, but the love I feel for my sister. I would not for anything hurt her feelings." Jane wrote that Terry had reported McKinstry was telling people in St. Louis

> that you are a man of intemperate habits and they consequently establish the conclusion that you are not reliable. He also tells Mr. Terry that you borrowed four thousand dollars of him and have never paid him a cent. I think that you made a great mistake in your communication by expressing the scandal as coming from another person. When the matter is investigated, it will merely be said that you expressed what I had written, and the blow will fall on me and cause a breach between Sue and me that can never be healed. Your own personal knowledge of his vile conduct while in Cal. and his treachery toward you would have been sufficient to condemn him. I cannot blame you for the desire to revenge yourself. I am grieved that I am brought into question and blame myself for writing the affair to you. I would not have done so, had I not become exasperated by what you had written to me, his treachery towards you and the great harm he has done his wife by leading so profligate a life. Had it not been for her, I would state that I knew what his character was and I despised him. For her sake, I was obliged to be civil.

Jane expressed her sadness that things had gone the way they had. Her main concern, she wrote, was that the affectionate relationship between herself and Susan would cease and that would cause her great sorrow. "Many things will be said to injure you," she wrote, "and you will have to vindicate your cause, and alienate a wife who is ever ready to come to his rescue. Strange as it may seem, she is ready to hate the one who says a word against him. Notwithstanding she is a woman of so much sense, she is completely under his influence and duped by him in all things. I cannot blame you. His conduct toward you is unpardonable. The rascal slips through the fingers of all that attempt to touch him." Jane did not define the incident she had written to George about but it was something that had come to light while Justus and Susan were living with Augustus and herself the previous summer, and something Jane had elaborated upon in response to George's telling of the difficulties that had arisen between himself and Justus.[8]

McKinstry reported at St. Louis on January 5, 1860, accompanied by Susan and the boys. Charles was now a young man of 17, James a lad of 15, and Carlisle, "Cy," a youngster of six. The family settled at 59 South 5th Street. On January

9, McKinstry formally relieved Captain Clary. His offices were on the second floor of a building at 4th Street and Washington Avenue. McKinstry moved in and began to make himself known to the merchants of the city. He renewed an acquaintance with Charles M. Elleard, a dealer with whom he had done business in San Francisco. He also introduced himself to the principals of the firm of Child, Pratt & Fox, merchants in hardware, and provided the a list of articles the quartermaster's department might need. Child, Pratt & Fox was the largest dealer in hardware west of the Mississippi River. McKinstry installed H. W. G. Clements, who was with him in California, as his chief clerk, and William L. Hahn, who had been with him in Tampa, as his cashier.[9]

Matters were relatively quiet for the chief quartermaster of the Department of the West during 1860. There were no major expeditions setting out from distant posts nor large campaigns afoot in the west although Brigadier General Harney only recently had completed confrontations with Sioux Indians on the plains, Mormons in Utah Territory, and the British in Oregon. For now, small garrisons of regular soldiers stationed at isolated forts and posts patrolled vast areas of barren country or escorted caravans of heavy wagons hauling emigrants or freight long distances. Occasionally, commands were transferred to relieve other commands. McKinstry signed a contract shortly after assuming office with Captain J. Throckmorton, owner and master of the river steamboat *Florence* "to carry two officers and twenty-seven men and their transportation to Fort Leavenworth." Witnesses to the signatures on this contract were Edward G. Terry, the clerk who would visit Augustus McKinstry in Hudson later in the year, and H. W. G. Clements. On the same day, McKinstry signed another contract with Throckmorton, presumably for the same trip up the Missouri River, "to receive on board a detachment of U. S. troops consisting of three officers and sixty enlisted men ... and four horses and such equipment as might be sent forward," and transport them further along to Omaha. Witness to this contract was Terry.[10]

Although military matters were quiet in the Department of the West in 1860, in marked contrast, political matters across the nation were reaching the point of boiling over. There were strong disagreements over the continuing existence of slavery in the southern states and whether slavery would be allowed in the new territories in the west. The waning powers of old coalitions in the south in the face of newer and stronger alliances in the north held the attention of the people of the nation. The fledgling Republican party fielded its first presidential candidate, John Charles Frémont, in the 1856 election, the first Republican-Democratic election in the nation's history. Frémont ran a close second to James Buchanan, gathering 1,400,000 votes to 1,800,000. Frémont's surprising results suggested the Republican party might be expected to do better the next time in the 1860 election. It also brought John Charles Frémont, explorer, millionaire, the "Pathfinder," to the forefront on a national level. Fremont was especially popular among the German populations of St. Louis and the Midwest.[11]

Within Missouri, people were struggling over the issues of union or secession, and freedom or slavery. Missouri had been settled by people who in their politics and their lifestyles were southern-thinking and slave-holding. With a population of 1,182,317 in the census of 1860, almost ten percent of the population of the state was listed as being slave. However, major changes began to take place in the 1840s when revolution and political displacement in Europe resulted in a large migration to Missouri, primarily Germans and Irish. Settling in St. Louis and its environs, this group who believed strongly in union and freedom was living in what had become the political, financial, social, and commercial center of the state. In that same census of 1860 that showed ten percent of the population of the state of Missouri to be slaves, the city of St. Louis reported a population of 166,733, but only 1,542, or less than one percent, were listed as slaves. The rural, agricultural population of the state and the urban, commercial population of its principle city were at odds over the volatile issues of slavery and union. In national and state elections, a strong majority of the voters in Missouri indicated the desire for compromise on the issues tearing at the fabric of the nation and the state rather than the desire to follow the more radical lead of their brethren further south. Missouri's voters fell into three groups of political philosophy. The older families, politically powerful, slave holding, and closely connected with the people of the states of the south, saw no alternative to the growing pressures within the nation other than immediate secession when and if the rest of the states of the south went out of the Union. Then there were those who favored remaining in the Union so long as there was no coercion by the federal government of southern states that did secede. Finally, there were those in Missouri who were in favor of remaining within the Union under any and all circumstances.[12]

On November 6, 1860, Abraham Lincoln of Illinois, the second candidate ever put forward by the Republican party, was elected to the presidency of the United States, an office to which he would not ascend until March 4 of the following year, a long four months off. The day following Lincoln's election, the palmetto flag was raised at Charleston, South Carolina, and on December 17, that state withdrew from the Union. The governors of the other southern states, initially those of the lower tier of slave states, began to correspond and discuss whether to follow the Palmetto State's lead. As the nation divided itself into opposing camps, nowhere was its agony more evident in splitting people apart and setting them against each other than in Missouri.

In November, 1860, the War Department ordered General Harney to the command of the Department of the West with headquarters at St. Louis. By now the fifth senior officer in the United States Army, Harney had enlisted at 18 in 1818 when McKinstry, his departmental quartermaster, was four. Harney married into the wealthy Mullanphy family of St. Louis and became closely involved with the members of St. Louis's social elite.[13]

Representing the people of St. Louis at Washington was Francis Preston Blair, Jr., St. Louis attorney and United States Congressman. Blair's father, Francis Preston Blair, Sr., had been the advisor and confidante to presidents since the administration of Andrew Jackson. Old Man Blair traveled from his home at Silver Spring, Maryland, to confer with President-elect Lincoln at his home at Springfield, Illinois, on December 11, 1860. In that conference, the two men agreed that Blair's eldest son, Montgomery, would serve in Lincoln's cabinet as postmaster general while the younger son, Frank, would see to affairs at St. Louis. Lincoln was intensely interested in ensuring that Missouri remained firmly within the Union. He counted on the Blair family, a powerful force in the state, to see to this. Many thought Lincoln's confidence was well placed: it was said that when the Blairs went out to a fight, the Blairs went out to a funeral.[14]

Earlier in 1860, Frank Blair became alarmed at the secessionist activities in the city of St. Louis and throughout Missouri. To counter this, he formed an association of citizens, known as the Safety Committee, consisting of himself, Samuel T. Glover, James O. Broadhead, John How, Oliver D. Filley, Peter I. Foy, and Julius J. Whitzig among others. All were popular among the city's Unionist German and Irish populations. The Safety Committee's responsibility was to do whatever was necessary to hold Missouri within the Union. The committee was to meet, discuss strategy, offer advice, and act in Frank Blair's stead during his frequent absences at Washington or on the political circuit. Blair also formed organizations of Union supporters first known as Wide Awakes, and later as Home Guards, in response to Minute Men clubs forming in support of the secessionist faction in the city. Blair's Home Guards began meeting and drilling in secret in halls and warehouses throughout the city. McKinstry was aware of these events but, since the army had no role in them, he was not involved.[15]

Missouri's legislature met at the state capital, Jefferson City, on the last day of 1860. The legislature's makeup did not reflect the political persuasions of the majority of the people of the state. With only a few Unionists from St. Louis present, Missouri's law-making body consisted primarily of men who were deeply southern-leaning in their politics. Incoming Governor Claiborne E. Jackson and Lieutenant Governor Thomas C. Reynolds were outspoken secessionists. The legislature passed and the governor signed into law a series of bills to arm the state militia, to curtail the power of the mayor of St. Louis, to expand the authority of the governor, and to create a police board for the city of St. Louis with appointments thereto made by the governor. The legislature also passed a bill calling for the election of delegates to a convention to consider Missouri's secession from the Union. Because of the strong feeling of the majority of the electorate to consider compromise before precipitate action, this legislation required a referendum before an act of secession could be validated.[16]

The legislature then adjourned, feeling that the outcome of the election of delegates to the convention which would take place on February 28 would result in a strong message from the citizenry that would send Missouri into the ranks of secession beside her southern sister states. The Democratic leadership of the legislature overlooked the growing political stature and the determination of Frank Blair, his local organizations, and the strong Unionist sentiment in the major cities of the state.[17]

Brigadier General David M. Frost, commander of the state's militia at St. Louis, issued an order on January 8, 1861, directing the members of his organization to muster at their armories upon hearing the pealing of the city's church bells for a period of five minutes. In one of its first overt acts, the Safety Committee discovered the bells were those of the city's Catholic churches. Oliver D. Filley and Peter I. Foy called upon Archbishop Peter R. Kenrick to protest. The two were assured by the prelate that the order had been given during his absence from the city and that he had already prohibited the use of the bells of the archdiocese for any such purpose. There was no doubt that, upon mustering in response to the pealing of the bells, the militia companies would have been ordered to seize the United States Arsenal at St. Louis which contained the largest supply of munitions and materials of war west of the Mississippi River including 60,000 muskets and accouterments, 1.5 million cartridges, and 90,000 pounds of gunpowder. In addition to the arsenal, the sub-treasury of the United States at St. Louis contained $400,000 in specie that attracted the attention of the secessionist leaders. State forces throughout the south had by this time begun seizing federal forts, arsenals, and treasuries after the secession of South Carolina, many of these state forces doing so well ahead of the formal secession of their own states. The leaders of the secessionist movement in Missouri intended to appropriate the ordnance at the arsenal and the specie at the sub-treasury as soon as practicable. The commandant at the arsenal, Major William H. Bell, a native of North Carolina, was a man with strong and open secession sympathies, who had already secretly agreed to turn the arsenal and its contents over to state authorities upon their specific demand he do so, under the presumption the arsenal's contents would be state property once the facility stood on state soil after secession. Frank Blair and the members of the Safety Committee clamored over the telegraph wires to Washington to demand the Buchanan administration replace Bell at the arsenal. This finally did take place but the belated success brought little satisfaction since Bell's replacement was Brevet Major Peter V. Hagner, a native of the District of Columbia, whose wife was the daughter of a slave-owning family and who associated with secession-minded men in the city. Blair was not satisfied with Hagner who was deemed to be "wholly out of the court," according to one of Blair's staff members. Blair unjustly doubted Hagner's loyalty. Hagner was eventually transferred to New York City where he served the nation faithfully and retired from the United States Army as a brevet brigadier general after a career of 45 years. Hagner and McKinstry had been classmates at West Point.[18]

As 1861 began, Blair belabored the Buchanan administration at Washington with letters and telegrams describing the unsettled situation in the city and the open efforts of secessionists to take the state out of the Union. He reported on the organizing and recruiting activities of secessionist leaders that were openly taking place and the lack of any visible response on the part of the administration to support the efforts of loyal men to offset these conditions. Matters in St. Louis and Missouri were approaching a crisis, the congressman claimed. On February 12, McKinstry notified Harney's adjutant, Captain Seth Williams, at headquarters in St. Louis, that two shipments of ordnance stores he had shipped to Fort Smith, Arkansas, one of cavalry equipment via the steamer *Napoleon* on January 15, and one of cartridges via the steamer *Southwester* on January 21, had been seized by persons claiming to act for the state of Arkansas. McKinstry advised Williams that Arkansas had passed no ordinance of secession nor announced a withdrawal from the Union. Because of the unsettled times, McKinstry recommended that he be authorized to instruct his agents to take legal steps to recover the lost stores rather than initiate a military response. On the following day, in response to one of Frank Blair's continuing complaints, General-in-Chief Winfield Scott telegraphed Harney from Washington asking whether Harney had enough men to defend the St. Louis Arsenal against attack. Scott asked whether Harney ought to order additional men from Jefferson Barracks, located several miles down the Mississippi River from St. Louis. Harney answered by assuring the general-in-chief that apprehensions about demonstrations against the arsenal were unfounded and that the secession party was in the minority in St. Louis. Harney closed his communication by declaring his complete confidence in Major Hagner, in command at the arsenal. This was not the message Frank Blair wanted transmitted to the administration at Washington. In fact, Harney's response was totally unacceptable to the fiery congressman. Blair thought Harney was ignoring what he thought was so obvious. On February 13, the adjutant general's office telegraphed Harney to issue orders for the garrison to abandon Fort Scott, Kansas, since it could not be supplied in safety. Harney replied that he would do so, but closed with further assurances regarding the safety of the St. Louis Arsenal. He had Hagner report to the chief of ordinance on conditions at the facility, stating that there was a garrison of 488 officers and men, that field works had been thrown up on all sides of the place, and guns had been mounted to command the interior faces of the walls. Hagner closed his report by assuring his chief that these arrangements still permitted the regular work of the arsenal to proceed without inconvenience.[19]

At the nation's capital, President James Buchanan was serving out the final months of his administration. A bachelor of 62, the Pennsylvanian was a conscientious politician considered by many to be evasive and irresolute. With dis-

Brig. Gen. William S. Harney served with McKinstry in Florida and Mexico and was his commanding officer in the Department of the West at St. Louis. (National Archives)

union looming, Buchanan declared that he was powerless to oppose it. No state had the right under the Constitution to secede from the Union, he explained, but were one to do so, as South Carolina had done and as others were threatening to do, he had no power under the Constitution to bring that state back to the Union by force of arms. Congress, he declared as he side-stepped his responsibility and his oath, was the only tribunal with the power to address this exigency. Rather than initiate any action, Buchanan lamely suggested: "Time is a great conservative power. Let us pause at this momentous point and afford the people, both North and South, an opportunity for reflection." Buchanan's attention during the remaining months of his administration would be directed at avoiding conflict between secession leaders and federal authorities until he could hand the presidency and the executive authority to Abraham Lincoln on March 4. Even when Frank Blair insisted that attention had to be given to the situation in Missouri, Buchanan was distracted by what he considered more pressing problems that had developed at two federal installations in the south, Fort Sumter in the harbor at Charleston, South Carolina, and Fort Pickens in the harbor at Pensacola, Florida. Both facilities were now under siege by state forces.[20]

Buchanan's cabinet was in turmoil as the crisis mounted and the new year commenced. With the end of his administration in sight, Buchanan's cabinet positions were almost all in transition. Lewis Cass of Michigan, McKinstry's benefactor earlier in his army career, now an aged, revered, and feeble man, had resigned as secretary of state on December 12. He was replaced by Jeremiah Black of Pennsylvania, formerly the attorney general. Black had been replaced on December 20 by Edwin M. Stanton, originally of Ohio. Howell Cobb of Georgia resigned as secretary of the treasury on December 8 and was replaced by Philip F. Thomas of Maryland. Jacob M. Thompson of Mississippi would resign as secretary of the interior on January 8. Secretary of war John B. Floyd of Virginia resigned under a cloud of accusations on December 29 and was replaced by Joseph Holt of Kentucky. Holt's former position as postmaster general was taken by Horatio King of Maine on February 12. The one consistent portfolio throughout this major shuffling in the cabinet was that of Secretary of the Navy Isaac Toucey of Connecticut.[21]

At St. Louis, Blair and the members of the Safety Committee saw in Harney a departmental commander who continued to assure the administration at Washington that all was well in Missouri. Blair was not the calmest of politicians when things did go his way and things were not going his way in Missouri. During this difficult time, Captain Nathaniel Lyon arrived at St. Louis with his company of 80 men of the 2nd Infantry on February 6 from Fort Riley, Kansas. Lyon and McKinstry by now had known each other more than 20 years, having served in the 2nd Infantry in Florida, along the Niagara frontier, in Mexico, and in California. Lyon sat on McKinstry's court-martial in Mexico City and during their time in California relieved McKinstry of his quartermaster's responsibilities at San Diego during McKinstry's suspension in September, 1850. The intense, righteous Lyon never tried to conceal his lack of trust or respect for McKinstry. In return, the quartermaster carried a strong grudge against the infantry officer. Doctor William A. Hammond, an army surgeon at Fort Riley and one of Lyon's associates at the time, wrote of the Connecticut native, "I have never in the whole course of my life met a man as fearless and uncompromising in the expression

Short, red-haired, fiery-tempered, Nathanial Lyon knew and served with McKinstry from their time at West Point until Lyon's death at Wilson's Creek on August 10, 1861. There was bad blood between the two men throughout their relationship. (Massachusetts Commandery Military Order of the Loyal Legion and the United States Army Military History Institute)

of his opinions, and at the same time so intolerant of the views of others, as was he. If he had lived four hundred years ago, he would have been burned at the stake as a pestilent and altogether incorrigible person, whose removal was demanded in the interests of the peace of society." Lyon's greatest fault was his uncontrollable temper which had caused him problems throughout his military career. Often others suffered severe consequences of his outburst. Just ten years before his arrival at St. Louis, Lyon led his company in pursuit of a band of renegade Indians in northern California. Closing on the fugitives at Clear Lake, Lyon was under orders from General Persifor Smith to bring the Indians to account. The natives put up a resistance that infuriated Lyon. He ordered his regulars to fix bayonets and follow the fleeing Indians into the rushes and reeds on the shore of the lake. Somewhere between 60 and 100 men were killed without mercy. Still angered and unsatisfied, Lyon then turned his men on the native women and children who were bayoneted and shot to death until the water of the lake was said to have run red with their blood. Somewhere between 200 and 400 natives were butchered without Lyon's command suffering a single loss. While stationed at Fort Riley, Lyon had witnessed the tragic results of political efforts to force slavery onto the people of Kansas. What he saw there infuriated him. He was fiercely patriotic, Unionist, anti-slavery, and sure of himself. As soon as he arrived at St. Louis, Lyon confronted Major Hagner at the arsenal and demanded the right to command by claiming his permanent rank of captain preceded Hagner's permanent rank. While so embroiled, 203 additional regulars of the 2nd Infantry arrived in the city and a few days later another 102, bringing the number of regulars under Lyon's command to 385. Lyon had his men take up quarters within the arsenal grounds and in private homes and commercial buildings close to its walls. He made no attempt to apply to McKinstry for quarters for the troops.[22]

Late in March, as one of his final acts as a member of the Buchanan administration, Secretary of War Joseph Holt ordered Colonel George H. Crosman to replace McKinstry as chief quartermaster of the Department of the West at St. Louis. Whether McKinstry's history and reputation had anything to do with Holt's decision is not clear. Gossip about the quartermaster's past had made the rounds at St. Louis. Much of it was based on the contents of the letters written to people in the city by his brother-in-law, George, in California. McKinstry was unpopular throughout the officer corps of the army yet Holt had no reason to question McKinstry's loyalty or ability. Regardless, Holt ordered Crosman to take McKinstry's place. Holt's order was immediately countermanded when Charles M. Elleard, the dealer from California, and Edward F. Fox, one of the partners in the St. Louis firm of Child, Pratt & Fox, who were present at Washington for the inauguration of President Lincoln, called upon the new Secretary of War Simon Cameron and assured the Pennsylvanian that "McKinstry was a good, loyal man; that the business of his office had been divided amongst the business houses without regard to friends or friendship." They noted that in his former positions, Colonel Crosman had repeatedly given contracts to his particular friends who managed to get almost all of his business. Frank Blair supported Elleard and Fox, writing to Cameron: "McKinstry is heartily disposed to do all that he can for the maintenance of the Government, and there is no ground for the nonsense that has been put afloat by those who want his position here." McKinstry remained in place at St. Louis but with the suggestion, proffered by those who opposed him, that he had been retained so that Frank Blair and Edward F. Fox "might have an available man."[23]

On March 11, 1861, one week after President Lincoln's inauguration, Frank Blair wrote to Secretary of War Cameron demanding that Lyon be given command of all troops at the St. Louis Arsenal and that Hagner's responsibilities be restricted to those matters that pertained only to his realm, the ordnance department. Nine days later, Harney, the departmental commander, wrote to the office of the adjutant general at Washington confirming that he had assigned Lyon to command all the troops in the city. Harney and the administration were only now becoming aware of the strong bond that had developed between Congressman Frank Blair and Captain Nathaniel Lyon, two dedicated and temperamental men who were determined to hold St. Louis and Missouri within the Union. Harney was a strict disciplinarian, an officer set in the army's ways, and he did not see the dangers that aroused Blair and Lyon. Only a few months earlier, Harney had assured Salmon P. Chase, now Lincoln's secretary of the treasury, that the army would not need to fire a gun to keep Missouri safely in the Union. Also, Harney was indignant that a congressman and a subordinate officer were imposing their wishes within the area of his command. He limited Lyon's authority to the control of the arsenal, its occupants, weapons, cartridges, and powder. Then, disregarding his subordinate's concern over the political turmoil taking place around him, Harney reverted to army business and ordered Lyon to Fort Leavenworth to sit before a court of inquiry called to look into charges brought against him for actions during his years at Fort Riley. This order was rescinded by the War Department and Lyon remained at St. Louis but with that order Harney had shown his displeasure at Lyon's attitude and manner.[24]

Matters on the national front continued to slide rapidly toward disunion. Following closely behind South Carolina, the lower tier of slave-holding states seceded in rapid order so that, by the first of February, 1861, the legislatures of Mississippi, Florida, Alabama, Georgia, Louisiana, and Texas had adopted ordinances of secession. Without a plan of organization or concerted action at first, these newly independent entities sent representatives to a convention at Montgomery, Alabama, on February 4 where they formed a provisional confederation. Ironically, the meeting at Montgomery took place on the same day another meeting, hosted by Virginia and involving representatives from the other states, met at Washington, D. C. in an attempt to find a path toward reconciliation and peace. The meeting at Washington was unsuccessful because representative from the seceded states boycotted the session. Then, on Friday, April 12, 1861, South Carolina batteries opened fire on the federal fort in Charleston Harbor, Fort Sumter, which was commanded by former West Point artillery instructor Major Robert Anderson who had been one of the members of McKinstry's court-martial there. Fort Sumter was able to hold out for only two days until it was forced to lower its flag. Civil war then swept over the land. That day the regular army of the United States numbered some 1,080 officers and 15,135 enlisted men, a force spread thinly along the borders and frontiers of the nation. The United States Army was a force far too small to provide the manpower that would be needed if the federal government were to try to restore the Union by force of arms. On April 15, three days after the firing on Fort Sumter, President Lincoln, in office a mere six weeks, called upon the governors of the loyal states to furnish 75,000 volunteers to put down what he termed a rebellion in the seceded states. Governor Claiborne Jackson's response was that Missouri would not furnish a man to what he described as an illegal, unconstitutional, and revolutionary proclamation. Frank Blair countered that with the offer to muster his Home Guards as Missouri's response to the president's call.[25]

The federal government was unprepared to respond to the sudden demands made by the governors of the loyal states who were rapidly recruiting their volunteers. The Lincoln administration was new to office, in place only a few weeks. The president's cabinet secretaries, some not yet ensconced in their positions and unfamiliar with the operations of their departments, were not used to working together nor with the executive. Many of them had not met Lincoln before being notified they had been chosen to assume their new responsibilities. The War Department under Secretary of War Simon Cameron was shaken by the defection of experienced officers and clerks who supported their seceding states. Cameron himself, inept and unable, initially abdicated most of his authority to Secretary of the Treasury Salmon P. Chase who stepped into the void and began issuing military orders and approving organizational planning.[26]

The army's quartermaster department consisted of 35 officers, ten of whom resigned to follow their home states out of the Union. Quartermaster General Thomas S. Jesup, after 45 years of service in office, died on June 10, 1860. He was replaced by Brigadier General Joseph E. Johnston, a Virginian. After ten months in office, Johnston resigned on the secession of his home state. It would not be until May 15 that Brigadier General Montgomery C. Meigs—a classmate of McKinstry's at West Point—was appointed quartermaster general, a post he would occupy for more than 20 years. Until Meigs took office and during the hectic months when the states of the north recruited and sent forward their thousands of volunteers in response to the president's call, the department responsible for clothing, equipping, housing, and transporting them was without a permanent commander.[27]

On April 16, Harney, belatedly concerned about the security of the St. Louis

Arsenal and in response to the telegraphed news received from Charleston Harbor and Washington, wrote to the adjutant general. He reported the arsenal grounds at St. Louis were surrounded by hills and he understood Governor Jackson intended to order state militia batteries mounted on the hills and on an island in the Mississippi River opposite the arsenal. In the event of Missouri's secession, Harney wrote, he predicted state authorities would demand the surrender of the arsenal with its ordnance treasures. "Under these circumstances, I respectfully request instructions for my guidance," Harney closed his communication. Captain Nathaniel Lyon did not waste time asking for instructions from a distant and unresponsive War Department. Without communicating with Harney, Lyon gave a note to an aide who was about to visit Springfield, Illinois, addressed to Governor Richard Yates. Lyon recommended in his note that the six regiments of volunteers called for from Illinois be held back for service at St. Louis and he urged the governor to requisition a large portion of the arms stored at the arsenal and have them shipped to safety in Illinois. As a result, 10,000 muskets and accouterments were shipped within ten days. Lyon took further steps on his own authority. In a meeting that ran late into the night of April 12, he conferred with the officers at St. Louis whom he trusted about specific steps he wanted taken to further fortify and defend the arsenal grounds. When asked what to do if Hagner interfered while they were carrying out the assignments Lyon gave them, he told the officers to put Hagner in irons and take him to the guard house. "If he interferes with me," Lyon told them, "I'll shoot him in his tracks!" Four senior army officers stationed at St. Louis were missing from this meeting. Two of these were know to be disloyal; one soon resigned and joined the secessionist forces and the other was arrested and charged with helping secessionist spies. The other two were McKinstry and Hagner, neither of whom Lyon trusted to support him or safeguard his plans.[28]

In the midst of the fury and rancor of looming civil strife, the routine of the quartermaster's department at St. Louis continued without interruption. McKinstry solicited bids for picket pins for cavalry operating in distant New Mexico. On April 19, Thomas Hood offered to furnish the pins at the lowest price submitted. McKinstry rejected this bid on the grounds that Hood's pins did not have the swivel heads specified and therefore were not suitable for use by the cavalry. McKinstry accepted a bid that was three times higher than Hood's. McKinstry sent all the proposals to the quartermaster's department at Washington from where contracts were issued. This, it turned out, was one of the last transactions by the office of the chief quartermaster, Department of the West at St. Louis, that was conducted under the rigid and specific rules and regulations of the army that governed procurements.[29]

On April 20, Secretary of War Cameron instructed Governor Yates to send "two or three of his regiments of Illinois volunteers" to St. Louis in response to Lyon's suggestion and ordered Harney to report in person to General-in-Chief

Scott at Washington. Without specific authority from the War Department, and upon hearing of Harney's orders, Frank Blair and Nathaniel Lyon began mustering and arming four regiments of Blair's St. Louis Home Guards. Harney departed from the city by rail on April 23. His journey proved eventful: early in the morning of April 26 as his train was passing through Harper's Ferry, Virginia, it was stopped and boarded by Virginia state troops. Harney was taken to Richmond and brought before Governor Robert Letcher where he was urged to resign his commission in the United States Army and accept an equal position in the Confederate service as had many of his friends and colleagues. Harney, a stubborn man but a staunch patriot, refused and was permitted to continue his journey.

After Harney's departure from St. Louis, McKinstry was without a commanding officer to shield him from the pressures and influences brought to bear by others. McKinstry was a senior army officer, albeit one without a command or troops to call upon, and he was now drawn daily into contact with Blair, Lyon, and their colleagues. Volunteers began to arrive at St. Louis. First were the local Home Guards, men without uniforms, equipment, and bereft of experienced officers and capable leadership. Companies from the environs of the city, and soon battalions and regiments from within Missouri and from Illinois, Iowa, and Kansas, and eventually from most of the states of the northwest began to arrive at and around St. Louis. The volunteers were enthusiastic, filled with patriotism and loyalty to the Union and, generally, to Frank Blair, but they were woefully lacking in organization, discipline, and the most basic camp equipment, uniforms, and arms. The federal War Department was unable to respond to the sudden massive demands made upon it. The staff departments, used to responding to the needs of the small regular establishment of less than 16,000 men, were suddenly faced with the immediate demands of 75,000 volunteers, then 350,000, and eventually 500,000. Clothing on hand at army depots when the president made his proclamation was adequate to meet the needs of the regulars but the estimated four million yards of blue cloth required to make just one uniform for each of the first wave of volunteers was nowhere available. McKinstry wired Colonel Charles Thomas, assistant quartermaster in charge of the clothing bureau at Philadelphia, asking how he was to supply the needs of the volunteers at St. Louis since his instructions and the army's regulations covered only the needs of the regulars. Thomas wired back that his orders were to supply the volunteers with such clothing as could be spared from existing stocks but that he could not send McKinstry the thousand uniforms he requested and he did not know when he would be able to in the future. "You are hereby authorized to furnish the regular supplies of camp equipage, including tents," Thomas wrote. He did not explain where McKinstry was to obtain the camp equipage and tents he was authorized to furnish the volunteers.[30]

Harsh reality became clear to McKinstry when he received further telegrams from the quartermaster's department in response to other queries and as he read the newspaper reports of the events taking place in the east. While there was a risk to the security of the Union in St. Louis and in the west, that risk was half a continent away from the imminent peril facing the new administration at Washington. In the dark hours the president, this cabinet, and the members of Congress could look out the windows of their government buildings and see Confederate picket fires burning among the hills and ridges of northern Virginia just across the Potomac River. Men, munitions, and supplies would be directed to the armies forming in the east to protect the nation's capital before they would be sent to armies forming elsewhere. This was made clear to McKinstry and the Union leaders at St. Louis when Secretary of War Cameron wrote to Frank Blair on May 9 that the needs of the forces at St. Louis would be met "as soon as the troops in this city and those under the command of General Patterson and Butler are supplied. It will be impossible to furnish clothing to your troops promptly. In New York and Pennsylvania their troops have either furnished themselves or been furnished, relying on reimbursement of the expenditures by the General Government." McKinstry wrote to the quartermaster's department on April 29, sending what he considered a major request for funds and asking for authority to operate independently of the established lines of supply and the policies and procedures of the quartermaster's department. "Demands are daily being made upon me by the volunteer regiments mustered into service in this city and the state of Illinois," he reported. The following day, McKinstry recalled the solution to the shortage of uniforms he faced while in Mexico City 14 years earlier. He telegraphed Colonel Thomas at Philadelphia: "Clothing could be manufactured here by the wives and daughters of the volunteers in the service, at reasonable rates, provided the materials be sent me, from your city or New York. I understand from the Honorable Mr. Blair that he has suggested the arrangement to the Secretary of War ... I can get to work immediately upon receipt of the first shipment of cloth."[31]

Pressures continued to build within St. Louis. Secretary of War Cameron telegraphed Lyon the authority to declare martial law in the city if he deemed it necessary. The governor's police commissioner at St. Louis called upon Lyon and directed him to remove the men of the 2nd Infantry from private homes and commercial buildings near the arsenal the regulars had occupied for quarters; Lyon refused. Governor Jackson ordered several companies of state militia from St. Louis to muster for their annual training in a camp to be set up on the hills overlooking the arsenal; Lyon put four companies of his regulars in tents up there. General Frost, a classmate of Lyon's at West Point, ordered the militia into an encampment at Lindell Grove on the western end of the city which he named Camp Jackson in honor of the governor. Lyon drilled his regulars at the arsenal and watched the activities at Lindell Grove. Frank Blair urged patriotic men of the city to form additional Home Guard companies. McKinstry struggled to address the overwhelming tasks suddenly appearing before him.[32]

While all of this was taking place, the river steamer *J. C. Swan* arrived at the St. Louis levee during the night of May 8 and unloaded heavy cases of goods that were hurriedly hauled in wagons to Camp Jackson. Marked to contain "marble Tamaroa," the cases actually contained two 12-pounder howitzers, two 32-pounder siege guns, 500 muskets, and a sizeable amount of ammunition, all recently taken when Louisiana state troops seized the federal arsenal at Baton Rouge on January 10.[33]

Responding to the threat he clearly saw when he learned the identity of the cargo from the *J. C. Swan*, the hot-tempered Lyon decided to move against Camp Jackson on his own authority. He organized, equipped, and partially armed some 70 officers and 3,400 men of the Home Guards but he needed more weapons for the men and he lacked horses to draw his artillery pieces. Lyon felt it would be unwise to apply for arms to Hagner at the arsenal who still exercised control over the ordnance there. Instead, he went to the Safety Committee. Frank Blair asked the brothers Oliver D. and Giles R. Filley to supply Lyon with muskets and shotguns they had in stock at their store and to contribute funds for the purchase of additional weapons. Governor Yates returned 200 muskets to Giles Filley from the shipment that had gone across the river to Illinois several days earlier and the brothers purchased with their own funds 70 Sharps rifles from a local gun dealer. Lyon needed 36 horses to haul his artillery pieces and caissons. By purchasing and borrowing from loyal citizens, the Filleys gathered the number of horses needed and sent them to the arsenal. Lyon was violating army regulations but applying to Hagner for weapons would have meant exposing his plans and his personal distrust of McKinstry kept him from asking the quartermaster to procure the draft animals. With his volunteer force backed by four artillery pieces and a strong contingent of regulars from the 2nd Infantry, Lyon marched to Lindell Grove and sent forward Major Benjamin Farrar, of the recently mustered 1st Missouri Volunteer Regiment, with a letter demanding the surrender of Frost and his entire command of 50 officers and 639 men. Outnumbered and outgunned, and protesting that his militia encampment was a lawful assembly called into being by the governor of the state — in fact, due to disband the following morning — Frost surrendered. One of the militiamen at Camp Jackson was 24-year-old Oliver McKinstry, the son of Alexander McKinstry, Susan's oldest brother. Alexander, his wife, Angelina, and their three children had lived at St. Louis for several years. Fortunately, Oliver was at home, off duty, when Lyon struck at Camp Jackson and thus avoided capture.[34]

As Lyon's force marched back to the arsenal grounds with its prisoners, a mob surrounded the column, shouting at the predominately German volunteers. Shots were fired by angry citizens and volleys were returned by the volunteers. Twenty-eight people were killed; the number of wounded, although much higher, was unknown. Riots erupted in the city that night as mobs rushed through the streets. Municipal authorities ordered all the saloons closed. Fighting and firing broke out in the city parks and at intersections. The citizens of St. Louis had already taken sides and now they had an excuse to move openly against each other. The following day mobs still milled and threatened. Within hearing of the house where Susan McKinstry and the three boys huddled behind locked doors, Unionists fired into a crows of secessionists at the corner of 5th and Walton Streets leaving seven bodies lying in the intersection. The city suffered unrest for days. The mayor appealed to its citizens for calm.[35]

On May 17, the War Department appointed Lyon a brigadier general of volunteers and named him Harney's successor as commander of the Department of the West, making him McKinstry's immediate superior.[36]

Volunteers had been swarming to St. Louis as early as April 22 when the 1st, 2nd, and 3rd Missouri Volunteer Regiments were mustered into federal service from the Home Guard companies. In the following 90 days, six more Missouri regiments arrived as well as regiments from neighboring states to bring the number to almost 40,000 men between May and September. "A few weeks would suffice to crowd the city and the arsenal with new levies who were entirely unequipped and for whose unexpected necessities no preparations had been made," McKinstry reported. "I was destitute of everything for their use." He could expect no assistance from the east as the government's first priority was to supply the armies gathering in Virginia and the District of Columbia for the defense of the capital. "I had not clothing, camp or garrison equipment on hand, and not horses, mules, or wagons for the supply of these troops. I had no money with which to make purchases, and the Government could not go into the market and buy on credit as responsible individuals could."[37]

The War Department made no attempt to meet the immediate and unprecedented demands of the thousands of volunteers suddenly sprung into being. The department did attempt to address the problem by instructing the state governments to house, feed, clothe, and equip their volunteers and to send the bills for that to Washington for reimbursement. Most of the loyal states were able to do this but Missouri had difficulties. Governor Claiborne Jackson, Lieutenant Governor Thomas Reynolds, and the state's legislature were solidly secessionist. Jackson had proudly rejected the call of President Lincoln for troops to suppress the rebellion of the seceding states and he boasted that he would do nothing to help those organizations being formed in St. Louis in defiance of his political position. Without a loyal state government to provide for Missouri's volunteers, the responsibility for clothing and equipping the men flooding into St. Louis fell on McKinstry who was without the means to do so.[38]

McKinstry first tried to find a source for uniforms. He again telegraphed the quartermaster's department on May 1 saying, "If you can furnish the cloth, I can clothe them at prices approximating very closely the Philadelphia standard; and its making up will materially aid the wives and families of the volunteers whom I propose to employ." On May 25, he telegraphed, "I have the honor to enclose herewith an estimate of funds required at this station. The large number of troops stationed here require large amounts of supplies and, in the present depressed state of affairs, they can be purchased for cash far below the market. If I have to purchase on credit, another ten percent will have to be added. So you will readily perceive the advantage for the Government in purchasing for cash." On June 4, Major Ebenezer S. Sibley, acting as interim quartermaster general after the resignation of Joseph E. Johnston and before the appointment of Montgomery C. Meigs, telegraphed McKinstry, "You are authorized without reference to this office, under the Commanding General's direction, to procure such means of transportation as he may deem necessary, practicing a sound economy in making your purchases, and if the exigency is not immediate or pressing, conforming to the law and regulations in relation to the manner of making purchases or contracts for supplies." On June 25, newly-appointed Quartermaster General Meigs wrote McKinstry, "The Department approves of your course ... but desires that while economy is right, there be no room left for charging the failure of any military movement upon a want of promptness and efficiency in the Quartermaster's Department."[39]

Early in the year, Congress had restated the policies that governed military procurement. Purchases and contracts for supplies and services were to be made after advertising for proposals, waiting a sufficient time for submission of bids, and then awarding the contracts to the lowest bidder. Usually instead of a written specification, a sample of the required item was exhibited as a standard. Delivered goods were compared to the standard and accepted or rejected based on whether they met all the requirements of government use. Paragraph 1048 of Army Regulations permitted a deviation from this rule: "When immediate delivery or performance is required by the public exigency, the article or service required may be procured by open purchase or contract, at the price and in the mode in which such articles are usually bought and sold, or such services engaged, between individuals." The quartermaster on the scene was authorized to determine which method to follow after analyzing the urgency and the duration of the exigency. Thus, by the end of June, 1861, McKinstry had in his possession written authority from the acting quartermaster general to purchase or contract for services and supplies under the direction of the commanding officer of the department without the approval of the quartermaster general's department at Washington. He had written instructions from the quartermaster general himself that economy or a lack of promptness and efficiency on the part of the quartermaster's department should not interfere with military movements. This authority, along with provisions by army regulations for situations when purchases and contracts needed to be made immediately in the face of a public exigency, suddenly gave broad discretion to the chief quartermaster at St. Louis.[40]

On June 10, 1861, Blair and Lyon met Governor Jackson, Brigadier General Sterling Price, named to command Missouri's state troops; Thomas L. Snead, the secessionist editor of the *St. Louis Bulletin* serving as the governor's aide and the general's secretary; and other secessionist officials at the Planter's House at St. Louis. Bad blood already existed between Lyon and Jackson stemming from the 1850s when each had served on opposite sides of the territorial struggle taking place over slavery in Kansas Territory. Earlier, Price and Harney had made an agreement while Harney commanded at St. Louis that state forces would preserve order throughout the state and, in turn, federal troops would not recruit in, pass through, or operate from the state if Price's state troops did preserve order. Lyon rejected this agreement in its entirety. In a profound display of his uncontrollable temper, Lyon shouted at Jackson, "Rather than concede to the state of Missouri the right to demand that my government shall not enlist troops within her limits, or bring troops of its own in, or out of, or through the state; rather than concede to any government in any matter, however unimportant, I would see you! and you! and you! and every man and woman and child in the state dead and buried!" Lyon said to Blair as the two stormed out of the hotel, "This means war!"[41]

Jackson and Price immediately left for the state capital at Jefferson City and Price ordered the burning of the railroad bridges over the Gasconade and Osage rivers between St. Louis and the capital. Jackson called to service 50,000 militia to protect Missouri from what he described as the federal government's intent to overthrow the state's government. On July 12, two days after the confrontation at the Planter's House, Lyon ordered a column of troops to move by rail from St. Louis to Rolla, Missouri, under Brigadier General Franz Sigel, a former officer in the army of the German confederation and recently director of public schools in St. Louis. Marching overland from the railhead at Rolla, Sigel advanced in the direction of Springfield. On June 13, Lyon started with another armed force on steamboats up the Missouri River in the direction of Jefferson City. Behind him at St. Louis, Lyon left his assistant adjutant general, Colonel Chester Harding, and his chief quartermaster, Brevet Major Justus McKinstry. Harding had complete authority to act in Lyon's name.[42]

On June 18, Quartermaster General Meigs telegraphed McKinstry: "Support General Lyon's movements by all necessary aid from the Quartermaster's Department." Meigs wrote the same day, "An order from a commanding officer to pay an account will put the responsibility on him who gives the order ... Consult and advise with the Assistant Adjutant General who doubtless only seeks the public good and thus avoid collisions, prevent improper orders being given through lack of experience, and save public money."[43]

On the authority provided in the quartermaster general's letter, McKinstry purchased without advertising or allowing time for the submission of bids "four thousand canteens, eight hundred and forty-seven mess pans, some axes and other hardware." The demand was so sudden and pressing, he explained, that a day's delay would have caused suffering and would have retarded Lyon's military operations and "the public exigency was such that I would have violated my duty had I not bought them as I did." He had hoped to have time to build stocks of equipment and clothing and to arrange for transportation before Lyon ordered his columns to march," he explained. "There appeared to be no probability that he would take to the field until after these supplies could have been obtained in the ordinary manner," McKinstry wrote. When Lyon sent Sigel toward Springfield on June 12 and then went himself up the Missouri River on the 13th, officers in both columns opted to hire their own wagon drivers, so urgent did they feel was the need. "Few tents and no clothing had been issued to them ... and from that time onward, their requisitions called for such immediate attention that there was not time at which the 'public exigencies' did not demand the purchase of the articles they needed, as quickly as I could procure them ... It invariably happened that the first intimation I would receive of a contemplated movement would be a requisition and order for the instant supply of quartermaster stores," wrote McKinstry.[44]

On June 15, Lyon and 2,000 men on three steamboats landed and took possession of Jefferson City, the state capital. Governor Jackson and the state legislature followed Sterling Price and the state militia to Boonville, some 40 miles westward up the river, which Price considered a better defensive position. The legally elected secessionist government of Missouri would be a government-in-exile thereafter. Following closely behind, Lyon's men approached and occupied Boonville on June 17 after a minor skirmish, but Lyon was forced to halt and wait there. He was not able to advance further against Price until June 27 due to the lack of wagon transportation, the need for provisions, and because he had to leave troops behind to garrison key points along the river. South and west of where Lyon impatiently waited, Sigel had been marching from the railhead at Rolla in the general direction of Springfield. On July 5, he skirmished with Confederate forces near Carthage. Outnumbered, Sigel fell back and then linked up with Lyon, who had taken Springfield on July 13. In Springfield, Lyon's force found itself unpaid, ill-fed, in dilapidated clothing, in part shoeless, and many without the most basic of military accouterments such as cartridge boxes, haversacks, canteens, and tents. On the day his forces took Springfield, Lyon telegraphed Postmaster General Montgomery Blair at Washington regarding the failure to get supplies to his army. Two days later, Lyon wrote to Chester Harding about the lack of clothing, rations, and field equipment for his men.[45]

On July 21, Harding wrote to Lyon from St. Louis regarding problems with the movement of supplies, claiming mismanagement at Rolla. A large number of wagons had been purchased at St. Louis and sent down the line of the railroad with 250,000 rations and 4,000 sets of clothing and shoes but only a part of this had been forwarded to the army in the field. When Sigel's column left St. Louis, his officers had hired their teamsters themselves in order to avoid going through McKinstry's office. When the wagons returned to Rolla after having made the journey to Springfield, McKinstry discharged the teamsters. Harding forcefully reminded McKinstry of his responsibilities and the fact that he had orders from the quartermaster general at Washington to support Lyon's movements. McKinstry then sent Thomas O'Brien to Rolla to straighten out the problems there and to act as an agent for the quartermaster's department. He instructed O'Brien to give his undivided attention to his duties and to adhere strictly to the rules laid down in army regulations when conducting business. By claiming adherence to army regulations as his justification for discharging the improperly hired teamsters, McKinstry was maliciously getting back at Lyon.[46]

On July 22, the Missouri state convention met at Jefferson City and affirmed the loyalty of the state to the Union, declaring that, with the flight of the established government under Claiborne Jackson from the capital, the state offices were vacant. A new provisional government was established under Hamilton R. Gamble and the state's capital was relocated to St. Louis. Missouri now had two governments, one pro-Confederate under Jackson west of Boonville and one pro-Union under Gamble at St. Louis.[47]

8

The Hundred Days

On July 25, 1861, Major General John Charles Frémont replaced Brigadier General Nathaniel Lyon in command of the Department of the West with his headquarters at St. Louis. Lyon remained in the field at the head of his troops at Springfield.[1]

Frémont was 48 years old when he arrived in the city accompanied by his wife, Jessie Benton Frémont, the daughter of Missouri's former Senator Thomas Hart Benton. Twenty years before, Frémont and the lovely Jessie eloped at St. Louis in October, 1841. Both knew the city and were well known there.[2]

Frémont had risen above the stigma of an illegitimate birth to an appointment in 1838 to the army's prestigious corps of topographical engineers. This was the same year McKinstry entered the officer corps of the army from West Point. Frémont earned the sobriquet "Pathfinder" from several exploring expeditions through the passes of the Rocky Mountains into Oregon and California, all of which began at St. Louis. During his service in California during the war with Mexico, the headstrong Frémont became embroiled with his superior officer, Brigadier General Stephen Watts Kearny, and was court-martialed on charges of mutiny, disobedience, and conduct prejudicial to military order. Found guilty of the last two charges, he impetuously resigned his commission. Frémont and Jessie settled in California after it achieved territorial status and, with statehood on September 11, 1850, Frémont was elected one of California's first United States Senators. His *las Mariposas* ranch in California held one of the richest producing gold mines in the state, making him a millionaire several times over. Had the new Republican party carried Pennsylvania and either Illinois or Indiana in the1856 presidential election, John Charles Frémont would have become the fifteenth president of the United States instead of Democrat James Buchanan.[3]

Frémont had recently returned from Europe where he had been seeking investors for his California holdings. Upon learning that he had been commissioned a major general in the United States Army and assigned to command the Department of the West, Frémont took the next ship from England to New York.

He was joined there by Jessie and their three children who had arrived by sea from California. Meeting at the executive mansion with President Lincoln and Postmaster General Montgomery Blair, his personal attorney and close friend, the three discussed the problems Frémont would face in Missouri and the west. Lincoln expressed his faith in Frémont; on parting, when Frémont asked if there were specific instructions, Lincoln's reply was, "No, I give you *carte blanche.* You must use your judgment and do the best you can." This was not an indication of a lack of concern on the part of the president; he was distracted by other pressing problems. On that same day, within miles of where the three men stood talking, the eastern army under Brigadier General Irvin McDowell was preparing to take the roads from Washington toward Confederate forces under General Pierre G. T. Beauregard which were emplaced behind Bull Run 26 miles to the west.[4]

Instead of hastening to St. Louis as the president urged him, Frémont went to New York City where he dallied for more than three weeks forming a staff, arranging for arms and munitions for his forces in the west, and meeting with influential men. During this time, Postmaster General Blair and Adjutant General Lorenzo Thomas repeatedly urged him by telegraph and messenger to move promptly to St. Louis to assume his command. The administration was barraged by alarming and conflicting messages from the west and Lincoln was anxious to have Frémont there to bring resolution and calm to the troubled region. It was not until the third week in July that Frémont finally left New York City.[5]

Frémont was not the first choice for the command of the Department of the West by the Blairs and their supporters. They wanted the man already on the scene, Nathaniel Lyon. Frank Blair and Lyon were kindred souls who shared the same fervor and patriotism that had carried them through the stressful months of late winter and early summer. Conservatives in Missouri, however, were concerned that Lyon was too brash, too fiery for the position. He had done well in the weeks since he arrived at St. Louis saving the city and its arsenal, capturing the state militia that threatened the city and the arsenal, organizing and moving an army into the field, beating state forces at Boonville, and capturing and holding Springfield. Yet Lyon was an outsider, an unknown to the conservative powers in the state and a man who seemed more intent on destroying the enemy than on restoring peace and security within the state. In a move led by Lincoln's attorney general, Edward Bates, himself a conservative Missourian, Frémont was chosen instead of Lyon for the departmental command. Frémont was a compromise candidate who was acceptable to the conservatives of Missouri and who was expected to work out well. Frémont was nationally known, his reputation as the explorer was well founded, and his strong showing in the 1856 election put him in good standing with the Republican leadership nationally and with the local German population of the city and the state. Lincoln had no second thoughts when he named Frémont to be one of the second highest ranking general officers in the United States Army, commissioned of equal date with George B.

John Charles Frémont commanded the Department of the West at St. Louis. Frémont was described by an associate who knew him as "possessing all the qualities of genius except ability." (Collection of the *New York Historical Society*; photograph by Root, 1856 or earlier, negative #37625)

McClellan. The two of them were junior only to 75-year-old Major General Winfield Scott who had held the position of general-in-chief since 1841.[6]

Frémont arrived at St. Louis in the heat of an oppressive summer morning and in the midst of a city that was divided, frightened, and suffering from the turmoil taking place throughout the state. Shops were closed, men were out of work, steamboats were tied up at the levee, and commerce had come to a halt as producers, merchants, and brokers watched and waited. Secessionist flags flew from prominent buildings in the city while recruiting officers actively signed men into the Confederate service or the secessionist Missouri state militia. Frémont was shocked by what he encountered. The day of his arrival, ignoring the army's regular channels of communication, he telegraphed his friend, Postmaster General Blair, a long list of problems he faced and what he considered to be his most urgent needs. But few in Washington concerned themselves with issues rising far to the west at that time. After its shattering defeat on the banks of Bull Run on July 21, the scattered remnants of Irvin McDowell's broken eastern army still wandered the streets of Washington and no one knew when Confederate cavalry might descent on the city from the ridges across the Potomac River. Blair was unable to help his friend, replying by telegraph, "I find it impossible to get any attention to Missouri or western matters from the authorities here. You will have to do the best you can and take all needful responsibility to defend and protect the people over whom you are especially set." The response might have turned the soul of another man toward despair but John Charles Frémont was more than just another man. Because of the president's *carte blanche*, he did not feel that he was cut off from succor and support from the seat of government in the east but rather that he was in a position of sole authority and power over matters in the west. He was in command of an area that took in half the continent, an area he knew well and where he had earned fame and fortune. Massive forces looked to him for command, discipline, and direction. Ironically, John Charles Frémont, pathfinder, millionaire, and politician, had never commanded a force of more than a few soldiers in his life. He did have the ability to make people believe in him, often before he had to prove himself to them. Josiah Royce, philosopher and historian, wrote of Frémont, "He possessed all the qualities of genius, except ability." Frémont's London financial agent wrote that he "had a bit of humbug in him." Elizabeth Blair Lee, daughter of the Blair family, openly accused him of being an opium addict. An associate who had met John and Jessie in California considered that "she was the better man of the two."[7]

With the arrival of his new commanding officer, McKinstry was still trying to find ways to fill the needs of thousands of volunteers arriving at and operating from St. Louis. Officers in command of regiments, battalions, and companies were demanding clothing, shoes, tentage, camp equipment, horses, mules, and wagons from him daily. These were supplies he did not have on hand and he saw no means of obtaining them through regular channels. On July 27, Quartermaster General Meigs learned from Postmaster General Blair at Washington, through whom Frémont continued to communicate outside army channels, that in Frémont's opinion the public service in Missouri needed three times the amount of funds that McKinstry had asked for in his most recent requisition.

Meigs asked Secretary of War Cameron to request Secretary of the Treasury Chase to increase the remittance. Meigs reminded McKinstry in a letter that it was necessary for him to support the needs of the service but he preferred to have purchases made through the established method of advertising for proposals, even under very trying circumstances. "The laws, the necessity, are fully met," Meigs wrote, "by putting a notice in the paper and purchasing as fast as offers come in, the next day, or the same day; take the then lowest bid or the then most advantageous offer. The next day after, you will have a still lower offer; take that for a portion of your supplies, and so on until you have all you need."[8]

McKinstry's day-to-day situation was far from the condition the quartermaster general indicated he thought existed at St. Louis. McKinstry described some of what he had to face, using as an example a situation that arose four days after Frémont and his staff arrived upon the scene. "On the 29th of July, 1861, I was ordered to have at command 'during the next fortnight,' clothing, camp and garrison equipage, for twenty-three regiments of infantry, three regiments of cavalry, and one regiment of artillery. On the same day, I was directed to purchase five hundred sets of cavalry equipments 'for tomorrow.' August 20th, I was ordered to purchase in this city and have ready to forward at once, clothing for six thousand men. August 21st, to purchase one thousand pairs of pants and the same number of jackets. September 4th, to contract for not less than one thousand wagons and the mules required to drive them, with the least possible delay. When I received the first order, I telegraphed the Quartermaster General in regard to the matter and received a reply, in substance, that impossibilities could not be performed, and that the Department could not fill the requisitions in the time allowed. General Frémont directed me to take immediate steps to furnish the articles called for in the most expeditious manner." McKinstry went on, describing a new complication to the difficulties he already faced. "It was the policy of the Government, and I was so instructed, to exclude all but men of known loyalty from the benefits of Government business. In a community like this, where a large part of the mercantile class was accused of entertaining disloyal sentiments, this policy, the wisdom of which had never been doubted, imposed still another restriction upon competition; and political cormorants did not hesitate to take advantage of these embarrassments to direct those benefits into their own pockets or the purses of their friends, so far as they had the power to do so. Notwithstanding all this, I made purchases and contracts without advertising only when the necessity for supplies was apparent or pressing, or when acting under the orders of the General Commanding." He gave a further example of the pressures

Opposite: Francis Preston Blair, Jr., St. Louis lawyer, congressman, and general, was McKinstry's supporter until he turned against Frémont and McKinstry. Blair was one of the few political generals who became a successful corps commander in the Civil War. (Massachusetts Commandery Military Order of the Loyal Legion and the United States Army Military History Institute)

under which he labored in the form of two letters written to him concerning James L. Lamb of Springfield, Illinois. Both letters praised Lamb's integrity and stated that purchases made from Lamb would oblige the writers. Both letters were dated September 9, 1861, and were signed, one "Simon Cameron, Secretary of War," and the other simply "A. Lincoln."[9]

Dealer in horseflesh Jim Neill was a stranger to McKinstry until Frank Blair introduced him as a personal friend and a sound Union man. Blair also recommended John A. Bowen and Charles M. Elleard, the latter whom McKinstry already knew. "In fact, the Representative of the St. Louis District sent more applicants to me than any other ten men in the country," McKinstry stated later. Blair even went the long way around to direct patronage where he wanted it. He wrote to Quartermaster General Meigs from St. Louis, sending along a letter from Major Benjamin Farrar, his close friend, who had written on behalf of his brother, John, asking for a contract to furnish horses. John Farrar was "about busted up financially, and very much in need of the kind to help him get through." Ben Farrar had appealed to Blair rather than to the quartermaster at St. Louis because, he wrote, "It is more necessary to have something of the kind from you to McKinstry, as I fear he is prejudiced against me because of my letter to the judge, which fell into his hands." John Farrar, Ben wrote, had been a steadfast friend to the Republican party and, he ended, "The contracts will be let and somebody will get the profits, and certainly no one deserves more than John." Farrar was referring to an earlier confrontation with McKinstry that had resulted in open enmity on the quartermaster's part with Farrar accusing McKinstry of favoring certain suppliers in St. Louis.[10]

McKinstry's offices were now constantly troubled by seekers, sellers, and clerks. At times, he was forced to post guards to keep the hallways clear so that officers from the arriving regiments could make their way in with their requisitions and lists of their requirements. Up to this time, McKinstry tried to meet the needs of the service using every means he had at hand and by generally adhering to the requirements established in army rules and regulations. At the same time, he exercised the broad discretion that his instructions and the regulations provided under conditions of exigency. With the arrival of Frémont, McKinstry's methods of operating changed and reverted to those of the past. All the justifications were in place. The immediate public need demanded that rules and regulations be set aside for the good of the national cause, as the commanding general of the department had ordered. The limited resources of the quartermaster's department were stretched so thin that McKinstry could not find relief through normal channels of supply. Delays due to competitive bidding would not be acceptable to the commanders of willing, loyal men who had arrived unprepared for military service in the field. These men were without uniforms, shoes, knapsacks, canteens, blankets, and even pots and pans. Any hesitation or reluctance on McKinstry's part to do everything conceivable to alleviate their needs would

Brig. Gen. Montgomery C. Meigs, quartermaster general during the Civil War, was behind the drawing of charges that led to McKinstry's St. Louis court-martial. (Library of Congress)

be taken as an indication of incompetence if not disloyalty. Conditions were perfect for fraud, waste, and abuse at St. Louis in the summer of 1861.

On his arrival at St. Louis, Frémont established his residence and his headquarters in the opulent home of Jessie's cousin, the widow Sarah Brant, on Chouteau Avenue. Fremont ordered McKinstry to rent the place for the government at the exorbitant sum of $6,000 a year. The walled mansion was guarded and access was limited by sentries to staff members and selected associates of the general, much to the complaint of public officials and military officers who felt they needed access to the departmental commander. Frémont's staff included a few officers appointed by the government and bearing commissions signed by the president which included McKinstry, the departmental chief quartermaster; Captain Chauncey McKeever, Frémont's adjutant; Lieutenant Colonel James Totten, his chief of artillery; Lieutenant Colonel Timothy P. Andrews, his paymaster; and Colonel Gustav Koerner, his aide. The remainder of Frémont's 28 staff officers held irregular appointments from Frémont, and many bore titles never seen on the army's table of organization such as an *adlatus* to the chief of staff; a military registrator and expeditor; a postal director; a music director, a police director, and more than a dozen assorted aides. Frémont's staff officers were, for the most part, foreigners and outsiders to Missouri and, therefore, to local affairs. They did more to insulate the general commanding the Department of the West from what was taking place rather than help him see and understand it. One historian described this collection as an "uncounted and glittering staff, which seemed to have received the Pentecostal gift of tongues—in which English was not included." Some of Frémont's appointees duplicated the role of officers already in place. Captain Edward M. Davis was appointed by Frémont as an assistant quartermaster even though he was a supplier of blankets to McKinstry, the department's chief quartermaster. Frémont organized and equipped a squadron of cavalry as his personal bodyguard under the command of Colonel Charles Zagonyi, a Hungarian refugee and solider of fortune. Observers reported confusion at the headquarters, a lack of direction and oversight. Frémont himself became involved in the issuance of contracts that should have been delegated to subordinates authorized to handle such matters. The general commanding gave orders that the city of St. Louis be fortified. Instead of turning to the army's corps of engineers to design and oversee the work, he told McKinstry to issue the contract to the firm of Beard & Palmer. One of the principles, E. L. Beard, a Frémont friend and neighbor from California, had managed the quartz mine at *las Mariposas*. The other, Joseph Palmer, was a long-time business associate of Frémont's from the Golden State. Both were members of what was referred to as the "California gang" at headquarters. McKinstry issued the contract to Beard & Palmer on September 25, 1861, without advertising or soliciting bids. The fortifications were already substantially complete, having progressed under the supervision of

Major Franz Kappner, an engineer with experience in the construction of European military fortifications, whom Frémont appointed. Between August 29 and September 6, three weeks before the contract was written, Beard had already received payments totaling $151,000. Estimates later by experienced engineers indicated that the cost of the work should have amounted to no more than $60,000. When the secretary of war visited St. Louis shortly thereafter, he determined that the work never should have been done in the first place. At Frémont's direction, the funds used to pay Beard & Palmer were diverted from an appropriation made by Congress to pay, clothe, and feed the volunteers at St. Louis. Paymaster Andrews was ordered by Frémont at one time under threat of arrest to turn over payroll funds to be used to pay Beard & Palmer. The payments were made on vouchers submitted by the contractor and approved by McKinstry. The total amount of the contract, $180,000, was never completely paid because the department actually ran out of cash. Frémont also ordered McKinstry to contract locally for the construction of 38 wooden mortar boats at $8,250 each for use on the Mississippi River. Commanders were later grateful for the boats when fighting moved down the river but experienced builders estimated the proper cost of the boats should have been in the range of $4,000 each.[11]

After the initial public exigency ceased to provide justification for extraordinary processes and long after established procedures for soliciting proposals and awarding contracts to the lowest or most responsive bidder should have been in place, McKinstry installed a method of procuring clothing and other supplies known as purchasing on requisition. He did this on his own and without instructions from Frémont. Early in September, without soliciting competitive bids, he issued a contract to the firm of Livingston, Bell & Co., for thousands of sets of uniforms, shoes, hats, overcoats, knapsacks, socks, and undershirts, "all to be made of the best army materials, and to conform to army regulations and requirements; the cost of manufacture, material, and transportation to be furnished to this department, upon which the department will allow a fair mercantile profit to the contractors." Itemized prices were not established ahead of the contract. There was no cost limit. There was no determination of what a fair mercantile profit was or how it would be determined. There was no delivery schedule. And, finally, there was no bond required to guarantee the performance and compliance of Livingston, Bell & Co. Under the same conditions, the St. Louis firm of Child, Pratt & Fox furnished army supplies between May and September, 1861, to the value of more than $800,000 without the price of a single item being determined beforehand, without competition, without a limit to the government's cost, and without a definition of what the contractor's profit was or how it would be determined.[12]

Child, Pratt & Fox became the prime supplier for the quartermaster's department at St. Louis without submitting competitive bids or establishing the prices of articles beforehand. It also became obvious that Child, Pratt & Fox was brokering most of the material it furnished to McKinstry. The agent for the firm of Stringer, Allen & Van Nostrand stated that his firm sold $2,599 worth of drawers to Child, Pratt & Fox for resale to the quartermaster's department at higher prices. The firm of Fiske, Knight & Co., sold $4,845 worth of brogans to Child, Pratt & Fox for mark-up and resale. Giles F. Filley, a member of Frank Blair's Safety Committed, reported offering camp kettles and mess pans manufactured by the firm he and his brother owned to McKinstry and being directed instead to sell them to Child, Pratt & Fox for resale. Filley reported he sold camp kettles at 42½ cents each and mess pans at 27½ cents each; Child, Pratt & Fox resold them to the quartermaster's department at 65 cents and 35 cents each, respectively. Filley testified later that he understood Child, Pratt & Fox had no written contract with the government for the products involved nor had it submitted itemized prices to McKinstry beforehand. The firm was operating on an open order for whatever supplies and materials it could provide. Filley also complained about the method of payment he received. Child, Pratt & Fox was paid by the government in gold coins or in United States Treasury certificates that could be redeemed for gold coins. Yet the firm paid its suppliers, such as the Filleys, with Missouri state script which ran at a discount of ten percent below gold coins or treasury certificates. Filley estimated that Child, Pratt & Fox was earning between 50 and 55 percent reselling items to McKinstry, between the mark up over its cost and the discount involved in state script. Filley would have gladly sold the goods directly to McKinstry at cost, he testified. Child, Pratt & Fox was in the hardware business, not in the clothing, mess pan, camp kettle, or shoe trade. One of the partners, Edward F. Fox, had been instrumental in retaining McKinstry in the position of chief quartermaster of the Department of the West by convincing in-coming Secretary of War Simon Cameron to reverse the order of out-going Secretary of War Joseph Holt in March. James P. Coghan, bookkeeper at Child, Pratt & Fox, admitted subsequently in testimony that the profits made by his firm through its monopoly on supplying the quartermaster's department at St. Louis were enormous, approaching 35 to 40 percent without taking into consideration the discount on Missouri state script. It was established later that an agreement to pay cost plus a fair mercantile profit was unknown in army procurement procedures. Experienced quartermaster officers testified they had never done business on these terms.[13]

In similar cases, merchants offered to sell tents to the quartermaster's department at St. Louis. All quickly learned that they could only sell to Joseph S. Pease who marked his costs up five percent or more before he resold to McKinstry. The firm of Clements & Co. sold Pease 100 tents for $22; Pease then resold them to the quartermaster for $30, making a profit of over 36 percent. There were rumors that Pease was related to McKinstry, which the quartermaster strongly denied. "They know better," he insisted, "for it was in proof before them that he was not connected with me by blood or marriage, and that I had no acquaintance with him before I was stationed here." McKinstry was factually correct that Pease was not related to him by blood or marriage but Pease's sister, Angelina, was married to Alexander McKinstry, Susan's brother. They were the parents of Oliver McKinstry, the young militiaman who closely escaped capture by Lyon's force earlier in the year. There was not a blood or marriage relationship between Pease and McKinstry but there was a definite and obvious family relationship.[14]

In another case of brokerage, Alexander Largue, agent for the firm of Code, Hopper & Gratz, offered McKinstry several thousand covered canteens at 36½ cents. McKinstry refused the offer, referring Largue to Samuel P. Brady, who bought the canteens and immediately resold them to the quartermaster's department at 44 cents. Brady described himself as a commission merchant and broker from Detroit and claimed to have known McKinstry since childhood. He was, in fact, the son of Colonel Hugh Brady who had commanded the 2nd Infantry from his home in Detroit and who had held the second lieutenancy open for McKinstry until he graduated from West Point. Brady later testified that McKinstry had contacted him for advice and assistance on prices and sources of items that were not available at St. Louis. Brady said that he was engaged in business, specializing in purchasing for the government certain army supplies with which he was familiar and which he furnished at a moderate profit no greater than he would have charged in trade with individuals or corporations. Brady's profit on the sale of the canteens to the quartermaster's department was 20 percent.[15]

With all the buying and selling and reselling taking place, two associates of Frank Blair, John How, former mayor of St. Louis and a member of the Safety Committee, and Walter S. Gurnee, a merchant from Chicago, approached Blair with an offer. They would contract to supply all the needs of up to 40,000 men in return for three-quarters of a million dollars. Blair was in favor of the proposal and encouraged the men to approach Frémont, the departmental commander. Frémont recommended the proposal to McKinstry who rejected it, based on the lack of public competition the arrangement would entail. McKinstry was aware that How and Gurnee intended to procure the majority of the materials involved at locations other then St. Louis. McKinstry wrote to How that he doubted the established firms in the city would concur with this divergence of fortune to outsiders. Frank Blair became furious at McKinstry for using the lack of competition to obstruct what the Congressman considered a done deal, knowing full well that McKinstry was blatantly avoiding competitive bidding himself. In a complete reversal, McKinstry then outlined to Frémont a similar transaction which involved himself entering into agreements with parties who would proceed to New York City to contract for quantities and materials matching those offered by How and Gurnee. He proposed that this be done without competition, but at established prices. McKinstry later thought better of the idea and withdrew it.[16]

The most flagrant abuse of established practices and procedures occurred in the procurement of horses and mules for the army. When the volunteers began flooding into the city, there were no animals within the quartermaster's control. Early on, Lyon had to go searching for the 36 horses he needed to pull his guns when he made the move on Camp Jackson. St. Louis was not well-equipped to supply all the materials of war that the forming organizations would require but it was beneficially located in the heart of the nation's horse and mule country. Farms abounded in Missouri and throughout Illinois, Wisconsin, and Iowa. Stock markets were held regularly and stock dealers did business in every city, county, town, and hamlet throughout the Midwest. McKinstry avoided the quartermaster department's established practice that required advertising for specific numbers of various types of horses and mules which would be inspected at identified locations on certain dates and would be accepted at the lowest prices. Instead, McKinstry set up a hand-picked corps of agents who would inspect, accept, and pay for horses and mules as they were offered. He published the prices the government would pay: $110 for mules, $119 for cavalry horses, and $150 for larger artillery horses. Traders were pleased to discover these prices which were well above the market prices at and around St. Louis until they tried to sell their animals. James Everett, a farmer and horse dealer, arrived in the city with a small herd and a note of recommendation from Frank Blair. On presenting his stock, he was told by McKinstry that no inspectors were available that day and, as it turned out, for the next four days. Before long, Everett came to understand the only way he was going to see his stock was to sell it first to Charles M. Elleard, one of the "California gang." Elleard bought Everett's stock well below the prices the government had published and resold the animals to the government at a mark-up of close to 40 percent. McKinstry also turned down an offer of horses from Frederick M. Colburn, yet bought equivalent animals from Jim Neil and Charles M. Elleard at prices higher than those Colburn was willing to accept. Leonidas Haskell, who had been Frémont's neighbor in California and was now serving on Frémont's staff as his police director, purchased and resold thousands of mules to the government for $110 when the local market was below $100. John Farrar received two contracts after his brother's solicitation, one for cavalry horses and one for artillery horses. Farrar had angered McKinstry by going over his head to Frank Blair. When Farrar arrived in the city with the cavalry horses, he was informed by the quartermaster that only artillery horses were being inspected that day. When he returned the following day with larger, stronger artillery horses, he was told that only cavalry horses were being inspected. This continued until Farrar gave up and sold the remainder of his contracts to Samuel A. Buckmaster who inherited the same problems that had driven Farrar away. Buckmaster eventually sold his stock to Jim Neil. While this was taking place, McKinstry's agents were inspecting and purchasing at several locations in the city, one of which was the Abbey Track, a race course owned and managed by Charles M. Elleard. When horses were inspected and accepted at any of the several locations, cavalry horses were immediately branded with US on the left shoulder and artillery horses were branded on the left shoulder and left flank. Thomas Dunn, a dealer in horseflesh, testified to seeing Elleard close the gates to the Abbey Track after the business of the day ended and brand cavalry horses he had accepted from sellers at a price well below the $119 the government would pay with a second brand on the flank, thereby raising the cost to the government to $150 and significantly increasing his profits. At about this time, Robert T. Coffey, a citizen of St. Louis, reported a conversation with Jim Neil during which the dealer bragged that he had a good thing going: on the same day, he was able to inspect, sell, and accept his own horses on behalf of the quartermaster's department. Coffey admitted, though, that "Neil had good stock."[17]

Animals were issued to army units as their requirements were made known, but the purchasing of animals went on without regard to whether there was a need pending. Sellers brought their stock to an inspection station where one of McKinstry's agents would inspect and accept or, more often, demand the seller accept a price substantially lower than what the government had advertised, Sellers had little choice, especially when bringing in a large herd. There were significant costs involved in rounding up and driving a herd of horses or mules from the country and there was no inexpensive way to hold stock in the city while the disappointed sellers tried to make sense of the bizarre manner of doing business. Most of them soon realized what they were up against and took the prices offered, generally in the range of $60 to $85 a head. The procurement of horses and mules was driven by the greed of the fortunate few who had McKinstry's blessing, regardless of the need for more animals or the numbers on hand at the moment. James Harkness, a dealer, reported seeing unfed, un-watered, and mistreated horses and mules dying in fields, corrals, and along the roads leading to the city. Harkness later testified that, in his opinion, McKinstry's agents purchased four or more times the amount of livestock needed by the army, much of which had to be held for months before being requisitioned and issued to the troops, or left to perish of neglect. Between May 23 and September 25, Frémont's California associate, Charles M. Elleard, purchased and resold 2,800 horses to the quartermaster's department at St. Louis for more than $310,000. Frank Blair's friend, Jim Neil, sold about 1,200 horses and mules for more than $140,000. Leonidas Haskell furnished approximately 2,300 mules to the government at a cost of more than $280,000. In the four months between May and September, 1861, McKinstry's department issued vouchers for more than 21,000 horses and mules at a cost to the government of more than $2.6 million. In almost every case, the government paid prices made higher than the market by the greed of the fortunate few.[18]

To express appreciation and to maintain favor, Elleard provided a horse and carriage for McKinstry's personal use. Several of McKinstry's agents were approached by Jim Neil and asked to contribute between $150 and $200 each toward the cost of this transportation. McKinstry accepted the horse and carriage without argument. Yet when Josephus Irvine offered a pair of carriage horses for McKinstry's use, a dealer named John Brown described the result. McKinstry and Irvine were conversing in low tones at McKinstry's desk when McKinstry rose, very excited, and shouted, "You damned scoundrel!" He ordered Irvine out of his office. Brown stated that he thought McKinstry was going to inflict harm on Irvine and stepped between the men, taking McKinstry by the arm. "This damned scoundrel wants to bribe me to give him a contract by offering to make me a present of a pair of fine carriage horses!" the quartermaster shouted. McKinstry ordered Irvine out of his office and threatened that if he was not gone immediately, he would have the guard throw him out. McKinstry's outburst was not untypical. John Allen offered to split the profits of a contract with Charles, McKinstry's son, claiming he had heard this was the accepted manner of gaining preference in obtaining contracts. McKinstry ordered Allen from his office and refused to have anything to do with the merchant thereafter. These incidents indicate that McKinstry was willing to go along with improprieties among his inner circle, but was strongly adverse to having anything to do with outsiders.[19]

In a more violent confrontation, Henry Clapp, a roofing contractor, testified that he was arrested by armed soldiers and taken to McKinstry's office where the quartermaster demanded of him whether he had made accusations against Alfred B. Ogden, the architect responsible for the construction of Benton Barracks in the city. McKinstry claimed to have heard that Clapp had accused Ogden of soliciting bribes when awarding contracts for the work on the facility. When Clapp denied the accusation, McKinstry called him damned liar and threatened to throw Clapp into prison on bread and water, insisting that he was determined to stop people from making accusations against the officers of his department. Charles H. Pond, another St. Louis architect and Clapp's father-in-law, witnessed this confrontation. "When he got Clapp before him," Pond later testified, "he cursed him up hill and down, and scared him so that he could not say a single word, a file of soldiers being around him." Pond interceded, explaining there were rumors Clapp had offered Ogden $700 to get the roofing work. Pond asked Clapp if that were true. McKinstry interrupted: "Stop! Don't answer that question! I am lawyer enough to ask this man all the questions I want him to answer!" McKinstry then demanded of Clapp, "Did you give Ogden any money, five hundred dollars or one dollar?" Clapp admitted he had offered Ogden an advance draft in the amount of $700 on the quartermaster's department, assuming that he would get the contract for the work. McKinstry demanded a yes-or-no reply to the amounts he had specified: $500 or one dollar. Clapp answered no, pleading that he be allowed to explain what had happened. "You stop!" McKinstry shouted at the frightened man. "Did you agree to give him $500, or one dollar?" Again, Clapp answered no. "Then," McKinstry shouted, "I will confine you five days on bread and water unless you recant that thing immediately!" At the same time, he called for the sergeant, threatening to have Clapp taken away. McKinstry handed Clapp a paper on which was written a recantation of the charges of fraud and bribery against Ogden, saying Clapp could sign it or go to prison. Pond and others present talked Clapp into signing the paper and leaving McKinstry's office. The recantation was published in the newspapers the following day. McKinstry subsequently awarded the contract for the roofing of Benton Barracks to a contractor named Thompson who had submitted a bid of $3.50 per hundred square feet of roofing. An experienced roofer, one Cristy, had submitted a bid of $2.20 per hundred square feet. A Congressional investigating committee's report later declared, "The consequence is that the government got a poor roof at a big price, the result of corrupt official action."[20]

At the same time, Nathaniel Lyon was on the move in central Missouri. Lyon and Frémont had never met. Frémont arrived at St. Louis after Lyon had taken to the field. The day Frémont did arrive, Captain John S. Cavender and Major Ben Farrar, emissaries from Lyon at Springfield, met Frémont and pleaded for reinforcements and supplies for Lyon's column. Frémont had the resources available to send to Lyon's support: there were nine regiments in northern Missouri under Brigadier General John Pope that were not opposed by a hostile force and two regiments at Rolla under Sigel, again not opposed by a hostile force. Frémont refused to send reinforcements from either column. Instead, he ordered four of Pope's regiments to St. Louis where they became part of an expedition Frémont personally led down the Mississippi River on steamboats to Cairo, Illinois, to reinforce Brigadier General Benjamin Prentiss against a Confederate threat that never materialized. Sigel's regiments were unable to move from Rolla because of a lack of transportation since McKinstry had dismissed the teamsters there. Before Cavender left for St. Louis, Lyon instructed him not to divulge any of his plans or conditions to McKinstry. Lyon suspected McKinstry would go out of his way to thwart him. Shortly after Cavender and Farrar arrived in the city, Dr. Frank Porter, another emissary from Lyon, arrived in the city and went immediately to McKinstry, asking for teams, wagons, and drivers to move the 13th Illinois and the 7th Missouri regiments from Rolla to Springfield. Porter later reported to Adjutant General Thomas that McKinstry "did not seem at all anxious about the matter, and stated the impossibility of furnishing those regiments with transportation." McKinstry told the doctor he had plenty of mules available but lacked wagons. When Porter met with Frémont and repeated the request he had made of McKinstry, he told Frémont that Lyon was going to fight the Confederate force in front of him with or without the support of his commanding general. Frémont told Porter he had ordered Lyon to fall back from Springfield to Rolla, adding, "If [Lyon] fights, it will be on his own responsibility."[21]

Lyon, headstrong as ever, moved from Springfield and on August 10, 1861, pitched into Sterling Price's much larger Confederate army near Wilson's Creek.

The battle was a disaster with untrained and inexperienced troops going into battle on both sides. Lyon's army lost a quarter of its strength but, of greater importance, while leading a movement that should have been delegated to a subordinate, Lyon was killed. Sigel, who finally managed to come up from Rolla, and Lyon's second in command, Brigadier General John M. Schofield, brought the survivors back to the rail head at Rolla. Price, after resting his victorious Confederates and gleaning the battlefield of abandoned arms and equipment, turned his attention toward a small federal garrison defending the Missouri River town of Lexington. Unknown to McKinstry, on the battlefield at Wilson's Creek lay Colonel Richard H. Weightman, mortally wounded while leading his brigade of Brigadier General James S. Raines's division of Price's Confederate army. Weightman was the cadet who attacked McKinstry at West Point 24 years earlier.[22]

The news of the disaster at Wilson's Creek did not reach St. Louis until August 13, but when it did, Frémont became alarmed. He did not know where Price and his Confederates would turn next. He was also aware that the nation and the Blairs would hold him responsible for the decision not to send reinforcements and supplies to Lyon at Springfield, and for Lyon's death. He was so concerned about the effect the news would have on the population of St. Louis that he declared martial law in the city and county and appointed McKinstry as provost marshal to enforce it. McKinstry declared that civil law would remain in effect but, at his discretion, martial law would be applied when necessary. This confused and infuriated many citizens of the city and county who could not predict which force the provost marshal might choose to send against them. Jessie Frémont wrote of the times, "These were wearing days and anxious nights, but the city learned to rest in peace, trusting to the watchfulness of Provost Marshal McKinstry and Colonel Neil." Frémont had named Colonel John Neil to command the city garrison and to serve as McKinstry's assistant provost marshal.[23]

Frémont directed McKinstry to suppress newspapers he felt were publishing information injurious to the Union cause, or to the Frémont cause. McKinstry banned the sale of the *New York News,* the *Journal of Commerce,* the *Day Book,* the *Freeman's Journal,* and the *Brooklyn Eagle.* In McKinstry's own mind, the *St. Louis Republican* which, in spite of its name, was the Democratic party's sheet, was pro-southern. Using the enticement of federal advertising revenue, McKinstry coerced its editor into supporting Frémont and allowed the paper to continue publishing to its more than 7,000 subscribers. On his own, McKinstry suppressed the *St. Louis Evening News,* a paper published by friends of Frank Blair and supported financially and editorially by the Congressman. The *St. Louis Daily Missouri Democrat* which, again in spite of its name, was the Republican party's sheet, continued to support Frémont and was allowed to publish unhindered.[24]

Colonel Gustav Koerner, one of the few of Frémont's staff properly appointed and commissioned by the government, wrote that McKinstry at this time was

PROCLAMATION

Head Quarters Western Department,

ST. LOUIS, MO., August 14, 1861.

I hereby declare and establish

Martial Law

In the City and County of St. Louis.

Major J. McKINSTRY, U. S. Army, is appointed Provost Marshal. All orders and regulations issued by him will be respected and obeyed.

J. C. FRÉMONT,

Major General Commanding.

Broadside announcement of martial Law in the city and county of St. Louis by Frémont, appointing McKinstry as Provost Marshal. (Missouri Historical Society, St. Louis)

"unpopular in the regular army and as provost marshal made himself perfectly odious by his vexatious measures. No one was allowed to leave the city of St. Louis or St. Louis County without a pass ... All saloons had to be closed by dark, and all persons found in the streets after nine o'clock were arrested by the patrols. Numerous arrests were made of citizens suspected to be disloyal, and no redress could be had in the courts, as martial law had been proclaimed. A great deal of dissatisfaction with Frémont was owing to McKinstry. I believe him to have been a brave and dashing soldier. He was more than six feet high and of corresponding robustness, of dark complexion and features indicating resolution and energy. He had 'an eye like Mars to threaten or command,' When in full regi-

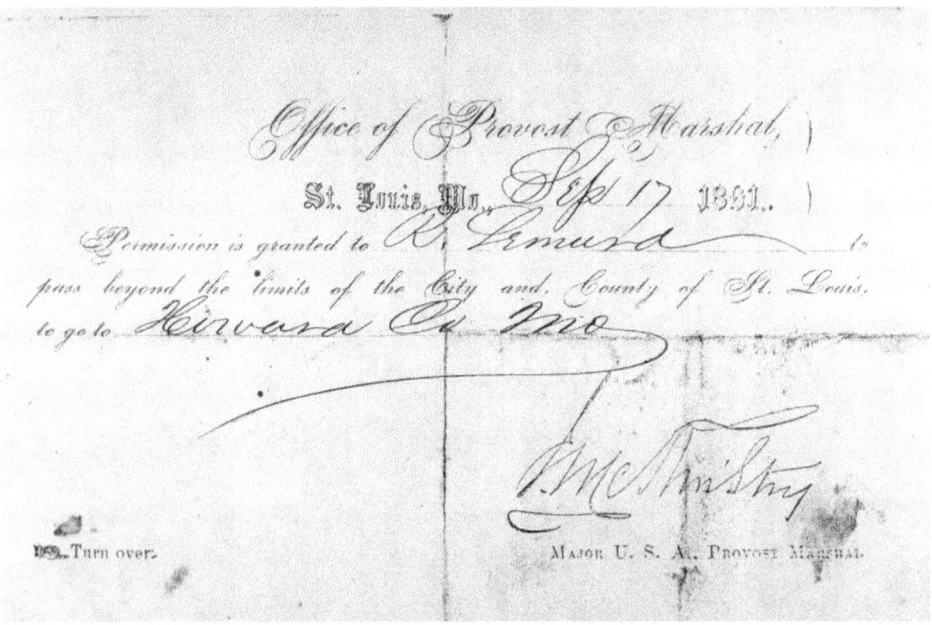

Provost marshal's office pass issued to Reeves Leonard September 17, 1862, signed by McKinstry. (Abiel Leonard Papers, 1782–1932, n.d., Western Historical Manuscript Collection — Columbia, MO)

mentals, on a black charger, he paraded the streets, he looked like the very ideal of a soldier."[25]

About the middle of August, 1861, Frank Blair returned to St. Louis from Washington in time to take part in the impressive funeral the city gave as the remains of Nathaniel Lyon were carried through. Shortly after Blair's arrival, he and Schofield called on Frémont. They were kept waiting in an anteroom for several hours before being ushered into the general's presence. Schofield was prepared to give a report of what had taken place at Wilson's Creek but, instead of listening or even indicating an interest, Frémont launched into a long oration on the campaign he intended to open against the enemy in southwestern Missouri. Blair and Schofield were amazed at Frémont's "egotistical insensitivity" and his lack of subjectivity. Blair later wrote his brother, the postmaster general, that he was quickly losing confidence in Frémont's capability and his observations, since his return to the city, "have shaken my faith in him to the very foundation." Frémont, Blair wrote, "talks of the vigor he is going to use, but I can see none of it, and I fear it will turn out to be some rash and inconsiderate move — adopted in haste to make head against a formidable force which could not have accumulated except through gross and inexcusable negligence ... My decided opinion is that he should be relieved ... the sooner, the better." Montgomery Blair shared the letter with the president, as his brother in St. Louis intended. Frank Blair was completely at enmity with McKinstry by now. It was partially because of the cor-

Montgomery Blair, St. Louis lawyer and Lincoln's postmaster general, was one of the first to see the faults and shortcomings of Frémont, and thus began working for the downfall of Frémont and his quartermaster, McKinstry. (Massachusetts Commandery Military Order of the Loyal Legion and the United States Army Military History Institute)

ruption that attended the workings of the provost marshal's office against many of Blair's constituents and followers, and partly because of McKinstry's refusal to put much of the patronage of the quartermaster's department where Blair wanted it. McKinstry's fate was now decidedly linked to that of Frémont, his commander.[26]

Frémont spent the night of August 29, 1861, awake, alone, thinking, and writing. The startling document he read to his wife and his friend, Edward M. Davis, the following morning extended martial law throughout the state of Missouri. It announced that persons taken within the lines of the army with guns in their hands would be shot if found guilty by a court-martial; the property of persons found to have taken up arms against the United States would be confiscated and their slaves set free; and all persons away from their homes would forthwith return to them or their continued absence would be held as presumptive evidence against them. When Abraham Lincoln read the telegraphed copy of the proclamation, he was alarmed. The possibility of citizens being shot by order of military tribunals was bad, Lincoln thought, but the concept of emancipation in a sensitive border state such as Missouri was not only inflammatory, but plainly encroached on the presidential prerogative. By telegraph, Lincoln suggested that Frémont withdraw the document "as of your own volition." When Frémont refused, the president responded that Frémont's reply "expressed the preference on your part that I should make an open order for the modification, which I cheerfully do."[27]

Frémont's detachment from reality became more evident in meetings he held with two officers of the paymaster general's department in late August and early September. Lieutenant Colonel Timothy P. Andrews, who had been forced to surrender payroll funds to be used to pay Beard & Palmer for work on the city's fortifications, testified to the presidential committee investigating war claims at St. Louis that Frémont, accompanied by McKinstry, had come to his office and, without preamble, told Andrews that as far as he was concerned, "the people of the United States were in the field, that he was at their head, that he meant to carry out such measures as they expected him to carry out, without regard to the red tape of the Washington people." When Andrews suggested that the term "red tape" usually described the system of governmental operations which, in the main, were tried and proven, Frémont repeated his words about the people being in the field, adding, "Now we have only extra-constitutional government; no civil rights, so to speak; all ordinary peaceful rules were to be set aside, and all of this thing of 'red tape' must give way very shortly to what the people required of him." The members of the committee investigating war claims pursued this matter further, interviewing Andrews's assistant paymaster, Major Chauncey C. P. Johnson, who told them in sworn testimony that Frémont had repeatedly in his presence said, "He did not intend, in the administration of this department, to be governed by the rules and regulations that were laid down by others." Several orders from Frémont to Andrews for payments that the paymaster considered illegal or improper had been passed to Johnson who came in contact with Frémont in the process of handling the transactions. Johnson added to his testimony that Frémont had told him, in response to his questioning the propriety of some orders, that he "intended to do what he considered best for the service, without regard to law or regulations; that he intended to cut 'red tape' and arrive at the end without reference to order or system, and directed me to pay these orders."[28]

Frémont's lack of restraint in the matter of finances was exemplified by his efforts to raise money locally. Prior to Frémont's arrival at St. Louis, Lyon, during his advance on Springfield, negotiated and obtained a loan backed by a claim against the federal treasury of $10,000 from the Bank of Springfield. This was added to the amount of $245,730 given to Lyon by the directors of the bank for transfer to St. Louis for safekeeping. These funds were appropriated by Frémont on August 7, 1861, and thrown into the coffers for use at his discretion. On August 13, the day prior to Frémont's declaration of martial law in the city, McKinstry called the directors of the major banks at St. Louis together and ordered them to loan Frémont $250,000. McKinstry made clear to the directors that the funds would be obtained; if they did not agree to the loan, the funds would be seized. Even small local banks experienced Frémont's extortion. The Bank of Missouri had a branch at Canton and the Union Bank had a branch at La Grange. The two banks sent specie in the amount of $68,250 to General John Pope who forwarded the money to their parent organizations at St. Louis for safekeeping. On Frémont's orders, these funds were seized and turned over to Frémont's assistant quartermaster, Edward M. Davis, who used them to pay for purchases of clothing, the greater portion of which went to Davis's son-in-law, Hallowell, a clothing contractor. Later, it was the determination of the committee investigating war claims at St. Louis that these loans and seizures were made without the authority of the government, without the government being informed about them, and that they had all taken place at a time when the federal treasury was meeting its obligations and were, therefore, unnecessary and illegal.[29]

On August 3, 1861, McKinstry was promoted because of seniority to the permanent rank of major in the quartermaster's department, displacing his brevet rank. On September 2, a day short of a month later, Frémont appointed him a brigadier general of volunteers and named him to command the Fifth Division of the army the Pathfinder was bringing together at and around St. Louis. The commanders of the other four divisions were Brigadier Generals Alexander Asboth, Franz Sigel, David Hunter, and John Pope. McKinstry's appointment was temporary; it would expire on July 17, 1862, unless confirmed by the United States Senate. McKinstry donned his new shoulder straps, each bearing the single silver star of his rank. On September 12, with Frémont's reluctant concurrence resulting from strong pressure from the administration at Washington,

McKinstry was replaced as chief quartermaster, Department of the West, by Colonel John Neil. He continued in his role of provost marshal for the city and county of St. Louis in addition to his division command. Less than a month later, the reliable Major Robert Allen was ordered to St. Louis to permanently assume the position of chief quartermaster. Allen was given specific instructions by Quartermaster General Meigs to exercise his judgment in managing the department and to suspend questionable contracts and vouchers. In doing so, Meigs assured Allen, he would be sustained by the department.[30]

Toward the end of August, 1861, Major A. A. Selover, one of the "California gang"; Samuel P. Brady, McKinstry's boyhood friend from Detroit; Charles M. Elleard; and Judge John J. Krum met at the firm of E. Jaccard & Co., dealers in silverware and jewelry, to take delivery of a presentation flag Jaccard had made for one of Frémont's artillery batteries. McKinstry joined the four men, agreeing with them that the flag Jaccard made was exactly what they had in mind. Selover agreed to pay for the flag, the others promising to settle with him later. Selover then asked Jaccard's clerk, Charles L. Spencer, to let them see some silverware. Selover told Spencer he had in mind a complete silver service which Spencer laid out for them. "I carried the set all through," Spencer later testified, "with a number of side pieces, desert knives and cases, oyster ladle, preserve spoons, and some extra pieces. The set, the cases, and the flag, which was priced at $90, were all included in one bill which was in excess of $3,000." Selover told Spencer that the silver service was for Mrs. McKinstry, every piece of which was to be engraved, "Mrs. General McKinstry." Smaller pieces would be engraved, "McK." The salver was engraved "Presented to Mrs. General McKinstry by friends of General Justus McKinstry, as a token of their respect for his distinguished zeal, and the eminent services rendered to his country while acting as provost marshal of the city and country of St. Louis, September 18, A. D., 1861." This took place several days before McKinstry was appointed a brigadier general and indicated that the four men were aware of his pending promotion. They agreed that Selover would be compensated for the cost of the flag and the silver service by subscriptions. Spencer testified that among the subscribers were Edward F. Fox, Jim Neil, Almon Thompson, Asa Jones, and Samuel P. Brady, all beneficiaries of McKinstry's largess. Spencer, on behalf of E. Jaccard & Co., subscribed $100 himself, hoping, he testified, "to make a good thing of it." Charles M. Elleard refused to pay the $250 Selover demanded of him, declaring, "No, sir, not a cent!" He had already paid the full $1,500 for a horse and carriage that the clique had presented to Jessie Frémont. McKinstry was chosen to make that presentation, saying that the horse and carriage were from friends of Frank Blair. When Jessie consulted Blair on whether she should accept the gift, he told her she had better not, and the horse and rig were sent back to the livery stable. Elleard noted, however, a few days later that the horse and carriage had been taken to the Brant mansion where the Frémonts resided. McKinstry and Frémont often socialized during these months in St. Louis in addition to the time they spend together on official business. On September 6, the nephew of the French Emperor Napoleon was scheduled to visit the city. "Well, they waited and waited and scowled and swore," commented an observer. "When 10 o'clock came, without any Prince, a precipitate retreat ... took place." The prince had arrived by railroad instead of by river steamer, and had originally been announced, and was asleep at the Planters House while the commanding general and his quartermaster waited on the levee.[31]

Frémont became acutely aware of Frank Blair's negative attitude toward him when the Congressman returned from Washington. Frémont chafed under what he considered Blair's unwarranted positions and statements. On September 18, Frémont ordered Provost Marshal McKinstry to arrest Blair on charges of "insidious and dishonorable efforts to bring my authority into contempt with the government and to undermine my influence as an officer." On his release from confinement at the arsenal a few days later, a furious Blair filed charges against Frémont with Adjutant General Thomas at Washington on September 26. He charged "tardy reporting for duty at St. Louis; poor tactics in trying to reinforce General Lyon; refusal to see those who sought an audience on important business; violation of the President's offers by issuing the Emancipation Proclamation; the employ of disreputable persons such as McKinstry," and so on. Blair, in his anger, overlooked the fact that he, not Frémont, was responsible for the employ of McKinstry. Blair and Frémont were feuding like adolescents and dividing the Union people of St. Louis into opposing camps when each should have been doing everything possible to unite the factions and solidify the Union cause. The squabble in Missouri was noted in Washington and the president was aware that he soon would have to step in. Lincoln, the ultimate politician, weighed the strength of the following that Frémont still commanded in the nation against the power of the Blair family in the volatile politics of this border state.[32]

On September 20, Colonel James Mulligan, commanding the small federal garrison at Lexington on the Missouri River, was forced after a valiant fight against odds of four to one to surrender the town to Sterling Price and his Confederates. At any time during the siege, Frémont could have sent an expedition on steamboats up the river to reinforce Mulligan or to evacuate him and his men. Frémont did neither.[33]

On September 26, a full two months after he arrived and assumed command of the Department of the West, Frémont left St. Louis at the head of an army of 21,000 men. He moved into the field, heading westward. Sterling Price, after his victory at Lexington, had begun a slow withdrawal heading southward in the direction of Arkansas. The main theater of operations for the remainder of the war would be southward and eastward from St. Louis. Frémont was marching in the wrong direction. On September 24, just before the movement, Frémont's aide, Gustav Koerner, wrote to his wife, Sophie, "Chaos reigns here. I will go with this expedition; and if things do not improve, I will resign. I have already talked very freely about the mismanagement of many things. [Frémont's] surroundings are good for nothing. Only an important victory can save him." By October 7, Frémont's five divisions were on the road for Tipton, Missouri. Price's Confederate army made it a point to stay well out in front of and away from the much larger Union column.[34]

Even before Frémont took command at St. Louis, a congressional committee chaired by New York's Charles Van Wyck began holding hearings on how government officials were distributing war contracts for services and supplies nationwide. The committee's creation was one of the first acts of Congress after convening the special session called by Lincoln that met on July 4, 1861. Members of the committee, in addition to Van Wyck, its chair, were Congressmen Elihu B. Washburne, of Illinois; William S. Hoffman, of Indiana; Reuben E. Fenton, of New York; Henry L. Dawes, of Massachusetts; William G. Steele, of New Jersey; and James S. Jackson, of Kentucky. The war was barely 75 days old when the Van Wyck Committee began holding hearings which it would continue to do well into April of the following year. After meeting in New York, Boston, and New Bedford, the committee moved to St. Louis.[35]

As the committee moved its hearings to St. Louis, Lincoln was meeting with General-in-Chief Scott at Washington to discuss the military situation in Missouri and the future of Frémont. Major General George B. McClellan telegraphed the president his advice, "I would suggest for your consideration E. A. Hitchcock, late of the army ... now a resident of St. Louis, as probably eminently qualified [to serve as Frémont's chief of staff.]" In line with the president's concerns, Quartermaster General Meigs and Postmaster General Blair, who were brothers-in-law, arrived at St. Louis on September 12. They had been sent by the president to observe what was taking place in the west with orders to report back. Meigs, of course, was most interested in the operations of the quartermaster's department there. He was not impressed with what he saw. He reported that McKinstry was a rapid talker whose glibness struck Meigs as rooted in the fear that his statements would not bear examination. The quartermaster general did admit McKinstry had shown energy and resourcefulness in fulfilling his responsibilities but his contracts were confusing and showed extravagance. As to Frémont, Meigs reported, "I do not think he is fit for his place; he is prodigal of money, unscrupulous, surrounded by villains, inacceptable to the people, and ambitious; should he see the opportunity, he would not hesitate to play Aaron Burr."[36]

Secretary of War Cameron and Adjutant General Thomas were dispatched by the president to St. Louis to observe and advise. Showing his continuing concern with affairs in the Department of the West, Lincoln wrote to Brigadier General — former Congressman — Samuel R. Curtis regarding whether he thought it necessary to replace Frémont. On October 7, this was the major topic at the administration's cabinet meeting at Washington.[37]

Charles H. Van Wyck, New York congressman and chair of the congressional committee looking into charges of waste, fraud, and abuse at St. Louis which helped bring about McKinstry's final court-martial. (National Archives)

The Van Wyck Committee opened hearings on October 15 at Barnum's Hotel in St. Louis, sitting "in secret session, examining witnesses and taking testimony relative to the contracts, orders, and expenditures for the public service by the Quartermaster's Department in this place." Immediately upon learning of the committee's presence, McKinstry's clerk, H. W. G. Clements, wrote to Chairman

Van Wyck and offered in the absence of McKinstry, who was with his division in the field on the road to Tipton, "to attend upon your Committee at any time with all the papers needful for your examination, and trust you will, at any time, call upon me as representing General McKinstry, for any explanation of any transaction which may appear to you to require explanation. All papers and documents in this office will be most cheerfully presented for your examination and inspection. Justice to General McKinstry, and a desire to aid your Committee by every means in my power, has induced me to make this communication." Clements was not called to testify until well toward the end of the committee's hearings and, by then, the members were no longer looking for justification or explanation of what had taken place at St. Louis during McKinstry's term in office. The committee members were men of prominence from both parties, experienced politicians who had seen much during their days in public office. They were not interested in embarrassing the Lincoln administration or hindering the Union war effort, yet their findings appalled them. Congressman Dawes wrote to his wife about his horror at "the stupendous frauds practiced upon the gov't." Congressman Washburne was dumbfounded at what he called the unblushing robbery he found everywhere he looked. "There never was so glorious a cause so poorly served, so utterly ruined through the instrumentality in about equal degrees of incompetence and knavery," Dawes protested. The committee's final report called the deplorable conditions "a tax upon the treasury of the United States which nothing but the most controlling reason of military necessity would ever justify. So far as the examination of the committee threw any light upon the question of profits, they were led to believe that the sum was much larger than is here admitted. But this sum is enough to call for an explanation from those to whom the funds of the government were entrusted. When the public credit is strained to its utmost tension, and the patriotism of the capitalist appealed to for means to meet the exigencies that press upon the government, the country has a right to know why this enormous amount has been diverted from the legitimate expenditure into the pockets of private individuals. The committee sought in vain for any satisfactory explanation. They regret to believe that none exists. It appeared that much of the expenditure, and that where the largest profits were paid, was upon those articles which, without the slightest difficulty, the quartermaster could have obtained at first hand from the merchants, manufacturers, and furnishers of St. Louis and its vicinity. This he persistently refused to do." The committed castigated Frémont as well in its report and in testimony before Congress, in which Congressman Dawes described Frémont's rule as one during which "an almost unprecedented waste of public money" occurred. However, throughout the committee's report of its findings, the members identified McKinstry as the primary source of the problems with government contracts at St. Louis.[38]

Another investigative body, the Commission of War Claims in St. Louis, was established by direction of the president and by order of the secretary of war to

Adjutant General Lorenzo Thomas knew McKinstry throughout his military career and was instrumental in bringing about Frémont's, and McKinstry's, downfall at St. Louis. (Massachusetts Commandery Military Order of the Loyal Legion and the United States Army Military History Institute)

investigate and settle claims arising from mismanagement and fraud in the Department of the West. The commission consisted of Hugh Campbell of St. Louis, a principal in the firm of R. Campbell & Co., which was a supplier of McKinstry; David Davis of Illinois, a close friend of the president and one of the men responsible for securing the nomination for Lincoln at the Chicago Republican convention in 1860; and Judge Joseph Holt of Kentucky who, as interim secretary of war in the final days of the Buchanan administration, had tried to replace McKinstry at St. Louis. The commission did not meet at St. Louis until November 6 but its existence and purpose were known and discussed throughout out the city and within the army in the field. The members of the commission had a harsh opinion of McKinstry. "Our investigations from day to day have afforded strong and ever-multiplying proofs that the administration of ... Quartermaster McKinstry was marked by personal favoritism, by a complete indifference to the public interests, and by an unceasing anxiety to fill at the expense of the nation the pockets of a clique of men who surrounded him and, enjoying the uninterrupted *entrée* to his office, ever stood between the government and the honest merchants and mechanics who sought to have dealings with it." The commission wrote in detail about how under McKinstry the system of advertising for bids and awarding to the lowest responsible bidder had been abandoned at St. Louis in favor of the use of middle-men, through whom purchases for the government were forced. They stated that the system, "if not an original device with Quartermaster McKinstry, was certainly pushed by him to an extent which has no parallel in the official delinquencies as connected with the military service of the country."[39]

Meanwhile, Frémont moved his column along the tracks of the Pacific Railroad, paralleling the southern bank of the Missouri River as far as Tipton, from where he intended to march overland in the direction of Springfield. He wrote to Jessie almost daily. On October 10, from Camp Asboth near Tipton, he complained to her that Secretary of War Cameron and Adjutant General Thomas were in St. Louis. "I want the Secretary of War to put an end to that kind of action which is impeding me by producing want of confidence. I think [Thomas] is not friendly to me." The following day, hearing that transfers of several senior officers of his command were pending, he wrote, "I don't think my dispatch to Cameron, requesting that McKinstry be left with me, reached him. Whether detained [by Thomas] or someone with him, he can find out. General Thomas, contrary to usage and regulation, ordered McKinstry and others from my department, without doing it through me — entirely overlooking and slighting me. It is a discourtesy and a military offense." By October 19, Frémont's army had reached the banks of the Osage River. Frémont wrote that transportation was the army's single most trying difficulty and asked his wife to do whatever was necessary to get wagons, mules, harness, and drivers sent to Tipton. He wrote that the divisions of Hunter, Pope, and McKinstry were "still alongside the railroad, transportation bound." He wrote Jessie that he was not sending orders to his staff at St. Louis because he did not feel they would have any force. The administration, he told her, "encourages all manner of disobedience with impunity." Fré-

Joseph Holt, interim secretary of war at the end of the Buchanan administration, tried to have McKinstry replaced at St. Louis. He later was one of three men named to the War Claims Commission that brought about McKinstry's final court-martial. (National Archives)

mont's October 24 letter had a more positive tone, advising Jessie that the van of his army was at Quincy with Sigel in the lead, Asboth next behind. He had "a good letter from General McKinstry. He is pressing forward; his advance will be in Warsaw today." On the 25th, from Hermansville, he wrote, "General Asboth's division is on the march, and will camp tonight seven miles in my rear, on open prairie ... and here, perhaps, the divisions which are behind — Hunter's, Pope's, and McKinstry's — will concentrate. General McKinstry is doing his best to get forward and so, I suppose, all are now."[40]

That same day, shouting "Frémont and the Union!" Colonel Zagonyi led the charge of Frémont's body guard into the streets of Springfield, skirmishing with and routing a small number of Confederate scouts and taking possession of the city. The main Confederate force was falling back from Lexington, its nearest column some 60 miles in front of Frémont's van. A week later, large portions of Frémont's army were still straggling along the road to Springfield, suffering from transportation shortages. "It would have been a good thing if Major Allen had gone to Tipton to push supplies forward," Frémont wrote Jessie. "McKinstry with his division will be in today. Pope ought to be here tomorrow."[41]

The day before Zagonyi led the charge into Springfield, President Lincoln mailed secret orders to General Curtis at St. Louis with instructions that they were to be delivered upon receipt to Frémont and to Hunter, Frémont's second in command, unless Frémont had recently won a battle or was in the immediate presence of the enemy and in expectation of fighting a battle. The orders relieved Frémont and put Hunter in his place. A subordinate of Curtis's carried the orders to the army, slipping past guards that Frémont had specifically charged with stopping any such messenger, and delivered the orders. When Frémont read the president's orders, he flew into a rage and gave orders to stop the march of all divisions immediately. He tore the shoulder straps bearing the two stars of his rank from the shoulders of his coat. At the urging of McKinstry, he replaced the insignia but insisted he would pass command immediately to General Pope, who was present. Again at the urging of McKinstry and others on his staff, he agreed to await the arrival of Hunter in the morning. When he did arrive, Hunter offered to delay the transfer of command if Frémont expected a battle in the immediate future. Hunter had no idea what Frémont's plans were, or where the Confederate forces under Sterling Price could be found. Frémont rejected Hunter's offer and at ten in the evening of November 2, 1861, Frémont turned command of the Department of the West over. Hunter called the division commanders to a conference. Learning that the closest elements of Price's army were at least 50 miles away, he asked for recommendations. Pope would not comment. Asboth, Sigel, and McKinstry urged continuing the advance. Hunter, however, followed the recommendations that accompanied his orders and turned the army back toward St. Louis. McKinstry received written orders to turn his division over to Curtis and to return to St. Louis ahead of the army. John Charles Frémont's command of the Department of the West had lasted exactly one hundred days.[42]

From Washington on November 11, having replaced General Scott and assumed the title general-in-chief himself, McClellan telegraphed in cipher to Curtis in St. Louis, "Have directed General Hunter to arrest McKinstry and send him to the Arsenal at St. Louis to report to you. Allow the least possible communications between him and his friends in the city." Unaware of the situation awaiting him, McKinstry rode on horseback to Rolla where he boarded the cars for St. Louis. On November, 13, at one of the stations along the way, he was arrested and taken into custody by a Captain Stendon. At the 13th Street Depot in St. Louis, he was removed from the cars by Captain Gordon Granger at the head of a body of cavalry, some 20 men. Granger, now in command at the St. Louis Arsenal, was one of the officers who had urged Garcia to bring his charges against McKinstry when Granger was a second lieutenant of mounted rifles in Mexico. Arriving at the arsenal, McKinstry was confined in a single room. Just prior to his arrest, his clerk, Clements, and his cashier, Hahn, were taken into custody and confined at Jefferson Barracks, ten miles down the Mississippi River from the city. The books and papers in McKinstry's office were seized and held.[43]

9

The Final Court

The Department of the West was discontinued and divided on November 9, 1861. Hunter was promoted to major general and given the Department of Kansas. McKinstry's former subordinate, Colonel Edward R. S. Canby, was given the Department of New Mexico. Major General Henry W. Halleck was given the Department of Missouri. Halleck's orders were to concentrate the forces therein southward and eastward in the direction that would become the major theater of war along the Mississippi and Tennessee rivers. Halleck's chief quartermaster, Major Robert Allen, was charged with restoring competence and confidence to a system of supply that was in deplorable condition. General-in-Chief McClellan minced no words when he told Halleck what he expected, "Reducing chaos to order ... and of reducing to a point of economy consistent with the interests of the State, a system of reckless expenditure and fraud perhaps unheard of in the history of the world." Halleck authorized Allen to annul contracts he determined fraudulent, to cancel the salaries of officers he deemed useless, to dismiss Frémont's "colossal staff hierarchy, with more titles than brains," and to stop further payments to Beard & Palmer for the fortification of the city.[1]

Immediately upon his return to St. Louis, Frémont reported by mail to the office of the adjutant general at Washington for further orders. When these were not forthcoming, he and the family left for New York City where they settled at the Astor House. Although tarnished by the administration's discontent with his performance in the west, Frémont still had a large following throughout the nation. Many of his supporters suspected political intrigue was a major part of his being left without a command. President Lincoln had to face the fact that Frémont was too popular to be arrested and brought up on charges, or even left sitting in New York awaiting orders. Two months later, Frémont was given command of the newly-created Mountain Department with headquarters at Wheeling, in western Virginia. It was a different story for Frémont's quartermaster. McKinstry was held in close confinement at the St. Louis arsenal for a week before he was permitted to telegraph Colonel Sibley at the quartermaster's department at Washington in response to Sibley's query about when the department could expect the submission of McKinstry's final accounting. "My papers have been seized and are in the possession of General Curtis," McKinstry wired back. "My clerk and myself are incarcerated like felons & myself forbidden communication with any one unless permissioned by Curtis. I cannot therefore comply with your order. As an officer of the Q. M. Dept., I protest against such treatment & demand an investigation by any tribunal my accusers may select."[2]

On November 22, nine days after his arrest and confinement, Curtis informed McKinstry that the Commission on War Claims was ready to begin the examination of his papers. He told McKinstry that he would not be released from custody to be present during the examination but that he could appoint someone to attend and act for him. "[I]t is important to me that my papers should be properly examined," he responded, "and I therefore request that my attorney, John M. Krum, Esq., be permitted, on my behalf, to be present ... If any examination is made, I hope it may be what I have been asking to have done — a full and fair one."[3]

On December 7, Adjutant General Thomas telegraphed Major Joseph Totten, assistant inspector general at St. Louis: "By direction of the general-in-chief, you are relieved from duty of making an investigation of the affairs of the Q. M. Dept. under Major McKinstry and will turn over your instructions of the 30th November to Samuel T. Glover, Esq., of St. Louis." McKinstry had not yet been charged with any impropriety or breach of regulations, nor had he been relieved of his temporary rank of brigadier general of volunteers, so it is significant that the adjutant general, the senior officer in the army responsible for keeping track of assignments and ranks, referred to McKinstry by his permanent rank of major rather than his still valid rank of brigadier general. The removal of Totten from the case is of added significance. Totten was the proper officer to begin the process of reviewing the circumstances and drawing up charges. His replacement by Glover, a prominent civilian lawyer of the city, a member of Blair's Safety Committee, and a close personal friend of Abraham Lincoln, indicated that serious charges would be forthcoming and these would not evolve from a simple military investigation. In his previous trials, McKinstry had been brought before the bar of justice within the jurisdiction of his military commands. At Mexico City, this was the area of authority of General Scott; in California, this was the area of the authority of the Pacific Division. Here at St. Louis, it became readily obvious that McKinstry was to be tried on a national scale wherein political forces would play as significant a role as alleged violations of the military code of conduct.[4]

On December 9, McKinstry's attorney, Krum, wrote a long letter to President Lincoln. Laying out the details of McKinstry's arrest and incarceration, Krum raised the issue that, almost a month after the fact, McKinstry still had not been informed of the grounds for his arrest nor the identities of his accusers. Krum wrote that he was prompted to communicate with the president, not only as McKinstry's attorney, but by other considerations. "There are peculiar circumstances attending the arrest and imprisonment of General McKinstry that savor of persecution and of an attempt to visit punishment upon him before conviction of any offense." Krum wrote, "He is kept under military surveillance and duress. He is not even allowed the privilege of visiting his wife and children, living in this city." The stringent and unusual course pursued by the government was the subject of frequent comment and severe criticism in St. Louis, Krum stated, and it was due to the administration and to the president that they be informed of these facts. "The friends of General McKinstry are ready (if the government will allow it to be done) to give bonds for his appearance to answer before any court or tribunal, civil or military, in any sum that may be required. Why may this not be done?" Krum received no response to his letter. On December 19, he was granted access to the room where McKinstry's books and papers were held and witnessed the investigation of those documents for three hours. Later in the week, he wrote to the members of the Commission on War Claims, addressing his letter, "To Messrs. Holt, Davis, and Campbell." He had been informed, he told them, that the commission contemplated taking a recess of a week or more over the Christmas holiday. He felt it his duty to call their special attention to McKinstry's papers which, according to what Krum had been told, contained a number of receipts, vouchers, and other written evidence of disbursement of public money made during McKinstry's term as quartermaster that involved large sums, "possibly a million of dollars in the aggregate." The receipts and vouchers were essential to McKinstry in rendering his accounts to the government and any loss would involve McKinstry and the persons holding his bond in great difficulty. Notwithstanding his imprisonment, Krum continued, McKinstry had been ordered to render his accounts to the quartermaster's department. In view of that, Krum asked, "respectfully but most earnestly that you will restore to the custody of General McKinstry all papers that have pecuniary value to him, and all others that you do not need in the course of your investigation." Krum wrote that he was authorized by McKinstry to say that his books and papers could be examined at any time by anyone representing the government, and there was nothing touching his official conduct that McKinstry wished to withhold or conceal, "and while he scorns the vile conspirators who have attempted to defame and ruin him, he does not believe the Government which he has served so long and faithfully will lend itself to their machinations." Davis and Campbell jointly signed a letter of response to Krum denying they had ordered the seizure of McKinstry's papers. "The Government did it," they advised. "It is for the Government to decide all questions growing out of their seizure. Mr. Glover is the counsel of the Government for our Commission. Whether he has the authority to do what you desire, you can readily ascertain by application to him."[5]

Krum then wrote to Glover: "When I consented a few weeks ago to be present at the examination of those books and papers, I supposed that some account of them had been taken when they were seized, and that they were under the control of the Commissioners, Messrs. Holt, Davis, and Campbell, and that such papers as were not needed to assist them in their investigation would be returned to Gen. McKinstry." Krum wrote that when he was let into the room in which the papers were held on December 19, he learned from General Curtis that no record of them had been made and that the officer in charge of seizing and holding the papers did not profess to know what had been taken. "Finding such to be the condition of things, and no one appearing to be in charge of the books and papers that had been seized, responsible for their safekeeping or restoration, I hesitated, when I receive your note, as to the propriety of my having anything to do with the proposed examination. On further reflection I have now to state that I am willing to be present, providing a schedule or list be made of the books and papers we examine. For this purpose, I will meet with you, with a competent clerk (Mr. Widgery) to assist at nine o'clock, Thursday morning, 26th inst." McKinstry's cashier, Hahn, later testified that McKinstry's office, with its books and papers, was taken possession of by the military "about the middle of November ... about the 21st of January, it was reopened; in the meanwhile the papers were much scattered about and some were now missing." When asked to state as nearly as he could the amount of business transacted in McKinstry's office from May until October, which was represented in the books and papers seized, Hahn answered, "I should say from five to seven millions of dollars."[6]

On January 2, 1862, McKinstry was given permission to write to Adjutant General Thomas at Washington. Reminding Thomas that he had not been informed of the accusations or grounds upon which the order for his arrest had been made, McKinstry wrote that it had just come to his attention that a committee of Congress under Chairman Van Wyck had made a report "in which serious implications are cast on my conduct while acting as Quartermaster of the Department of the West; and said committee accuse me, in various forms, of malversation in office." McKinstry demanded that a court of inquiry be ordered to examine the imputations and accusations of the committee and to review his conduct and the manner in which he had discharged his duties at St. Louis.[7]

On January 9, Krum wrote again to President Lincoln, reminding the chief executive of his letter of December 9 and stating that he had heard from contacts at Washington that his letter had received proper attention. The circumstances surrounding the arrest and imprisonment of McKinstry were so very unusual and altogether without precedent in the history of military or civil affairs, Krum wrote, that he hoped he would be pardoned for addressing the president directly as commander-in-chief of the army and as the political head of the nation. "A great wrong has been done General McKinstry, and if the military authorities were either misled or imposed upon when the orders were issued," Krum pleaded, "it now devolves upon the same authorities to make the only reparation in their power by giving the accused an opportunity to vindicate his conduct and character before a court of inquiry." Krum asked that the limits of arrest for McKinstry be extended to the city of St. Louis because no charges had been brought against him thus far. "The Government," Krum wrote, "by holding General McKinstry in his present limits at the Arsenal, and withholding his books and papers, prevents him from rendering his accounts as Quartermaster."[8]

On January 9, 1862, the Commission on War Claims at St. Louis began to transmit to the secretary of war at Washington a series of outstanding vouchers and invoices that had been submitted by merchants and contractors at St. Louis which had been reviewed and revised by Commissioners Campbell, Davis, and Holt. January 9 had been established as the final date claims could be presented to the commissioners. In his instructions to Major Allen who took over for McKinstry when Frémont's army marched from St. Louis, Quartermaster General Meigs had given specific directions on the procedure to be followed when reviewing questionable claims presented for payment. "Whenever a bill bears the aspect of jobbing, speculation, or illegality, set it aside as one of those to be deferred." Meigs was stating that claims against the government were to be deferred until resolved. There was no provision in army regulations for questionable claims to be revised, adjusted, or negotiated, yet the documents transmitted to Washington for payment by the three commissioners were revised. Each was made out originally in black ink, which was normal commercial practice. Each of them had been reviewed and approved by McKinstry. During the subsequent court-martial, the judge advocate would read into the record, "It appears that upon the face of some of said vouchers, there is writing in red ink; it is admitted by the prosecution, for the purposes of this trial, that it was put there by order of the War Claims Commission which sat in St. Louis in the winter of 1861–62; that said writing in red ink was placed upon them without the authority or consent of the accused; and the government has paid the amounts indicated in red ink and in the receipts interlined in red ink attached to them." For example, vouchers from Child, Pratt & Fox were revised in red ink from $20,388.90 to $14,881.05; from $13,006.50 to $9,493.70; from $15,282.97 to $11,751.27. A voucher from Charles M. Elleard for horses was revised from $16,209.00 to $15,957.00. Vouchers from other suppliers were similarly reviewed, revised, and paid. McKinstry was not consulted on what the revised amounts should be. There was no discussion with the claimants on how they had arrived at the original amounts. There was no public accounting of the basis on which the commissioners established the prices that subsequently were paid. There was no indication from the commissioners whether they considered any of the claims they revised and approved for payment to be fraudulent claims against the government. It is unconscionable that a commission of the federal government, charged by the president to investigate and correct so flagrant a robbery of the public purse, would approve the payment of those claims at all. Under the orders of the quartermaster general and under established army practice, the claims should have been set aside completely. Instead, they were reviewed, revised, and paid. The attention of the members of the commission was obviously focused on the amounts of the transactions and not on the propriety of the transactions themselves. Child, Pratt & Fox, Charles M. Elleard, and the other members of Frémont's and McKinstry's coterie of corruption were in fact rewarded by receiving payments that were only slightly less than the inflated and improper claims they had originally submitted. Justice would have been better served had Major Allen been allowed to implement the orders from Quartermaster General Meigs to defer questionable claims.[9]

Krum persisted on McKinstry's behalf. He wrote to Halleck at St. Louis, asking for the return of McKinstry's books and papers. He wrote to the new Secretary of War Edwin M. Stanton, pleading McKinstry's case and repeating his request that the limits of arrest be enlarged to the city of St. Louis. Halleck had by now agreed to release McKinstry's papers and books, granting permission for their transportation to the arsenal. But Krum argued in his letter to Stanton, "Even were it prudent, or practicable, to remove the books and papers referred to, of what advantage to General McKinstry can their removal to the Arsenal be, when his former clerks ... are imprisoned ten miles off, at Jefferson Barracks? My object in addressing you this communication and statement of facts, is to ask that the limits of arrest of General McKinstry, and of his clerks, may be extended, so as to allow them access to the offices where the books and papers of the late Quartermaster now are, in this city."[10]

While McKinstry was being held in close confinement at St. Louis, Frémont was organizing his new command at Wheeling. On February 14, 1862, Colonel Joseph W. Savage, a member of Frémont's staff, wrote his colleague, Colonel John Fiala, Frémont's former chief topographical engineer still at St. Louis. He said, among other things, "Should you have any means of communication with Gen. McKinstry, General Frémont would like to have you say to him that immediately upon the announcement that the Senate had recommended his rejection [of appointment to brigadier general of volunteers], Gen. Frémont visited the committee and insisted that, as he had recommended Gen. Mck., he had some right to know the grounds of his rejection. As they could, of course, give none except *ex parte* charges against him, they so far yielded to the representation of the general to withdraw the recommendation & agree that the nomination should hold over until the charges could be investigated."[11]

On February 22, 1862, as a result of Krum's perseverance, McKinstry was released from close confinement at the arsenal and the limits of his arrest were extended to the city of St. Louis. Clements, his clerk, and Hahn, his cashier, were released the same day under the same wider restrictions. At the time of his release, McKinstry had been held in close custody in cramped quarters at the arsenal for 101 days, prohibited from communicating with the outside world and unable to see Susan and the boys. Yet no charges had been brought against him. No accuser had confronted him. In one of his transmissions to the quartermaster general, he quoted Article 78 of the Articles of War which provided: "No officer or soldier who shall be put in arrest shall continue in confinement more than eight days, or until a court-martial can be assembled." McKinstry had requested a court of inquiry. He had requested a court-martial. He protested to Quartermaster General Meigs, "I asked for a trial, or a court of inquiry, immediately upon my arrest. Some weeks had elapsed and no response to my request being given, I again demanded a hearing in some form, and have since made repeated applications of the same import, through the agency of friends, to the President, the Secretary of War, and the Judge Advocate General. All these efforts to obtain a hearing have been in vain and I am still under arrest." McKinstry would continue under arrest, held by military orders to the city of St. Louis, until he was finally brought to trial by court-martial on September 10, 1862. It would not be until September 25 that he would hear for the first time the one charge and 61 specifications that were brought against him, more than ten months after his arrest.[12]

On March 30, 1862, Frémont wrote McKinstry from his headquarters at Wheeling regarding the contract with Beard & Palmer for the construction of the fortifications at St. Louis. "You were charged with acts which you did not commit, for the purpose of holding me responsible for them. The ground I have taken is, first, that our acts, not only undeserving of censure but were intended to be, and had proved to be, eminently right and useful to the public service." Further, Frémont wrote, "Another ground, which I have still more distinctly taken, is that I assume in the fullest manner, the entire responsibility for the contract." Frémont declared that he ordered Beard to perform the work before the contract was signed, "leaving it to be completed afterwards. I ordered money to be paid him in advance, as he required it." Beard had been referred to McKinstry when he brought the contract to Frémont for signature. Frémont stated that McKinstry claimed that Beard's prices were too high. "I told you to reduce them to what you considered reasonable, leaving for him a fair profit, having regard to the circumstances under which the works were built and the extraordinary labor and expense he underwent." Frémont added that he did not remember whether McKinstry objected to the orders involving Beard and the fortifications, but whether he had or not, Frémont declared that he would have overruled an objection. The general wrote that McKinstry was not responsible for the decision involving Beard and the fortifications at St. Louis other than in obeying Frémont's direct orders to do as he was told.[13]

As winter passed and spring arrived at St. Louis, McKinstry still did not receive notice of a court convening as he had repeatedly requested. He was certain that one would eventually be ordered, so he and Krum continued gathering evidence and taking depositions in preparation. On June 2, 1862, McKinstry con-

Charles P. Stone is best known for having been held under arrest for 189 days without charges being brought against him early in the Civil War. McKinstry, however, was held under arrest without charges being brought against him for 327 days. (Massachusetts commandery Military Order of the Loyal Legion and the United States Army Military History Institute)

tracted to have printed, bound, and distributed at his own expense a document addressed to Quartermaster General Meigs that ran in excess of one hundred typeset pages and included almost a hundred appended documents. The style and manner of the document were typical McKinstry, with bombast, accusation, and indignation apparent throughout. He opened by detailing the course of events that led to his present situation, including the fact that he had yet to be charged with anything. "In the meantime," he wrote, "besides individual assaults upon my character, portions of the public press have assailed me, and the most foul and malicious slanders concerning me have been made public by two Congressional reports—one being that of the Special Investigating Committee of the House of Representatives, known as the Van Wyck Committee, and the other that of the Commission on War Claims at St. Louis." He was content to rest no longer under such unjust and injurious imputations. He would, he wrote, avail himself of his official connection with the quartermaster's department to give Meigs, its chief, a brief history of his transactions and the persecutions to which he was being subjected.[14]

While composing this lengthy document and working with John Krum to gather materials for the time to come in court, McKinstry also supervised the work of Clements and Hahn in preparing his final accounting to the quartermaster's department. In spite of his arrest and the deplorable manner in which his records had been seized and handled, his final rendering was made on June 19, 1862, "an account for all the money that had come into his hands, to the dollar." The account consisted of McKinstry's detailed explanation of where the funds placed in his control had been expended. It did not address the loose and irresponsible manner in which those expenditures had been made.[15]

At about the same time, far to the east of St. Louis near the hamlet of Cross Keys in the Shenandoah Valley of Virginia, Frémont's command was routed after it attacked Confederate forces under the command of Major General Thomas Jonathan "Stonewall" Jackson. Frémont's force, one of three federal armies trying to trap and destroy Jackson, was sent flying even though it outnumbered its enemy by almost two to one. A little over a week later, Frémont left the army after learning he would have to serve under Major General John Pope, one of his former subordinates and a man Frémont despised. The "Pathfinder" would turn his attentions toward other endeavors. He and McKinstry remained in touch.[16]

In its issue of Saturday, September 10, 1862, the *St. Louis Daily Missouri Democrat* announced the convening of McKinstry's long-awaited general court-martial. The eleven officers ordered to the court were Brigadier General William S. Harney, Brigadier General Lawrence P. Graham, Brigadier General Philip St. G. Cooke, Colonel Carlos Waite, Colonel Joseph P. Taylor, Colonel Henry K. Craig, Colonel John S. Simonson, Lieutenant Colonel James D. Graham, Lieutenant Colonel Thomas L. Alexander, Lieutenant Colonel William. N. Grier, and Major Israel Vogdes. 1st Lieutenant Addison A. Hosmer was assigned as judge advocate. General Harney, the senior officer, was to be president of the court. The *Democrat* opened with an editorial opinion of regret that all the time he had been under arrest and requesting a court to investigate his official conduct, the nation had lost the services of "an officer possessing the experience and acknowledged ability of General McKinstry." That he would have a full and impartial trial, the editor could not doubt from the high character of the members of the court. "And, if honorably acquitted (as all impartial men must desire), we hope to see the energy and indomitable will, which distinguished the General, put in requisition in the field."[17]

On September 15, Harney asked to be excused from the court because of his involvement earlier as McKinstry's commanding officer. He was replaced by 70-year-old Colonel Benjamin L. E. Bonneville from Benton Barracks in the city. General Graham, the next senior officer to Harney, assumed his position as president of the court. Colonel Carlos Waite, now commanding the 1st Infantry Regiment, had commanded Company H of the 2nd Infantry as a captain when McKinstry joined that regiment in 1838. Waite had served in Mexico with McKinstry and knew him well. General Cooke, Colonel Craig, Colonel Simonson, and Lieutenant Colonel Grier all had served in Mexico and knew McKinstry. Major Vogdes had been a year behind McKinstry at West Point and knew him well. At least half the officers sitting on the court had been acquainted with McKinstry for 15 years and were familiar with his service and his reputation. Starting with the replacement of Harney, a great deal of shuffling took place as the officers of the court made arrangements to leave their commands for the time they would be sitting in judgment of McKinstry. Army Surgeon Madison Mills, St. Louis's medical director, wrote early on that Colonel Taylor was suffering from a severe case of piles and had become so weak and feeble that he could not serve; he was excused. Surgeon Mills also certified that General Graham would not be available for at least ten days due to ill health. General Crooke assumed Graham's role as president of the court. Major Vogdes, only recently released from a Confederate prisoner of war camp, telegraphed that he would be late in arriving, but would attend. Withal, the court convened one day later than ordered, on Thursday, September 25, 1862, at 9:00 a.m. in the building on the northeast corner of Locust and 4th streets in the city, two blocks from McKinstry's former offices.[18]

General Cooke called the court into session only to discover that the judge advocate was not present. Lieutenant Hosmer had been searching through the night of September 24 and the morning of September 25 to find the messenger from Washington who brought the written charge and specifications against McKinstry. When Hosmer did arrive in court, he explained, "He has the papers, the documentary evidence, and charges, and was sent from Washington a week ago. When I went to see him in Washington, he said I should find him here with the papers. They were not given into my charge. I made every effort I could last night to find him. I know him. His name is Botts—William B. Botts. He is a clerk in General Meigs's office in Washington. He has been here. He was here on Saturday ... I have applied to one of the detective police force and he said he will use all his powers to find him." A motion was made for the court to adjourn until noon. After some discussion, the decision was made that Botts probably would not be found in that short time so the court adjourned until 10:00 a. m. the following day. Lieutenant Hosmer worked through the night with the St. Louis police detective to track down the missing Botts.[19]

The court met the following morning with Botts present and opened with Judge Advocate Hosmer reading the order from General Halleck by which the court was called into session. He interrupted himself to remark at the presence of newspaper reporters in the room. Hosmer stated that it was most unusual to have the matters of a military court-martial brought before the public in the newspapers and ordered the reporters to leave. McKinstry was immediately on his feet, protesting emphatically. He insisted that, for the past year, his character had been reviled by reporters, newspapers, politicians, and others and this trial, which he had exerted himself so much to obtain, would prove useless unless its proceedings were laid before the public. He had been prosecuted for political purposes, he declared. Every agency had been employed to assail his integrity and character and he owed it to himself as well as to the citizens of St. Louis that this trial be made public. The court had it within its power to decide the question, McKinstry insisted, and he trusted it would do him the justice to decide in the affirmative. The judge advocate cleared the court in order to consider McKinstry's protest. When it reconvened, Hosmer announced that the court had decided to permit the presence of the reporters. Hosmer then read into the record the single charge against McKinstry: neglect and violation of duty to the prejudice of good order and military discipline. He then read into the record each of the 61 specifications that had been entered to support the charge.[20]

General Cooke asked who had signed the charge and specifications. The judge advocate answered that he had signed them. McKinstry interrupted, "Who had signed the charge?" The answer was of importance to him, he insisted, as the charge and specifications had been initiated by other parties and sent to St. Louis from Washington. It was important to him to know who his prosecutor was. "The Judge Advocate says he signed them. Is it he, then?" Hosmer explained that his signature was a formality. McKinstry considered this and stated, "I reply to the charge and all the specifications, not guilty." Hosmer requested an adjournment over the weekend until Monday, giving as his reason the fact that he had just come from the field and was not well acquainted with the case. McKinstry protested: the prosecution had arraigned him on the charge and the specifications and he objected to any postponement. It was nearly ten months since he had been ordered under arrest, he contended, reminding the court that for several months of that time he had been held in close confinement. One witness, Peter Wiles, named in one of the specifications and called by the court to establish the charge, was sitting in the room and prepared to testify. It was due to himself, McKinstry insisted, that the investigation proceed. The government had ample time — "Indeed, the delay on the part of the government in this case was without precedent!"— and the exigencies of the public service were such that there was danger even that this court might be dissolved before the investigation could be brought to a close. "It is all important," he concluded, "that no time should be lost by unnecessary postponement." McKinstry's objection was considered, and then overruled.[21]

Beginning with its issue of Tuesday, September 30, 1862, the *Daily Missouri Democrat* began to carry the transcript of the proceedings on its third page under the heading, *The Court Martial*. The court met six days each week from ten in the morning until about three in the afternoon. The *Democrat's* correspondent copied the two official court reporters' notes each evening — one reporter having written down the questions, the other the answers— and the *Democrat's* typesetters and printers worked into the early hours of the morning to set and print the previous day's testimony. On only one of the 65 days of hearings was the *Democrat's* correspondent unable, due to illness, to attend and transcribe; in that instance the paper ran a short summary of the previous day's activities in order to keep its readers current. For the citizens of St. Louis, the *Democrat's* daily reporting of the testimony, the charges and countercharges, the examinations and cross-examinations involving local personalities, all of whom were known to the citizenry and involving events they had witnessed, if not taken part in, made for popular reading and lively discussion.[22]

Samuel T. Glover was called by the prosecution. When asked at whose direction he had seized and examined McKinstry's books and papers, he replied, "By the request of the War Claims Commission ... Messrs. Joseph Holt, Hugh Campbell, and David Davis." Glover admitted that he was the individual who had drawn up the charge and the specifications under which the court was sitting. When asked who directed him to prepare the charge and the specifications, he answered, "I received a note from the Postmaster General, Montgomery Blair, informing me that the War Department would direct me to do so; the note from the Adjutant General came afterwards and assumed that I was doing so, and merely directed me to do so promptly."[23]

Colonel Chester Harding, who had served as Lyon's adjutant, testified giving general background on the conditions at St. Louis in the early months of 1861. Volunteers, he told the court, had begun arriving on April 22. Describing how these early volunteers were clothed and equipped, he testified, "They had nothing at all, and there was nothing, or little, in the quartermaster's department with which to supply them ... It was difficult to procure mess pans and camp kettles as rapidly as they were required; and these troops marched to the field in June only partially supplied with canteens and haversacks. None had knapsacks." Describing the difficulties and embarrassments of McKinstry during these months, Harding told the court that when the call for volunteers was made, the quartermaster's depot at St. Louis comprised little more than an office that had been used for making requisitions and forwarding supplies to frontier posts as they were received. For a long time after the volunteers began arriving in the city, no supplies were received from the east and the quartermaster was faced with either letting the troops go into the field without supplies or obtaining them locally in the best manner he could. During the early months, Harding said, "We thought he was unnecessarily careful, and adhered too much to the rules under the circumstances." When Frémont arrived and took command, a number of regiments were deficient in equipment to a lesser or greater extent. These deficiencies had to be supplied by the quartermaster at almost a moment's notice and, to Harding's knowledge, McKinstry never at any time had enough of anything on hand to supply the demands made upon him. It was frequently the case that portions of regiments which were not completely organized would unexpectedly be sent to the field for duty. Orders would come to McKinstry to furnish them with everything at any hour of the day or night. From his frequent visits to McKinstry's offices, Harding said he could state the amount of business was almost overwhelming. He noted that in addition to McKinstry's official duties as chief quartermaster, he was later named provost marshal of the city and county, and, he testified, the labors of that additional office itself "were enough for any one man." There were at least 40,000 troops who received their outfits from McKinstry during the months of May, June, July, August, and September, 1861, in whole or in part, Harding told the court.[24]

On Tuesday, November 21, 1862, after a month and a half of hearing the prosecution present witnesses and testimony in support of each of the specifications to the charge against McKinstry, on the 46th day of the court's sitting, the prosecution closed its presentation and McKinstry began his defense and, as was his wont, acting as his own counsel. He opened by asking the court to pardon him for presenting before introducing testimony some of the grounds of his defense, the facts that he intended to establish into evidence. At the same time, McKinstry directed the attention of the members to the particular exigencies under which he acted, "and to the difficulties, embarrassments and animosities, malevolence, and back-biting that beset my path during the considerable part of my services as Chief Quartermaster and Provost Marshal of the Department of the West." His defense, he told the court, would rest on simple and plain grounds. He then proceeded, in typical McKinstry fashion, to describe at length fourteen of these. First, all purchases of supplies and materials for the army were made in pursuance to law and in conformity with army regulations, which allowed for his discretion as to the mode of such purchases. Second, when he made purchases without soliciting proposals, he was justified in so doing by the exigencies of the service. Third, the course he pursued was recommended by his superior officer, the quartermaster general. Fourth, the method he adopted and followed in making purchases of supplies and materials was known at the time to the secretary of war and the quartermaster general, and neither objected. Fifth, in most instances, he acted under the specific orders of his superior officer, the commanding general of the department. Sixth, during the time the materials and supplies in question were purchased, an army of nearly 100,000 volunteers was being organized and when they assembled at St. Louis, they were lacking clothing and equipment. Seventh, at the time there were only a few manufacturers of the materials and supplies needed in St. Louis. Eighth, during the time the purchases were made, the government did not furnish him with sufficient money to enable him to pay cash on delivery for the supplies needed; since many dealers in St. Louis were adverse to selling to the government on credit at the time, he was obliged in many cases to accept higher prices. Ninth, when the larger part of the supplies were purchased, though he asked, he was not provided with the requisite number of assistant quartermasters familiar with the service to aid him in performing the duties suddenly imposed upon him. Tenth, inasmuch as he was comparatively a stranger in the St. Louis business community, he was dependent on the recommendations of public figures in his selection of employees, and he used his best judgment in hiring them. Eleventh, in view of the condition of the department during the time the supplies were purchased, the lack of ready money, and the urgent need to purchase supplies on short notice, the prices he paid were not unreasonable and he had not wasted public money. Twelfth, as to the oppression of Henry Clapp alleged in the 27th specification, he expected to disprove all the prosecution had introduced in support of the specification but, even if it were true, it did not prove the charge against him; he insisted that if the allegation were true, it was not cognizable before this court-martial. Thirteenth, if the allegations of the 43rd specification were not sufficiently refuted by the examination of Thomas Hood, the witness for the prosecution, he expected to rebut Hoods testimony *in toto*, In addition, he expected to show that the proposal he accepted to furnish picket pins, which was made at the same time Hood made his offer, was in due course reported to the quartermaster general, who approved it. He maintained that this matter was not open for further investigation. Lastly, fourteenth, he expected to show that there had been no motive on his part, either of interest, gain, or friendship, to the prejudice of the public service or the neglect and violation of his duty in the particulars alleged against him.[25]

Almost a month of examining and cross-examining the prosecution's witnesses and his own followed until on December 23, McKinstry called General Harney to the stand. Harney gave his rank and position during the spring of 1861. In response to McKinstry's question whether he had been diligent and attentive to the discharge of his duties as the department's chief quartermaster, Harney testified, "He was entirely to my satisfaction." McKinstry asked about interference by others with Harney's command while at St. Louis. The judge advocate interrupted Harney's response with the objection that the acts of others were not the subject of this court. McKinstry argued that the specifications to the charge covered the period from April 9 to October 6, 1861, and during that time Harney was his commanding officer. McKinstry proposed to show that, commencing with the command of Harney and throughout the summer and fall of 1861, persons holding official positions at Washington and at St. Louis exercised such influence on the president and the war department that a direct interference with the command of the Department of the West and with himself resulted, greatly influencing the operations and transactions of the quartermaster's department at St. Louis. McKinstry charged that these parties directed into the pockets of their adherents the patronage which was supposed to be discharged by his office. It was entirely proper for him, arraigned as he was on a charge of neglect of duty, to exhibit to the court the obstacles—"official, if you please!"—that he encountered at every point, preventing him from adhering to the regulations. "If the Government created or sanctioned the impediments to a proper discharge of duty on my part," he argued, "surely no court-martial will permit the persecution to avail himself of his own acts to convict me of neglect of duty." The conditions that existed during the summer and fall of 1861 were relevant to the case which he sought to prove through the testimony of Harney, and, later, of Frémont. "I struggled to prevent the fraud I clearly saw they were attempting upon the Government and the people," he claimed. "That struggle, gentlemen, has cost me my rank, position, and place, and submitted me to this persecution." The court closed to consider McKinstry's question to Harney and the judge advocate's objection to it. The court decided to allow the question and Harney immediately picked up where he had been interrupted. "Yes, this interference was exercised by Frank Blair to such an extent that it caused me to be removed from the command of the Department of the West," the old dragoon stated, "in consequence of the base falsehoods which he fabricated and communicated to the Administration through his brother, Montgomery Blair; his influence was such with General Lyon that I never communicated with General Lyon at all — I communicated with Frank Blair! I know General Lyon was entirely under the influence of Frank Blair—entirely!"[26]

McKinstry's clerk, Clements, was called and asked about McKinstry's financial standing. Clements answered that McKinstry never had much money at his disposal. "I have lived with him the better portion of the past ten years and have time and again known him to draw his pay in advance, and have on several occasions loaned him money."[27]

Frémont returned to St. Louis while the court was in session. One evening a large assembly of citizens called upon him and stood in front of his residence on Chouteau Street to hear him speak. "The occasion ... of my visit to your city," he addressed them, "is altogether personal. One of my principal objects in coming here is to be present during the trial with my friend, that true soldier and loyal citizen, General McKinstry. During the period which the prosecution against him is directed especially to cover, I was his commanding officer and, therefore, in a better position to become intimately acquainted with the nature, extent, and value of his services than any others ... Having the opportunity to be present here with him, I could not have reconciled it with my conscience to be absent, believing as I do that the assaults upon him were made solely because he felt it an honorable duty to stand faithfully by the side of his chief." Frémont took the stand on December 29, the 65th and final day of the court. When he assumed command in July of the prior year, he testified, the exigencies of the service in the department were great. Troops converging on St. Louis often had to be immediately sent into the field and he ordered McKinstry to furnish supplies and equipment to them. "I did give such orders to General McKinstry; they were frequent, urgent, and peremptory." He described McKinstry's performance in his role of quartermaster as "so diligent, attentive, and energetic, and performed his duties in such a way as to command my unqualified respect and approbation." McKinstry asked Frémont about the time he assumed command of the western department, whether troops were arriving daily during the months of August and September. "Almost daily, at the rate of 1,000 a day," Frémont answered. At the end of Frémont's testimony, McKinstry announced to the officers of the court that he had completed his defense.[28]

The court adjourned to meet the following morning, December 31. It continued to meet through January 9, 1863, reviewing the massive amount of testimony presented. The court went into closed session on January 10, and on January 15 announced it had arrived at its finding. On January 16, the court announced its verdicts. On the charge of neglect and violation of duty to the prejudice of good order and military discipline, the court found McKinstry guilty. On the 61 specifications to the charge, the court found him guilty on 27. The findings and the sentence of the court were promulgated in orders by army commander, Major General Halleck, now at Washington:

> ... and the court does therefore sentence Major Justus McKinstry, Quartermaster, United States Army, *"To be dismissed the service."*[29]

Under the discretion given by Article 89 of the Rules and Articles of War, Halleck suspended the sentence until the pleasure of the president could be determined, on the recommendation of several members of the court who hoped for a remission or mitigation of the sentence. That pleasure was made known two days later when Abraham Lincoln ordered the sentence of the court to be carried out.[30]

10.

Epitaph

Justus McKinstry at long last had put himself out of the United States Army. He had been tried and condemned by the officers of his final court-martial with a sentence confirmed by his commander-in-chief. McKinstry had earned the doubtful fame of being the only general officer on either side of the American Civil War court-martialed and dismissed for fraud. His career since his graduation at West Point had been directed by his own efforts toward that end, and from all of this there had been no material gain. He had nothing to show for his sins. The profits from his Mexican exploits were no more. Rancho Santa Ysabel was gone. The silver service remained for a while but for the rest of their lives, Susan and the boys would live in poverty and McKinstry, himself, would exist on dreams, schemes, and sinecures obtained through his former St. Louis associates.[1]

Others did gain. Frémont's "California gang" made large amounts of money from the departmental commander's disregard of propriety and his quartermaster's willingness to manage a program of waste, fraud, and abuse under Frémont's reign. Leonidas Haskell sold some 2,300 mules to the government in the single week between September 17 and 24, 1861. Buying from local farmers and herders at $95 a head on average, and selling to the quartermaster's department at $110 a head, Haskell pocketed profits of just under $100,000 for which he put forth no capital or effort, other than to observe farmers and herders as they drove their stock to the inspectors, transferring the title in passage. Child, Pratt & Fox was only the major example of the flagrant theft of public funds that took place under McKinstry's watch at St. Louis. If the amount of business the firm conducted was in fact only the $800,000 it admitted to, and the profits were merely the 40 percent its bookkeeper declared, the firm pocketed somewhere in the neighborhood of $320,000 in the five months of the summer of 1861 before the incompetence of McKinstry's commander and the outrage, envy, and anger toward himself brought this to an end. McKinstry's reputation in the army had long been tarnished, yet he never gave an indication that this troubled him. His manner was always one of confidence, that he could talk his way around, or bully his way through, any opposition he encountered. By the autumn of 1861, he had earned the enmity of most of the officer corps of the regular army as well as the citizenry of St. Louis, but neither fact seemed to bother him.

McKinstry was not the only example of a corrupt army officer. Serving with him throughout his career were other corrupt officers, some incompetent officers, and many officers long and flagrantly absent from their commands. But their existence demands comparison to the majority of the officers in the United States Army who were honest, capable, and present at their posts or stations, however distant,

Justus McKinstry at age 50 in a photograph taken after his St. Louis court-martial. (Library of Congress)

dangerous, or desolate those might be. The United States Army did not make Justus McKinstry into what he became but the United States Army did allow him to corrupt himself in plain sight of his fellow officers and his commanders. There was suspicion and often proof of illegitimacy at Mexico City, at San Diego, and at St. Louis. Yet other than his court-martial at West Point, every time McKinstry was brought before the bar of military justice to stand before a court of inquiry or a court-martial, it was because of an act originating outside the army command in which he served. In Mexico, it was Garcia's letter to Captain Irwin that led to the court of inquiry and the resulting court-martial. In California, it was the determined and continuing efforts of Cave Couts to rid himself, the army, and San Diego County of McKinstry's influence and presence. At St. Louis, it was political intrigue and the outrage of Frank Blair and other citizens and merchants of the city that brought him down among the ruins brought on by the incompetence of his commander, Frémont. The United States Army's chain of command, its professional officer corps, and its rank and file were observing and accepting the antics McKinstry was carrying on when they should have been roaring with rage. The United States Army did not make Justus McKinstry what he became but the United States Army stood aside and did little to challenge him as he did it. McKinstry was guilty of his own sins. The United States Army was guilty of allowing those sins to be committed so openly and flagrantly. But, for the first time, as a result of his St. Louis court-martial, McKinstry did not get away with it. Yet even his fall at St. Louis was based as much on the political tinge of his association with John Charles Frémont as on his own malfeasance.

Six months after his dismissal from the army, a convocation of anti-administration Democrats gathered at Springfield, Illinois. The *Illinois State Register* estimated between 75,000 and 100,000 persons attended and listened to more than 25 speakers orating from six podiums as they blasted the Republican administration, its president, and its conduct of the war. Listed among the speakers was "McKinstry ... of St. Louis." A record of McKinstry's speech has not been found, but he would have had much to say, and little of it would have been in support of those holding power in Washington.[2]

A little over a month later, Jane McKinstry wrote to George in San Diego mentioning that Susan planned a visit to Hudson in August. This was connected to McKinstry's relocation from St. Louis to New York City, where he would reside until 1867; Susan and the boys would maintain their residence at St. Louis. Coincidentally, the Frémonts were living at 21 West 19th Street in New York City. After waiting for orders that never came, Frémont had resigned his commission. He was one of the two highest ranking officers in the United States Army, standing at the time equal to George McClellan who, since November 7 of the previous year, was also without a command and awaiting orders that never came.[3]

A presidential election was to take place in November, 1864, and the Lincoln administration was not at all certain of re-election. The war was going badly. Draft riots in New York City brought the opposition to the loss of lives and treasure to the forefront. George McClellan was about to be nominated as the Democratic candidate to run for the presidency with a platform of ending the war quickly and bringing the states of the south back into the Union with slavery intact. As Lincoln and the Republicans prepared for a hard campaign against McClellan and the Democrats, Lincoln and his backers learned to their dismay that another Republican was about to enter the contest as a candidate. While he might not have large enough a following to ensure his election, John Charles Frémont did have the power to split the Republican vote and assure the election of McClellan. Frémont still held broad support from his 1856 campaign, especially among the voters in the western states. There were many in the Republican ranks, hard-line radical Republicans who saw Lincoln as leaning toward a soft peace with the states of the south after the war. Frémont, they recalled, was the general who had freed the slaves in Missouri and ordered rebels found with guns in their hands to be shot. As early as August, 1863, these radicals had determined they would have to replace Lincoln if they hoped to control the course of the war and

A brilliant engineer and organizer, McClellan as general-in-chief issued the telegraphic order for McKinstry's arrest at St. Louis. (Massachusetts Commandery Military Order of the Loyal Legion and the United States Army Military History Institute)

the reconstruction period that would follow the Union victory. They considered Frémont a formidable opponent to Lincoln and one who could be counted on to follow their political philosophy.[4]

The Democratic party opened its national convention at Chicago on August 24, 1864, intent on naming McClellan its candidate for president and George H. Pendleton, of Ohio, for vice president. To the surprise of the Democratic leadership, they found Frémont also was planning to stand in opposition to McClellan at Chicago. Even though he carried the standard of the radical Republicans, he sent his personal representative, McKinstry, to the Democratic convention with a letter of commitment to serve the party as its presidential candidate. Samuel L. M. Barlow, one of McClellan's managers, wrote from New York City, "McKinstry, of St. Louis, Frémont's agent, left yesterday for Chicago, where I believe he is a delegate. He takes with him a written pledge from Frémont to declare for an immediate armistice and a convention [of the states], and with this he proposes to secure the Democratic nomination." Understanding that McKinstry's presence at the convention with a single letter would probably not ensure a place on the ballot, yet hoping to gain something from his efforts, Frémont instructed McKinstry, "to make any arrangement which the Democrats determined to be best in regard to running or withdrawing from the Presidential contest." Under Frémont's instructions, McKinstry was to offer Frémont's withdrawal and his support of the McClellan ticket in return for restoration of his military command at St. Louis. Colonel Randall B. Marcy, McClellan's father-in-law and campaign advisor, telegraphed McClellan that he had met with McKinstry and discussed Frémont's withdrawal from the campaign. McClellan wrote back to Marcy referring to his father-in-law's meeting with McKinstry, "The interview was a strange one, & confirms many little hints that had reached my ears. We will talk more fully when we can."[5]

Frémont was working both political camps. Marcy later telegraphed McClellan, "McKinstry has just received Frémont's withdrawal from the canvas, to be published on telegraphic notice from him. Says Frémont had an interview with Chase and Wilson; they promised him a position in [Lincoln's] cabinet & dismissal of the two Blairs if he would withdraw from the [Republican] race and advocate Lincoln." Lincoln's emissaries referred to were Secretary of the Treasury Salmon P. Chase and Senator Henry Wilson, both staunch Lincoln supporters. It was to the favor of both parties that neither took Frémont up on his offer to throw the election for his own political gain.[6]

In the November 8, 1864 election, Lincoln got 2,330,552 votes to McClellan's 1,835,985, but of more import, Lincoln carried every loyal state with the exception of Delaware, Kentucky, and McClellan's home state of New Jersey. Although it did not change the result of any one state's electoral vote, Lincoln also carried the soldiers' votes by 116,887 to 33,748, this against the once-beloved general who had organized and led the Union armies. Lincoln's victory at the ballot box was aided to a great degree by the marching and fighting of 80,000 Union veterans under Major General William T. Sherman who were cutting a wide swath across the state of Georgia and the heart of the Confederacy, taking Atlanta on September 2, 1864. The fall of Atlanta contributed mightily to the restoration of confidence and faith throughout the north, happening a mere two months before the election. Significantly, Major General Frank P. Blair, Jr., marched with the Army of the Tennessee, one of the two field armies with Sherman, quite ably leading its XVII Corps.[7]

After his embarrassing rejection by both political parties, Frémont next turned toward what was in his mind the challenge of the future: the national interest in building railroads. He still had his personal fortune, although he was having trouble with uncontrolled operating costs at his California holdings and with unfaithful stewards. Focusing his efforts in New York City, he purchased a country estate nearby at Tarrytown which Jessie named *Pocaho*. At this time, McKinstry was listed as a stock broker in New York City.[8]

During the Springfield campaign in 1861 in Missouri, Franz Sigel's column of Lyon's army had been able to support and supply itself as it moved westward without relying on mules and wagons for transportation only as far as Rolla, a hundred miles from St. Louis where the tracks ended. Construction of the St. Louis & San Francisco Railway had reached Rolla on January 1, 1861, but there it stopped during the course of the war. In 1867, Frémont assumed control of the line and began trying to finance efforts to push the tracks westward in the direction of Springfield. Rolla, a backwater Missouri town until then, saw its fortunes climb; the residents of the settlement called it, "the child of the railroad." In 1867, McKinstry moved to Rolla and began doing business there as a land agent.[9]

Frémont's railroad interests were by now extensive. Investors convinced him to become involved in the Memphis, El Paso & Pacific Railroad based in Texas. The war had also interrupted the development of this line. Frémont leaped at the challenge of getting the operation up and running, using his name and his contacts to attract investors. Soon after he became involved, the company issued its first mortgage bonds for $5 million at 6 percent. Railroad charters and federal land grants were relatively easy to come by at the time but money from American investors was not. Railroad stocks had become notorious as excellent means for losing fortunes quickly. Frémont, however, had extensive European connections. He traveled to France to solicit investors for his new enterprises. The laws of France forbade brokers from presenting for sale on the Bourse, France's principal exchange, certificates of foreign corporations unless those certificates were regularly traded on the main exchanges in the home country. Frémont had to demonstrate in Paris that shares of the Memphis, El Paso & Pacific were being sold on the New York Stock Exchange in order to be allowed to offer these certificates on the Bourse. In line with that, the *New York Daily Tribune* carried an advertisement on October 1, 1868, "Memphis, El Paso & Pacific Railroad Company's six percent first land mortgage bonds, principal and interest payable in coin, for sale at 105, and accrued interest, in currency," by the brokerage houses of Hodgkin, Randall & Hobson, No. 14 Broad Street, and Corn & Auferman, No. 30 Broad Street, in New York. Frémont was successful in France using the *Tribune* ad and a fraudulent pamphlet that gave investors the impression that the Memphis, El Paso & Pacific bonds carried a guarantee backed by the United States government. Complaints were not raised and the true worth of the investments were not challenged until some $4.5 million had been collected from European investors. In 1873, Frémont's deceptive proposals were exposed and he was charged with fraud, tried *in absentia,* and convicted by the government of France. He was out of the country at the time and never returned. It is not clear how close McKinstry's New York stock brokerage and his Rolla land agency were involved in Frémont's manipulations, but there is a very strong coincidence there.[10]

McKinstry's fortunes, which never were bright at their best, sagged from this time. At some date between mid-1863 and 1865, Susan and the boys left him and moved from St. Louis to Ypsilanti, although correspondence shows the wife and sons maintained some contact with him. It is not clear why Susan and the boys did not move to Hudson to live with her brother and sister there. On December 16, 1864, Augustus wrote to George in California, "Susan is still at Ypsilanti, Michigan, with her boys. Her husband, I believe is in NY — not heard from lately. Last heard of him as being without business except some way connected with Gold and Silver mining in Colorado Territory, which I suppose is not giving him a living. I am told he expects to be reinstated in the army, which I suppose is the only occupation by which he can make a living for his family and, for their sakes, I hope he may." Augustus wrote to George on November 11, 1868, mentioning the death of their father, George, Sr., and referring to the settlement of his estate, "The immediate available funds of the Est. were consumed by the amt. paid to the heirs of our brother, Alexander, and the urgent need of our sister, Susan, who you are aware is entirely dependent on her own ... Only one of the boys had yet succeeded in finding something to do."[11]

Susan's financial condition did not improve. She wrote to George on December 2, 1869, from Ypsilanti, "Your description of the improvements in San Diego has given me California fever. I am living here in a very humble & poverty stricken way. With my three boys, trying to keep body and soul together, using the small means my father left me. Until Jus can get back in the Army or be able to do something in the support of his family. He is in New York working for the restoration to the Army. Whether he will succeed or not, God only knows. He has never met with any success in any business since he left the Army & probably never will." Susan reminded her brother of some wharf lots that McKinstry had bought

10. Epitaph

Susan McKinstry at age 60 in a photograph taken while she was living at Ypsilanti, Michigan. Susan was McKinstry's loyal supporter from their marriage in 1838 until she and the boys left him in 1865. (Columbia County Historical Society, Kinderhook, NY)

at San Diego just before they left there and wondered if they could be recovered by paying back taxes. She asked about Santa Ysabel, "The deed was in my name and as I have never signed any deed disposing of it, I should think it might be recovered. If you & I could, by working together, regain that property, it would be a handsome reward for both of us. Could you not induce some lawyer to undertake the thing by giving him a liberal interest in the property?" Susan apparently was unaware of the quitclaim element of the agreement to purchase Santa Ysabel that McKinstry had signed. Ortega and Stokes were unable to obtain clear title to the ranch until three years after Susan wrote to George and they eventually sold the ranch to other parties. She gave George news of the boys and asked, "What are the chances for young men in San Diego? I have half a mind to sell and hereby to go out there with the boys. If I were a few years younger, perhaps it would do to entertain such an idea seriously." Three years later she wrote to George, again from Ypsilanti. She was supporting herself and the boys by taking in boarders. "I seldom find time to write a reasonable letter; my time is so taken up with the cares & hard work of housekeeping ... I want to give up housekeeping and board for the rest of my days & I shall do so as soon as the boys are self-supporting." This is a significant statement for Susan to make since Charles at this time was 29, James was 27, and Cy was 18. "We are looking for Jus next week. He is in Ft. Yuma, has just gotten an interest in a large contract for filling in the 'slough ponds' about the city. You remember how many there are; he has one-fifth interest in the contract & expects to make money. I hope he may for his family's sake as much as for his own." The city directory for St. Louis for that same year, 1872, shows McKinstry living in the city at 710 Pine Street, and for 1873, there at the La Cleve Hotel. It is unclear why Susan wrote that he was at Fort Yuma. Jeannie McKinstry, Augustus's daughter, wrote George from Hudson on February 28, 1875, "My father had not heard from Aunt Sue in several weeks but at that time she was very well ... It is most astonishing that he can't find some sort of employment. I wish with all my heart that Aunt Sue's letters could be pleasanter and happier. She certainly deserves it after all these years of trial."[12]

On October 10, 1876, Susan, now 62, wrote to George bringing her brother up to date on her condition, "One day I fainted from the heat and my health is bad this fall, I am not well a day. The Dr. says my health is caused by all my bad feelings, though I think Drs. do a great deal of guessing." She told George about the boys. Cy was working in a railroad office in Toledo, Ohio. Jimmy had a cigar and tobacco store in Ypsilanti, although she wished he was in some other kind of business. "Elisha's wife is in the East," she wrote, "& is coming here on her way home to visit in November, I think. I shall not feel bound to be very attentive as E. has taken no notice of this family in years, not so much as to send his regards."[13]

McKinstry continued his efforts toward reinstatement in the army. Congressman Alpheus Williams of Michigan, working on his behalf, managed to get a committee of the House of Representatives to pass a resolution on January 9, 1877, calling for "a copy of all the proceedings of the court-martial in the case of Major Justus McKinstry, quartermaster, United States Army, convened at St.

Louis, Mo., September 24, 1862." Secretary of War J. D. Cameron replied on January 17 that the record was voluminous, containing more than 2,100 pages, and that a clerk working at the rate of 25 pages a day, could not copy the record in less than 84 days. It would be impossible to furnish the record before the close of the present session of Congress, Cameron wrote. If it were still the desire of the committee that the copy be furnished, he suggested that an appropriation of $250 be made for the necessary clerical work. The resolution was tabled by the committee and no further actions was taken on Congressman Williams's request.[14]

In 1878, McKinstry was listed in the St. Louis city directory as holding the position of inspector for the water department. In 1879, he was listed as holding the same position, living at 1609 Olive Street. By this time, McKinstry was 66 years old.[15]

On July 13, 1880, after a life filled with many glorious enterprises and a few successes, John Charles Frémont, the victim of his own visions and the greed of his associates, died in poverty in New York City.[16]

On January 29, 1887, Congress passed legislation providing that officers of the army and navy who had served prior to the commencement of the war with Mexico and had been dismissed after the close of that war, were entitled to receive the Mexican War pension. The obvious constituency behind this was the number of Mexican War veterans who, because of service in the armed forces of the Confederacy during the Civil War, were not eligible for any federal benefits from that conflict. McKinstry applied to the Department of the Interior, Bureau of Pensions, on June 8, 1877, claiming his Mexican War pension and stating, "[I was] engaged in the battles of Vera Cruz, Cerro Gordo, and in the battles in the Valley of Mexico and Churubusco, for which I was brevetted a major." Three days later he filed Claim 14019 applying for his Civil War pension but this claim was rejected in March of the following year with a hand-written endorsement, "Claimant was not honorably discharged but was dismissed the service by sentence of a General Court Martial." McKinstry did begin receiving his Mexican War pension of eight dollars a month at his 2647 Olive Street address. At age 73, he was listed in the St. Louis city directory as a sanitary officer with the St. Louis City Health Department.[17]

Susan died at Ypsilanti at the age of 77 on February 8, 1892. Some time before that, on August 28, 1865, McKinstry's oldest brother, retired Commodore James Patterson McKinstry, had purchased Lot 1 of Block 84 in the new Highland Cemetery at Ypsilanti, twelve graves in a circular plot at the intersection of several drives. The boys, probably in response to their mother's wish, purchased two other lots in Highland Cemetery in Susan's name shortly after her death. Susan was buried in Lot 9 of Block 99, apart from the McKinstry family and, eventually, from her husband.[18]

McKinstry was listed as living at Memorial House in St. Louis in 1895 at the

Obelisk marking the McKinstry family burial plot in Highland Cemetery at Ypsilanti, Michigan, where McKinstry is buried. (Author's photograph)

age of 81. That year he married Adelaide Dickinson. The two were united in matrimony by Reverend P. G. Robert, rector of the Church of Holy Communion. Adelaide was 41 years old. The couple moved into their home at 4360 Clayton Street, St. Louis.[19]

Two years later, on December 10, 1897, Justus McKinstry died at age 83 of senile debility. Undertakers Smithers & Wagoner held the body three days until McKinstry's sons could travel from Ypsilanti to claim the remains. Justus McKinstry was buried in his brother's lot in Highland Cemetery on January 4, 1898.[20]

Guardians had to be appointed for Adelaide shortly after McKinstry's death, initially because of a condition described as "unsound mind," and subsequently as "insane." Adelaide lived under guardianship until she died on September 20, 1909. Prior to her passing, in an effort to continue McKinstry's Mexican War pension on her behalf, affidavits regarding Adelaide's health and well-being were collected. Mary E. Van Sank of St. Louis, referring to McKinstry in her affidavit, stated what had to be defining epitaph of this rogue:

"Said soldier left no property."[21]

Chapter Notes

1. The First Court

1. Stephen E. Ambrose, *Duty, Honor, Country— The History of West Point*, The Johns Hopkins Press, Baltimore, MD, 1966, 40 [Ambrose].

2. National Archives, Office of the Judge Advocate General, Record Group 153, Box 93, Court-Martial Files, Washington, DC, [Archives, JAG, Court-Martial Files]; United States Military Academy, *Register of Officers and Cadets of the United States Military Academy*, West Point, New York, 1837 [Register of Offices and Cadets, 1837].

3. Archives, JAG, Court-Martial Files.

4. Ibid.; James Regan, *The Judge Advocate's Guide*, Beresford Printer, Washington, DC, 1877, 82 [Regan].

5. Gustav Koerner, *Memoirs of Gustav Koerner, 1809–1896, Life Sketches Written at the Suggestion of His Children*, Thomas McCormack, ed., The Torch Press, Cedar Rapids, IA, 1909, Vol. 1., 169 [Koerner]; Albert D. Richardson, *The Secret Service, the Field, the Dungeon, and the Escape*, The American Publishing Company, Hartford, CT., 1865, 196 [Richardson].

6. Archives, JAG, Court-Martial Files.

7. Francis S. Drake, ed., *Dictionary of American Biography*, James Osgood and Company, Boston, MA, 1872, 265 [Drake].

8. Archives, JAG, Court-Martial Files.

9. Ibid.

10. Ibid.

11. Ibid.; George W. Cullum, *Biographical Register of the Officers and Graduates of the U. S. Military Academy*, Houghton Mifflin Co., Boston, MA, 1891, 645 [Cullum]. Reference is to Cadet Christopher A. Green, class of 1836, who graduated from the academy ten months prior to the convening of this court.

12. Ibid.

13. Ibid.

14. James L. Morrison, Jr., *The Best School in the World, West Point, The Pre-Civil War Years, 1833–1866*, The Kent State University Press, Kent, OH, 1986, 39 [Morrison].

15. Drake, 265.

16. Morrison, 79.

17. Thomas J. Fleming, *West Point, The Men and the Times of the United States Military Academy*, William Morrow and Company, New York, NY, 1969, 91 [Fleming]; Morrison, 79.

18. Edward M. Coffman, *The Old Army, A Portrait of the American Army in Peacetime, 1784–1898*, Oxford University Press, New York, NY, 1986, 46 [Coffman]; Morrison, 79.

19. Morrison, 79.

20. United States Military Academy, *Regulations of the U. S. Military Academy at West Point*, J. and J. Harper, New York, NY, 1832, 30 [Regulations]: "119. All Cadets who shall combine or agree to hold no friendly or social intercourse with another, and any Cadet who shall endeavor to persuade others to enter into such combination or agreement, shall be dismissed the service, or otherwise severely punished."

21. United States Military Academy, Cadet Index Card File, Justus McKinstry, Class of 1838, West Point, NY, [Cadet Card File]; Emory Upton, *The Military Policy of the United States*, Government Printing Office, Washington, DC, 1912, 94 [Upton]. Federal law on April 29, 1812, established that the corps of cadets was not to exceed 250.

22. United States Military Academy, *Cadets Admitted to the United States Military Academy, No. 1, 1800–1845*, West Point, NY [Cadets Admitted].

2. The Michigan Frontier

1. William Willis, *Genealogy of the McKinstry Family with a Preliminary Essay on the Scotch-Irish Immigrants to America*, Henry Dalton and Son, Boston, MA, 1852, 5 [Willis]; James T. White, ed., *The National Cyclopedia of American Biography*, James T. White & Co., New York, NY, 1893–1919, Vol. 16, 57 [White]; Ann M. Micou, *Patriots and Pioneers: Five Generations of McKinstrys (1712–1961)*, no. loc., privately published, 2000, 1 [Micou]; Russell Seymour Hilbert, *A History of the Hilbert and McKinstry Families*, privately published, Brighton, MI, 1976, 110 [Hilbert]. Hilbert writes that there was a McKinstry family in Ballymena, Northern Ireland, listed in the 1619 census.

2. William Darby, *A Tour from the City of New York to Detroit, in Michigan Territory, etc., 1818*,

reprinted by Quadrangle Books, Inc., Chicago, IL, 1963, 37 [Darby]; Steven Bailey Miller, *Historical Sketches of Hudson, Embracing the Settlement of the City, Government, Business Enterprises, Churches, Press, Schools, Libraries, etc.*, Bryan and Webb, Printers, Hudson, NY, 1862, 6–35 [Miller]; Everts and Ensign, publ., *History of Columbia County, New York, with Illustrations and Biographical Sketches of Some of its Prominent Men and Pioneers*, Philadelphia, PA, 1878, 162 [Everts]; J. H. Lant, ed., *The Hudson Directory for 1874–75, etc.*, Bryan and Webb, Printers, Hudson, NY, 1874, 42 [Lant].

3. The *Hudson Bee*, issues from 1810 through 1818, The Columbia County Historical Society, Kinderhook, NY, [*Hudson Bee*]; Anna Rossman Bradley, *History of Columbia County, with Biographical Sketches, etc.*, Record Printing Co., Hudson, NY, 1908, 57 [Bradley]; Record Printing and Publishing Co., ed. and publ., *Columbia County at the End of the Century*, published under the auspices of the *Hudson Gazette*, Hudson, NY, 1900, 60–61 [Record Printing]; Lant, 43; Patricia Fenhoff, History Department, City of Hudson, NY, mss letter, September 26, 1990.

4. Willis, 24; Ypsilanti Historical Society Museum and Archives, mss index cards on members of the McKinstry family derived from The *Ypsilantian*, Ypsilanti, MI, var. dates [*Ypsilantian*].

5. Ira Rosenwaike, *Population History of New York City*, Syracuse University Press, Syracuse, NY, 1972, 17 [Rosenwaike]; Julius W. Pratt, "The War of 1812," *History of the State of New York*, Alexander C. Flick, ed., Columbia University Press, New York, NY, 1943, 243–244 [Pratt]; Everts, 16; Record Printing, 326.

6. Willis, 24; Archer Butler Hulbert, *The Niagara River*, G. P. Putnam's Sons, New York, NY, 1908, 6 [Hulbert].

7. Harvey C. Colburn, *The Story of Ypsilanti, Written for the Centennial Celebration of the Founding of the City, in Cooperation with the Committee on History*, Ypsilanti, MI, 1923, 64 [Colburn]; Francis Paul Prucha, *The Sword of the Republic, The United States Army on the Frontier, 1783–1846*, The Macmillan Company, Collier Macmillan, Canada, Ltd., Toronto, ON, 1969, 107 [Prucha, *Sword*] Upton, 98.

8. William Lee Jenks, *St. Clair County, Michigan, Its History and Its People, A Narrative Account of Its Historical Progress and Its Principal Interests*, The Lewis Publishing Company, Chicago, IL, 1912, 138 [Jenks]; Robert C. Nesbitt, *Wisconsin, A History*, The University of Wisconsin Press, Madison, WI, 1973,116 [Nesbitt]; Frederick B. Shaw, *One Hundred and Forty Years Service in Peace and War: History of the Second Infantry Regiment, United States Army*, The Strathmore Press, Detroit, MI, 1930, 116 [Shaw].

9. Clarence M. Burton and M. Agnes Burton, eds., *The History of Wayne County and the City of Detroit, Michigan*, The S. J. Clark Publishing Company, Detroit, MI, 1930, 246, 857 [Burton]; Robert B. Ross and George B. Catlin, *Landmarks of Wayne County and Detroit*, rev. by Clarence M. Burton, published under the auspices of the Evening News Association, Detroit, MI, 1898, 260, 595 [Robert Ross]; Jenks, 10, 25.

10. Burton, 857; Willis Frederick Dunbar, *Michigan, A History of the Wolverine State*, William B. Erdmans Publishing Co., Grand Rapids, MI, 1965, 267 [Dunbar].

11. Silas Farmer, *History of Detroit and Wayne County and Early Michigan, A Chronological Cyclopedia of the Past and Present*, Munsell & Co., New York, NY, 1890, 90, 98, 102, 770, 916 [Farmer]; Elisha McKinstry, *Some Reminiscences by Elisha Williams McKinstry*, Charles Hedges McKinstry, ed., no loc., 10, 13, 1983 [Elisha McKinstry].

12. Willis, 22–24.

13. National Archives, Official Records of the Navy Department, Records of Officers, James Patterson McKinstry, Record Group 42, Washington, DC [McKinstry, James, Officer's Record].

14. National Archives, Office of the Adjutant General, Cadet Application Papers, 1805–1866, Application and Endorsements of Justus McKinstry, Record Group 94, Roll 65, Frames 275–293, Washington, DC [Cadet Application].

15. Cadet Application; Elisha McKinstry, 9.

16. Cadet Application.

17. Cadet Card File.

3. Cadet Gray and Army Blue

1. National Archives, Office of the Chief of Engineers, Letters Received, Justus McKinstry to Charles Gratiot, December 18, 1832, Entry No. 18, M1066, Record Group 77, Washington, DC [McKinstry, Request to Resign].

2. Cadet Card File; Cadet Application.

3. Cadet Application. At this time, cadets were obligated to one year's active service after graduation which, added to the four years of academic study, came to the five years mentioned in the letter. Four days after McKinstry's graduation from the academy on July 1, 1838, an act of Congress would extend that obligation to eight years; Coffman, 47n.

4. Cadets Admitted.

5. Elizabeth Day Jenkins Waugh, *West Point, The Story of the United States Military Academy Which, Rising from the Revolutionary Forces, Has Taught American Soldiers the Art of Victory*, The Macmillan Company, New York, NY, 1942, 1–2 [Waugh]; Gene Gurney, *A Pictoral History of the United States Military Academy in War and Peace, From Colonial Times to Vietnam*, Crown Publishers, Inc., New York, NY, 1977, 7 [Gurney].

6. Richard H. Kohn, *Eagle and Sword, The Federalists and the Creation of Military Establishments in America, 1783–1802*, The Free Press, New York, NY, 1975, 303 [Kohn]; Morrison, 2; Russell F. Weigley, *History of the United States Army*, Macmillan Publishing Company, Inc., New York, NY, 1967, 105 [Weigley]; Ambrose, 40; Sidney Foreman, *West Point, A History of the United States Military Academy*, Columbia University Press, New York, NY, 1950, 35, 91 [Foreman].

7. Cullum, 89; Cadets Admitted.

8. Fleming, 47; Morrison, 65.

9. Ambrose, 150; Forman, 144; Morrison, 71.

10. Ambrose, 65; M. I. Luddington, *Uniforms of the United States from 1774 to 1880, Illustrated*, The Quartermaster General, Washington, DC, American Lithograph Company, publ., New York, NY, 1890, 210 [Luddington]; Waugh, 62.

11. Ambrose, 154; Fleming, 92.
12. Regulations.
13. Forman, 9; Stephen W. Sears, *George B. McClellan, The Young Napoleon,* Ticknor and Fields, New York, NY, 1988, 4 [Sears, *Napoleon*].
14. Morrison, 26, 41–42; Cullum, 694; United States Military Academy, *U. S. Military Academy Staff Records, 1835 to 1842,* vol. 2, West Point, NY, 18 [Academy Staff Records]; United States Military Academy, *Register of Officers and Cadets of the United States Military Academy, West Point, New York, 1835,* West Point, NY [Register of Cadets, 1835]. William A. Brown subsequently changed his name to William A. Austine for reasons not in evidence in the archives.
15. United States Military Academy, *Roll of Cadets Arranged According to Merit in Conduct for the Year Ending 1834,* West Point, NY, 16 [Roll of Cadets]; Forman, 230; United States Military Academy, *Register of Delinquencies, 1834–1838,* West Point, NY, 57. [Register of Delinquencies.]
16. Ambrose, 163; Fleming, 93.
17. Cullum, var.
18. Academy Staff Records.
19. Ambrose, 142; Cullum, 726; National Archives, Office of the Adjutant General, Orders Received, 2nd U. S. Infantry, *Description and Succession of Officers Book, 1825–1859,* Entry 1070, Record Group 391, Washington, DC [Officers Book]; George C. Saffarans, ed., *Historical Register of the Commissioned Officers of the Second U. S. Infantry, from its Organization, March 4, 1791, including Supplementary Tabulations of Historical Data Concerning the Regiment,* Regimental Press, Logan, CO, 1904, 12 [Saffarans].
20. John K. Mahon, *History of the Second Seminole War, 1835–1842,* University of Florida Press, Gainesville, FL, 1991, 104 [Mahon, *Seminole War*]; Edwin C McReynolds, *The Seminoles,* University of Oklahoma Press, Norman, OK, 1957, 154 [McReynolds]; Virginia Bergman Peters, *The Florida Wars,* The Shoestring Press, Hamden, CT, 1979, 195 [Peters]; George Walton, *Fearless and Free, The Seminole War, 1835–1842,* The Bobbs-Merrill Company, New York, NY, 1977, 18 [Walton]; John T. Sprague, *The Origins, Progress, and Conclusion of the Florida War, etc.,* D. Appleton and Co., Philadelphia, PA, 1848, 103 [Sprague].
21. Willia, 22–24.
22. R. Ernest Dupuy, *The Compact History of the United States Army,* Hawthorn Books, Inc., New York, NY, 1973, 77 [Dupuy]; Prucha, *Sword,* 6; Weigley, *Army,* 88.
23. Morrison, 8; Weigley, *Army,* 123. The staff consisted of the scientific departments: engineers, topographical engineers, and ordnance; and the general staff departments: adjutant general, inspector general, judge advocate general, commissary general, quartermaster general, surgeon general, and paymaster general. The line consisted of artillery, dragoons, infantry, and mounted rifles.
24. Coffman, 54.
25. Coffman, 45, 65; Morrison, 15–16; Officer's Book; Francis Paul Prucha, *Broadaxe and Bayonet, The Role of the United States Army in the Development of the Northwest, 1815–1860,* The State Historical Society of Wisconsin, Madison, WI, 1953, 54]Prucha, *Bayonet*]; Mark W. Summers, *The Plundering Generation, Corruption and the Crisis of the Union, 1849–1861,* Oxford University Press, New York, NY, 1987, 28 [Summers, *Generation*].
26. Coffman, 49; Thomas M. Exley, *A Compendium of the Pay of the Army from 1785 to 1888, Compiled under the Direction of the Paymaster General of the Army,* Paymaster General's Office, Government Printing Office, Washington, DC, 1888, 49 [Exley]; Morrison, 20.
27. Coffman, 22–23, 137; Prucha, *Bayonet,* 34; Prucha, *Sword,* 26; Shaw, 37; William Addleman Ganoe, *History of the United States Army,* Appleton-Century, New York, NY, 1936, 173; Weigley, *Army,*168.
28. Prucha, *Sword,* 1; Gary D. Ryan and Timothy K. Nenninger, *Soldiers and Civilians, The U. S. Army and the American People,* National Archives and Research Administration, Washington, DC, 1987, 27 [Ryan].
29. Weigley, *Army,* 170.
30. National Archives, *Returns from Regular Army Infantry Regiments, June, 1821– December, 1916, Second Infantry, January, 1833-December, 1848,* National Archives Microfilm Publications, Microcopy 665,m Rolls 16 and 17, Washington, DC [2nd Infantry, *Returns*].
31. Luddington, 11,15.
32. Saffarans, 23; Shaw, 208; *The Detroit Free Press,* June 1, 1868, Detroit, MI [Detroit Free Press]; Justus McKinstry, *Vindication of Brig. Gen. J. McKinstry, Formerly Quarter-Master, Western Department,* privately published, St. Louis, MO, 1862, 65 [McKinstry, *Vindication*].
33. Mahon, *Seminole War,* 287; Shaw, 440.
34. William Bridgwater and Seymour Kurtz, eds., *The Columbia Encyclopedia,* Columbia University Press, New York, NY, 3rd edition, 1968, 1859 [Bridgwater].
35. Ambrose, 116; Weigley, *Army,* 169; Erna Risch, *Quartermaster Support of the Army, A History of the Corps, 1775–1939,* Department of the Army, Quartermaster Historian's Office, Office of the Quartermaster General, U. S. Government Printing Office, Washington, DC, 1962, 198 [Risch]; National Archives, Office of the Quartermaster General, Record of Regular Officers, Quartermaster's Department, L-P, McKinstry, Justus, Boxes 219–225, Record Group 92, Washington, DC [McKinstry, Officer's Record].
36. 2nd Infantry, *Returns.*
37. Prucha, *Sword,* 183; 2nd Infantry, *Returns.*
38. 2nd Infantry, *Returns;*
39. McKinstry, Officer's Record; 2nd Infantry, *Returns.*

4. Swamps and Hammocks

1. Felix P. McGaughy, Jr., *The Squaw Kissing War: Bartholomew M. Lynch's Journal of the Second Seminole War, 1835–1839,* a thesis submitted to the graduate school of Florida State University in partial fulfillment of the requirements for the degree of master of science, April, 1965, The Florida State University, Tallahassee, FL, 1965, 164 [McGaughy]; 2nd Infantry, *Returns.*

2. 2nd Infantry, *Returns;* John K. Mahon, ed., *Reminiscences of the Second Seminole War, by John Bemrose,* University of Florida Press, Gainesville, FL, 1966, 34n [Mahon, *Bemrose*].
3. McKinstry, Officer's Record.
4. McGaughy, 25, 28; James A. Huston, *Army Historical Series, The Sinews of War: Army Logistics, 1775–1953,* Office of the Chief of Military History, United States Army, Washington, DC, 1966, 121 [Huston]; James F. Sunderman, ed., *Journey into the Wilderness, An Army Surgeon's Accont of Life in Camp and Field during the Creek and Seminole Wars, 1836–1838, by Jacob Rhett Mott,* University of Florida Press, Gainesville, FL, 1963, 275 [Sunderman]; Miles W. Schuh, mss letter January 1, 1992, Panama City Beach, FL, to the author [Schuh].
5. Peters, 7–11; Prucha, *Sword,* 270; Henrietta Buckmaster, *The Seminole Wars,* The Macmillan Company, New York, NY, 1966, 12 [Buckmaster].
6. 2nd Infantry, *Returns.*
7. 2nd Infantry, *Returns;* McGaughy, 29, 82.
8. Peters, 177; H. J. Chaffer, *Florida Forts Established Prior to 1860,* typescript in the P. K. Yonge Memorial Library, University of Florida, Gainesville, FL, n. d. [Chaffer[; 2nd Infantry, *Returns;* Sunderman, 276.
9. 2nd Infantry, *Returns.*
10. Dupuy, 87; 2nd Infantry, *Returns.*
11. McKinstry, Officer's Record.
12. 2nd Infantry, *Returns.*
13. John K. Mahon, ed., "Joseph R. Smith, Letters from the Second Seminole War," *The Florida Historical Quarterly,* XXXVI, 4, April, 1958, 331 [Mahon, *Smith*], Saffarans, 12.
14. Mahon, *Smith,* 347; 2nd Infantry, *Returns.*
15. Mahon, *Smith,* 347.
16. Willis, 22–24.
17. Sprague, 103.
18. Ganoe, 176.
19. Milton Metzer, *Hunted Like a Wolf— The Story of the Seminole War,* Farrar, Straus and Giroux, New York, NY, 1972, 187 [Metzer].
20. 2nd Infantry, *Returns.*
21. National Archives, Office of the Quartermaster General, Consolidated Correspondence File, 1794–1915, McKinstry, Lt., Record Group 92, Box 641, Washington, DC [Quartermaster General, *Correspondence*]; Risch, 198.
22. 2nd Infantry, *Returns.*
23. 2nd Infantry, *Returns;* Saffarans, 12.
24. Ganoe, 188; Walton, 224; Shaw, 222; 2nd Infantry, *Returns.*
25. McGaughy, 5; Peters, 236, 240; Prucha, *Sword,* 270; Walton, 11, 232; Sprague, 248; Mahon, 305; 2nd Infantry, *Returns;* Meltzer, 20.
26. Peters, 240; Shaw, 224; Sprague, 473.
27. 2nd Infantry, *Returns;* Robert West Howard, *Thundergate: The Forts of Niagara,* Prentice-Hall, Inc., Englewood Cliffs, NJ, 1968, 24–25 [Howard]; Nuala Drescher, *Engineers for the Public Good, A History of the Buffalo District, U. S. Army Corps of Engineers,* United States Army Corps of Engineers, Buffalo, NY, n. d., 2 [Drescher].

5. Halls of Montezuma

1. Brian Leigh Dunnigan, *History and Development of Old Fort Niagara,* Old Fort Niagara Association, Inc., Youngstown, NY, 1985, 1, 48 [Dunnigan, *History*]; Brian Leigh Dunnigan, *Glorious Relic, The French Castle and Old Fort Niagara,* Old Fort Niagara Association, Inc., Youngstown, NY, 1987, 70 [Dunnigan, *Relic*]; Brian Leigh Dunnigan and Patricia Kay Scott, *Old Fort Niagara in Four Centuries, A History of its Development,* Old Fort Niagara Association, Inc., Youngstown, NY, 1991, 46 [Dunnigan, *Development*], Brian Leigh Dunnigan, *A History and Guide to Old Fort Niagara,* Old Fort Niagara Associations, Inc., Youngstown, NY, 1985, 2 [Dunnigan, *Guide*].
2. Charles A. LeCount, "'I Have Not Seen Niagara Falls Yet,' Dr. James H. Sargent's Visit to Fort Niagara in 1846, James Hovey Sargent to Fanny Sargent, Fort Niagara, New York, July 5, 1846," *OFN— Now and Then, A Newspaper of the Old Fort Niagara Association, Inc.,* Vol. XLIII, Number 12, 1993, 2–3, [LeCount]; Willis, 22.
3. Brian Lee Dunnigan, *Forts within a Fort, Niagara's Redoubts,* Old Fort Niagara Association, Inc., Youngstown, NY, 1989, 96 [Dunnigan, *Redoubts*]; Dunnigan, *History,* 60.
4. Quartermaster General, *Correspondence.*
5. Quartermaster General, *Correspondence.*
6. Charles L. Dufour, *The Mexican War, A Compact History, 1846–1848,* Hawthorn Books, Inc., New York, NY, 1968, 11 [Dufour].
7. Robert Selph Henry, *The Story of the Mexican War,* The Bobbs-Merrill Company, Inc., New York, NY, 1950, 17 [Henry]; John S. D. Eisenhower, *So Far From God, The U. S. War with Mexico, 1846–1848,* Random House, New York, NY, 1989, xix [Eisenhower]; Samuel Eliot Morison, *The Oxford History of the American People,* Oxford University Press, New York, NY, 1965, 559 [Morison].
8. Eisenhower, 105; George Winston Smith and Charles Judah, *Chronicles of the Gringos, The U. S. Army in the Mexican War,* The University of New Mexico Press, New Mexico State University, Las Cruces, NM, 1968, 74 [George Smith].
9. Shaw, 229, 261; 2nd Infantry, *Returns.*
10. McKinstry, Officer's Record.
11. Quartermaster General, *Correspondence.*
12. McKinstry, Officer's Record; 2nd Infantry, *Returns;* Saffarans, 12.
13. Ganoe, 209; Weigley, *Army,* 181; Eisenhower, 110; Henry, 138–139; W. A. Croffut, ed., *Fifty Years in Camp and Field, The Diary of Major General Ethan Allen Hitchcock, U. S. A.,* Putnam's Sons, New York, NY, 1909, 234 [Croffut]; Joseph E. Chance, ed., *Mexico Under Fire, Being the Diary of Samuel Ryan Curtin, 3d Ohio Volunteer Regiment, During the American Military Occupation of Northern Mexico, 1846–1847,*Texas Christian University Press, Fort Worth, TX, 1994, 122 [Chance].
14. Risch, 237; K. Jack Bauer, *The Mexican War,* Macmillan Publishing Company, New York, NY, 1974, 33, 236 [Bauer]; Dufour, 43.
15. Shaw, 229.
16. Eisenhower, 161.
17. Eisenhower, 171, 226; Henry, 193.
18. Christopher Phillips, *Damned Yankee, The Life*

of General Nathaniel Lyon, University of Missouri Press, Columbia, MO, 1990, 43 [Phillips]; George Rollie Adams, General William S. Harney, Prince of Dragoons, University of Nebraska Press, Lincoln, NE, 2001, 94 [Adams]; Logan U. Reaves, The Life and Military History of Gen. William Selby Harney, Bryan, Brand & Co., St. Louis, MO, 1878, 1 [Reaves]; Robert McHenry, ed., Webster's American Biographies, Dover Publications, Inc., New York, NY, 1978, 250 [McHenry].

19. Risch, 240; Saffarans, 12; Quartermaster General, Correspondence.

20. Quartermaster General, Correspondence.

21. Eisenhower, 267.

22. Dufour, 202.

23. Dufour, 203; Henry, 262; William A. Austine, "Letter to Cousin," April 1, 1847, William A. Austine Papers, Southern Historical Collection, University of North Carolina Library, Chapel Hill, NC, [Austine].

24. Bauer, 246; Dufour, 202; The New Orleans Picayune, March 25, 1847; Risch, 25; George Smith, 183; Austine, April 1, 1847.

25. Eisenhower, 265; Henry, 269; Croffut, 249; United States Congress, Executive Documents Printed by Order of the House of Representatives during the Second Session of the Thirty-Seventh Congress, 1861–62, Executive Document 144, Government Printing Office, Washington, DC, 1862, 51 [Congress, Executive Document 144]; Austine, April 1, 1847.

26. Dufour, 213; Eisenhower, 269; Henry, 277.

27. Dufour, 255; Austine, April 23, 1847; Mark Mayo Boatner, The Civil War Dictionary, David McKay Company, Inc., New York, NY, 1959, 928 [Boatner]; Picayune, May 1–6, 1847; George Smith, 216; Huston, 150. Reference is to Captain Thomas Williams, West Point class of 1837, aide-de-camp to General Scott at the battle of Cerro Gordo.

28. Henry, 29; Eisenhower, 292; Congress, Executive Document 144, 55.

29. Croffut, 257; Henry, 318; Shaw, 238.

30. Henry, 319–320.

31. Eisenhower, 314; Shaw, 243; Croffut, 277; Henry, 329–331.

32. Henry, 342.

33. National Archives, Office of the Adjutant General, Letters Received, Capt. J. McKinstry, After-Action Report, Record Group 182, microfilm file S-5446–726, Frames 0835 et Seq, Washington, DC [McKinstry, After-Action Report]. Escopette is a Spanish term for a short rifle of carbine.

34. Ibid.

35. Francis B. Heitman, Historical Register and Dictionary of the United States Army, Government Printing Office, Washington, DC, 1903, 674 [Heitman].

36. Eisenhower, 330–343; George Smith, 247; Croffut, 29; Shaw, 254; Adams, 102.

37. Adams, 102–103; Austine, November 1, 1847; Seeman & Peters, Printers and Binders, Thirty-Sixth Annual Reunion of the Association of the Graduates of the United States Military Academy at West Point, New York, June 13th, 1905, 71–72, Saginaw, MI, 1905 [Seeman]; Huston, 150; Dennis J. Wynn, The San Patricio Soldiers, Mexico's Foreign Legion, Southern Studies Monograph No. 74, Texas Western Press, The University of Texas at El Paso, TX, 1984, 12–14 [Wynn]; Samuel E. Chamberlain, My Confessions, Written and Illustrated b Samuel E. Chamberlain, Harper Brothers, Publishers, New York, NY, 1956, n. p. [Chamberlain].

38. Croffut, 304; Henry, 367; Eisenhower, 346; George Smith, 266.

39. Risch, 295.

40. Bauer, 327; Dufour, 297; Henry, 369.

41. Congress, Executive Document 144, 3, 25, 27; Weigley, Army, 185; Risch, 225; Philip Katcher, The American Soldier, U. S. Armies, 1775 to the Present, Osprey Publishing, Ltd., London, England, 1990, 207 [Katcher]; United States Congress, Executive Documents Printed by Order of the House of Representatives during the Second Session of the Twenty-ninth Congress, 1847–48, Messages of the President of the United States, with Correspondence Therewith, Communicated between the Secretary of War and Other Officers of the Government, on the Subject of the Mexican War, House Executive Documents, Vol. 7, Wendell and van Benthuysen, Printers, Washington, DC, 1848, 1060 [Congress, Executive Documents, Vol. 7].

42. McKinstry, Officer's Record.

43. Congress, Executive Document 144, 108. In correspondence and discussion, Mexico City, the city of Mexico, is often referred to simply as Mexico.

44. Boatner, 354; Congress, Executive Document 144, 108.

45. Congress, Executive Document 144, 11, 22.

46. Congress, Executive Document 144, 2, 26.

47. Congress, Executive Document 144, 1, 2.

48. Congress, Executive Document 144, 3; Austine, November 1, 1847.

49. Congress, Executive Document 14, 3–8.

50. Risch, 25.

51. Congress, Executive Document 144, 22–23.

52. Congress, Executive Document 144, 86.

53. Congress, Executive Document 144, 25.

54. Congress, Executive Document 144, 61–67; Ramon Alcaraz, et al., "The Other Side," Notes from the History of the War between Mexico and the United States, translated and edited by Albert C. Ramsey, New York, NY, John Wiley, 1850, quoted in Eisenhower, 351.

55. Congress, Executive Document 144, 67.

56. Congress, Executive Document 144, 105; Philips, 56, 81; Patricia L. Faust, ed., Historical Times Illustrated Encyclopedia of the Civil War, Harper & Row, Publishers, New York, NY, 1986, 454, 790. Voltigeurs were a regiment of foot soldiers who were paired with a mounted rifleman, the two riding double while in transit, the voltigeur dismounting to go into action on foot as a skirmisher; during the war with Mexico, horses were never issued to the regiment which served as infantry and was disbanded at the end of the war.

57. Congress, Executive Document 144, 106–108.

58. Congress, Executive Document 144, 108.

59. McKinstry, Officer's Record.

60. Eisenhower, 363.

61. Mark W. Summers, The Era of Good Stealings, Oxford University Press, New York, NY, 1993 [Summers, Era], cf., for corruption in the army, in politics, in commerce, and in society.

62. Upton, 216–218.

63. Eisenhower, 363; Dufour, 280.

64. Johanna Cecelia Ross, George P. McKinstry, Jr., A Manuscript Collection, a theses presented to the fac-

ulty of the Department of Librarianship, California State University, San Jose, in partial fulfillment of the requirements for the degree of master of arts, California State University, San Jose, CA, 1972, 113 [Johanna Ross].

65. McKinstry, *Officer's Record*.

66. Bridgwater, 652; United States Congress, *Executive Documents Printed by Order of the House of Representatives during the Second Session of the Thirty-Fourth Congress, 1855–56, Executive Document 135*, "Report on the United States and Mexican Border Survey, Made under the Direction of the Secretary of the Interior, by William J. Emory, Major, First Cavalry, and United States Commissioner," Cornelius Wendell, Printer, Washington, DC, 1857, 3 [Congress, Executive Document 135]; McKinstry, *Officer's Record*.

6. The Golden Shore

1. White, 57; Ray Brandes, *San Diego, An Illustrated History*, A Rosebud Book, Los Angeles, CA, 1981, 51 [Brandes].

2. New York Historical Resources Center, Olin Library, Cornell University, *Guide to Historical Resources in Columbia County, New York, Repositories*, Ithaca, NY, n. d., 37 [Olin]; Johanna Ross, 4, 27,40; Lant, 63; Parmenter & Van Antwerp, publ., *Directory of the City of Hudson for the Years 1851–52*, Hudson, NY, 1851, 51 [Parmenter]; James E. Moss, ed., *The Journal of San Diego History*, Spring, 1970, Volume XVI, No. 2, San Diego Historical Society, San Diego, CA, 6 [Moss].

3. McKinstry, *Officer's Record*; Congress, *Executive Document 144*, 145. Emory was using McKinstry's brevet rank of Major in referring to him.

4. McKinstry, *Officer's Record*; Robert E. Mayer, comp. and ed., *San Diego, A Chronological and Documentary History, 1535–1976*, Howard Furer, Series Editor, Oceana Publications, Inc., Dobbs Ferry, NY, 1978, 24 [Mayer]. The Sandwich Islands were the contemporary name for the Hawaiian Islands.

5. Carl H. Heilbrom, ed., *History of San Diego County*, The San Diego Press Club, San Diego, CA, 1939, 80 [Heilbrom].

6. Boatner, 388; Shaw, 250; Saffarans, 24; Henry F. Dobyns, *Hepah, California! The Journal of Cave Johnson Couts, From Monterrey, Mexico, to Los Angeles, California, during the Years 1848–1849*, Arizona Pioneers Society, Tucson, AZ, 1962, 1, 109–113 [Dobyns]; Richard Joseph Coyer, "Cave Johnson Couts: On Both Sides of the Law,: *La Campana de Escuela, Annual Memorial History Awards*, Old School House Historians, Old Town, San Diego, California, James Robert Moriarty III, ed., University of San Diego History Department, Vol. 1, No. 1, San Diego, CA, 1974, 30 [Coyer].

7. Coyer, 20; Dobyns, 3.

8. Dobyns, 11.

9. McKinstry, *Officer's Record*. The mouth of the Gila River, where it flows into the Colorado River, is the site of present Yuma, Arizona. The commissioners intended to run their survey eastward from there to El Paso, Texas.

10. 2nd Infantry, *Returns*.

11. Congress, *Executive Document 144*, 137, 149; Emory, 4. Brag was a form of poker.

12. Coyer, 21; Dobyns, 97; Mayer, 24; Raymond G. Starr, *San Diego, A Pictoral History*, The Donning Company, Publishers, Norfolk, VA, 1937, 39 [Starr]; Congress, *Executive Document 144*, 142, 144, 159.

13. Congress, *Executive Document 144*, 145.

14. Congress, *Executive Document 144*, 145.

15. Congress, *Executive Document 144*, 145; McKinstry, *Officer's Record*; Robert B. Roberts, *Encyclopedia of Historic Forts, The Military, Pioneer, and Trading Posts in the United States*, Macmillan Publishing Company, New York, NY, n. d., 67 [Roberts]; Richard H. Coolidge, M. D., *Statistical Report of the Sickness and Mortality in the American Army, Compiled from the Records of the Surgeon General's Office: Embracing a Period of Sixteen Years, from January, 1839, to January, 1855*, A. O. P. Nicholson, Printer, Washington, DC, 1856, 449 [Coolidge].

16. Coffman, 178; Johanna Ross, 116. The council of administration at an army post appointed the sutler, selected the chaplain, and administered the post fund.

17. Coffman, 193; McKinstry, *Officer's Record*; Johanna Ross, 101; Congress, *Executive Document 144*, 1. The lure of the gold fields was so strong that in the eighteen months between July, 1848, and January, 1850, 716 men deserted from the army in California, leaving only 539 officers and men on duty in the Pacific Division.

18. Congress, *Executive Document 144*, 131; Boatner, 108; Saffarans, 12–13. Unlike the transcripts of the Mexico City courts, officers involved in this court-martial were referred to by their brevet ranks.

19. Congress, *Executive Document 144*, 132–139.

20. Congress, *Executive Document 144*, 132–139.

21. Congress, *Executive Document 144*, 155.

22. Congress, *Executive Document 144*, 161.

23. Congress, *Executive Document 144*, 161.

24. Boatner, 10; Faust, 8; Risch, 295; Elisha McKinstry, 13; Justus McKinstry, mss letter to Robert Allen, October 24, 1850, from San Francisco, CA, in McKinstry, *Officer's Record*.

25. Johanna Ross, 119.

26. Coyer, 20–21.

27. James Mitchell Clarke, "Antonio Melendez: Nemesis of William Walker in Baja California," *California Historical Quarterly*, Vol. 12, #4, December, 1933, 318 [Clarke]; McKinstry, *Officer's Record*.

28. Coyer, 20–21

29. Dobyns, 99; Clarence Allen McGrew, *City of San Diego and San Diego County: The Birthplace of California*, The American Historical Company, Chicago, IL, 1922, 72–79 [McGrew]; Leland E. Bibb, "William Marshall, 'The Wickedest Man in California,' A Reappraisal," *The Journal of San Diego History*, Winter, 1976, Volume 22, No. 1, 10–13, San Diego Historical Society, San Diego, CA, [Bibb].

30. Cecil C. Moyer, *Historic Ranches of San Diego County*, Union-Tribune Publishing Company, San Diego, CA, 1969, 56 [Moyer].

31. Rose Hollenbaugh Avina, *The Chicano Heritage, Spanish and Mexican Land Grants in California*, Arno Press, New York, NY, 1976, 100 [Avina]; Ferol Egan, *Frémont, Explorer for a Restless Nation*, Doubleday & Company, Inc., Garden City, NY, 1977, 311 [Egan]; Congress, *Executive Document 144*, 187; Moyer, 56.

32. Congress, *Executive Document 144*, 220, 237; Boatner, 210, 623; McKinstry, *Officer's Record;* United States Senate, *Executive Document No. 55,* 33rd Congress, 2nd Session, "Map of That Portion of the Boundary between the United States and Mexico, from the Pacific Coast to the Junction of the Gila and Colorado rivers, etc.," Ackerman Lith., New York, NY, 1855 [Senate, *Executive Document 55*].
33. Congress, *Executive Document 144,* 179, 205, 245, 276.
34. Samuel P. Heintzelman mss. letters to Justus McKinstry, September 3 and 17, 1853, from Fort Yuma Ceola, Arizona Territory, in McKinstry, *Officer's Record.*
35. Boatner, 108; Congress, *Executive Document 144,* 189.
36. Johanna Ross, 127.
37. Congress, *Executive Document 144,* 233.
38. Congress, *Executive Document 144,* 200, 233, 248.
39. Congress, *Executive Document 144,* 127, 249; Johanna Ross, 124.
40. Boatner, 259, 800, 901; Congress, *Executive Document 144,* 174, 245.
41. Congress, *Executive Document 144,* 247–249; Roberts, 84; Coolidge, 450.
42. Congress, *Executive Document 144,* 249.
43. McKinstry, *Officer's Record.*
44. Justus McKinstry, mss letter to H. W. G. Clements, February 11, 1855, from San Francisco, California, in McKinstry, *Officer's Record.*
45. Summers, *Generation,* 155; *New York Evening Post,* February 13, May 2, August 3, December 10, 1855.
46. Congress, *Executive Document 144,* 242; Johanna Ross, 25; 129; Robert C. Cowan, *Ranchos of California,* Academy Library Guild, Fresno, CA, 1961, 93 [Cowan].
47. Coyer, 23–28; Dobyns, 87, 100.

7. Wide Missouri

1. McKinstry, *Officer's Record.*
2. Adams, 149–155.
3. McKinstry, *Officer's Record; Ypsilantian;* Johanna Ross, 191; Willis, 23.
4. McKinstry, *Officer's Record;* Willis, 23; Peter M. Wilson, Ph. D., *John and Jane (Dickie) McKinstry,* privately published, Spotsvania, VA, 2000, 1 [Wilson].
5. McKinstry, *Officer's Record;* National Archives, Department of the Treasury, mss letter R. J. Zimmerman to Major Justus McKinstry, May 25, 1859, Washington, DC, [Zimmerman]; Charles E. Lyght, M. D., ed., *The Merck Manual of Diagnosis and Therapy,* Merck Sharp & Dohme Research Laboratories, Division of Merck & Co., Inc., Rahway, NJ, 1966, 1444 [Lyght].
6. McKinstry, *Officer's Record;* Johanna Ross, 147.
7. McKinstry, *Officer's Record.*
8. Johanna Ross, 146–147, 161.
9. McKinstry, *Officer's Record;* Johanna Ross, 14; Willis, 24; The *Daily Missouri Democrat,* St. Louis, MO, December 31, 1862 [*Democrat*]; The *St. Louis Republican,* St. Louis, MO, November 23, 1890 [*Republican*]; Ward S. Parker, mss letter, August 24, 1994, St. Louis, MO [Parker].
10. McKinstry, *Officer's Record;* Adams, 160, 192–197.
11. Pamela Herr and Mary Lee Spence, eds., *The Letters of Jessie Benton Frémont,* University of Illinois Press, Urbana, IL, 1993, 68 [Herr, *Letters*]; Charles N. Holmes, "The First Republican-Democratic Presidential Campaign," *Journal of American History,* Vol. VIV, 44, Organization of American Historians, Bloomington, IN, 1920 [Holmes].
12. William E. Parrish, ed., *A History of Missouri,* Volume III, 1860 to 1875, University of Missouri Press, Columbia, MO, 1973, 3 [Parrish, *Missouri*]; James Neal Primm, *Lion of the Valley, St. Louis, Missouri,* 2nd ed., Pruett Publishing Company, Boulder, CO, 1990, 246 [Primm] [. Robert Julius Rombauer, *The Union Cause in Missouri, An Historical Sketch,* Nixon-Jones Publishing Co., St. Louis, MO, 1909, 127 [Rombauer].
13. Boatner, 376; Rombauer, 126; Adams, 179; Reaves, 1.
14. Everett B. Long, with Barbara Long, *The Civil War Day by Day, An Almanac, 1861–1865,* Doubleday & Company, Garden City, NY, 1971, 19 [Everett Long]; William E. Parrish, *Frank Blair, Lincoln's Conservative,* University of Missouri Press, Columbia, MO, 1998, 88 [Parrish, *Blair*]; Lucy Louise Tasher, *The Missouri Democrat and the Civil War,* a dissertation submitted to the faculty of the Division of the Social Sciences in candidacy for the degree of Doctor of Philosophy, Department of History, University of Chicago, Chicago, IL, 1934, 45 [Tasher]; Walter B. Stevens, "Lincoln and Missouri," *The Missouri Historical Review,* Vol. X, January, 1916, State Historical Society of Missouri, Columbia, MO, 73–74 [Stevens]; Thomas J. Scharf, *History of St. Louis City and County,* Louis H. Everts Co., Philadelphia, PA, 1883, Vol. 1, 925 [Scharf]; Arthur M. Schlesinger, Jr., *The Age of Jackson,* Little, Brown and Company, Boston, MA, 1953, 76 [Schlesinger].
15. McKinstry, *Vindication,* 4; Parish, *Blair,* 87–88; Primm, 242.
16. Parrish, *Missouri,* 6; James Peckham, *Gen. Nathaniel Lyon and Missouri in 1861,* American News Company, Publishers, New York, NY, 1866, 25 [Peckham]; Rombauer, 123; William Ernest Smith, *The Francis Preston Blair Family in Politics,* Vol. II, The Macmillan Company, New York, NY, 1933, 19 [William Smith, *Blair Family*].
17. William Smith, *Blair Family,* 22.
18. Peckham, 43–45; Rombauer, 4, 138–139, 144; Primm, 247; Boatner, 365; Robert Underwood Johnson and Clarence Clough Buel, eds., *Battles and Leaders of the Civil War, From Sumter to Shiloh,* Vol. 1, "In Command in Missouri, by John C. Frémont, Major General, U. S. A.," Thomas Yoseloff, New York, NY, 1956, 279 [Johnson, *Battles and Leaders*]; Allan Nevins, *Frémont, Pathfinder of the West,* D. Appleton-Century Company, New York, NY, 1939, 624 [Nevins, *Pathfinder*]; Steven E. Woodworth, *Jefferson Davis and His Generals, The Failure of Confederate Command in the West,* University of Kansas Press, Lawrence, KS, 1990, 35 [Woodworth, *Jefferson Davis*]; Louis S. Gerteis, *Civil War St. Louis,* University Press of Kansas, Lawrence, KS, 2001, 82, 85, 89 [Gerteis];

Archdiocese of St. Louis, "About the Archdiocese," St. Louis, MO, 2001 [Archdiocese].

19. Department of War, Secretary of War, *The War of the Rebellion, A Compilation of the Official Records of the Union and Confederate Armies*, four series, 129 volumes, Government Printing Office, Washington, DC, 1880–1900, series 1, volume 1, 646 [*OR*, I, 1].

20. Margaret Leech, *Reveille at Washington, 1860–1865*, Harper & Brothers, Publishers, New York, NY, 1941, 3 [Leech]; John G. Nicolay and John Hay, eds., *Abraham Lincoln*, The Century Co., New York, NY, 1894, 336 [Nicolay, *Lincoln*]; Kenneth M. Stampp, *And the War Came, The North and the Secession Crisis, 1860–1861*, Louisiana State University Press, Baton Rouge, LA, 1950, 18 [Stampp, *War*].

21. Johnson, *Battles and Leaders*, 5; Ivan Musicant, *Divided Waters, The Naval History of the Civil War*, Harper Collins Publishers, Inc., New York, NY, 1995, 2 [Musicant]; Philip Gerald Auchampaugh, *James Buchanan and His Cabinet on the Eve of Secession*, privately printed, Lancaster, PA, 1926, 85 [Auchampaugh]; William M. Fowler, Jr., *Under Two Flags, The American Navy in the Civil War*, W. W. Norton & Company, New York, NY, 1990, 33 [Fowler].

22. Peckham, 141; Parrish, *Missouri*, 11; Rombauer, 153; Philips, 68, 82.

23. *Democrat*, October 2, 1862; McKinstry, *Vindication*, 34; *OR*, I, 1, 681; Boatner, 210.

24. *OR*, I, 1, 656–658; David Donald, ed., *Inside Lincoln's Cabinet, The Civil War Diaries of Salmon P. Chase*, Longmans, Green, and Co., New York, NY, 1954, 163 [Donald]; Donald C. Hinze and Karen Farnham, *The Battle of Carthage in Southwestern Missouri, July 5, 1861,* Savas Publishing Company, Campbell, CA, 1997, 19 [Hinze].

25. Parrish, *Missouri*, 10; Weigley, *Army*, 567.

26. Herman Hattaway and Archer Jones, *How the North Won, A Military History of the Civil War*, University of Illinois Press, Urbana, IL, 1991, 273; Donald, 12; Huston, 164.

27. Boatner, 542; Huston, 168; Risch, 332–334.

28. *OR* I, 1, 666–667; Parish, *Blair*, 96; Thomas L. Snead, *The Fight for Missouri: From the Election of Lincoln to the Death of Lyon*, Charles Scribner's Sons, New York, NY, 1886, 147 [Snead]; Ray W. Irwin, ed., "Missouri in Crisis, The Journal of Captain Albert Tracy, 1861," *Missouri Historical Review*, Vol. 51, October, 1956, 17–18 [Irwin]; Hattaway, 34. Moses Wright resigned his commission in the army to join the Confederacy; Richard B. Lee was arrested as a secessionist who was communicating with spies.

29. McKinstry, *Vindication*, 33.

30. Edward Hagerman, *The American Civil War and the Origins of Modern Warfare, Ideas, Organization, and Field Command*, Indiana University Press, Bloomington, IN, 1988, 45 [Hagerman]; Huston, 183; McKinstry, *Vindication*, 10; Steven E. Woodworth, ed., *The American Civil War, A Handbook of Literature and Research*, Greenwood Press, Westport, CT, 1999, 406 [Woodworth, *Civil War*].

31. McKinstry, *Vindication*, 10–11; *OR* I, 1, 681.

32. Long, 71–72; Parrish, *Blair*, 95; Rombauer, 219.

33. *OR* I, 1, 3, 4; Parish, *Blair*, 100.

34. Long, 73; Johanna Ross, 149; Willis, 24; John McElroy, *The Struggle for Missouri*, The National Tribune Company, Washington, DC, 1909, 73 [McElroy]. McKinstry later tried to refuse payment of the voucher submitted by the firm of Glasgow & Harkness that furnished many of the horses until Harkness went to Lyon, then in the field, who peremptorily ordered McKinstry to honor the voucher and process payment.

35. Long, 73; *OR* I, 1, 3, 4; John F. Marszalek, *Sherman, A Soldier's Passion for Order*, The Free Press, A Division of Macmillan, Inc., New York, NY, 1993, 145; [Marszalek]; Parrish, *Blair*, 102; Peckham, 155.

36. Boatner, 498; Long, 10.

37. Frederick H. Dyer, *A Compendium of the War of the Rebellion*, Thomas Yoseloff, New York, NY, 1909, 171 [Dyer]; *Democrat*, Friday, November 12, 1862; McKinstry, *Vindication*, 8.

38. Fred Albert Shannon, *The Organization and Administration of the Union Army, 1861–1865*, Arthur H. Clark, Co., Cleveland, OH, 1928, Vol. 1, 53 [Shannon]; Peckham, 27; Hagerman, 45.

39. McKinstry, *Vindication*, 11–12.

40. War Department, *Revised Regulations for the Army of the United States, with a Full Index, by Authority of the War Department*, J. G. L. Brown, Printer, Philadelphia, OA, 1861, 155 [Army, *Regulations*]; Risch, 342.

41. Cardinal Leonidas Goodwin, *John Charles Frémont, An Explanation of His Career*, Stanford University Press, Stanford, CA, 1930, 220 [Goodwin]; Peckham, 243; Primm, 252; William Smith, *Blair Family*, 51; Hans Christian Adamson, *Rebellion in Missouri, 1861, Nathaniel Lyon and the Army of the West*, Chilton Company, Book Division, Publishers, Philadelphia, PA, 1961, 7 [Adamson].

42. Long, 84; Parish, *Blair*, 109; Rombauer, 266; McKinstry, *Vindication*, 9.

43. National Archives, Office of the Judge Advocate General, Record Group 153, Boxes 409–410, mss. letter Montgomery Meigs to Justus McKinstry, June 18, 1861, Washington, DC.

44. McKinstry, *Vindication*, 9, 22.

45. Long, 85; Parrish, *Missouri*, 23; Rombauer, 277; Allan Nevins, *The War for the Union*, Charles Scribner's Sons, New York, NY, 1959, Vol. 1, 319 [Nevins, *War*]; McKinstry, *Vindication*, 90; Allan Nevins, *Frémont, The West's Great Adventurer, etc.*, Vol. 2, Harper and Brothers, Publishers, New York, NY, 1928, 544 [Nevins, *Great Adventurer*].

46. Peckham, 313; McKinstry, *Vindication*, 101; McKinstry, *Officer's Record;* Rombauer, 295; *OT* I, 3, 545; Edward G. Longacre, "A Profile of General Justus McKinstry,} *Civil War Times Illustrated*, July, 1978, Volume XVII, Number 4, Historical Times, Gettysburg, PA. [Longacre].

47. Long, 100.

8. The Hundred Days

1. Long, 101; Parrish, *Blair*, 115; Primm, 252.

2. Goodwin, 3; Pamela Herr, *Jessie Benton Frémont, American Woman of the 19th Century, A Biography*, Franklin Watts, New York, NY, 1987, 63, [Herr, *Frémont*].

3. Egan, 483; McHenry, 131; Andrew Rolle, *John Charles Frémont, Character as Destiny*, University of Oklahoma Press, Norman, OK, 1961, 5, 15, 134 [Rolle].

4. Rolle, 175; Herr, *Frémont*, xx; Herr, *Letters*, 243; William Smith, *Blair Family*, 55; *OR* I, 3, 395; Johnson, *Battles and Leaders*, I, 280.
5. Johnson, *Battles and Leaders*, I, 279,
6. Parrish, *Missouri*, 17–18; Nevins, *Great Adventurer*, Vol. , 534; Johnson, *Battles and Leaders*, I, 278.
7. Alice Eyer, *The Famous Frémonts and Their America*, revised edition, The Christopher Publishing House, Boston, MA, 1961, 285 [Eyer]; Johnson, *Battles and Leaders*, I, 280; Rolle, 175; Herr, *Letters*, xx and xvii, quoting Elisha O. Crosby, *Memoirs ... 1849 to 1864*, Charles Allen Barker, San Mateo, CA, Huntington Library, 1945, 35; Peckham, 291; William Smith, *Blair Family*, 57; *OR* I, 3, 406.
8. Russell F. Weigley, *Quartermaster General of the Union Army, A Biography of M. C. Meigs*, Columbia University Press, New York, NY, 1959, 188 [Weigley, *Meigs*].
9. McKinstry, *Vindication*, 15–17.
10. *Democrat*, December 22, 1862; McKinstry, *Vindication*, 23; United States Congress, Reports of Committees of the House of Representatives, Made during the Second Session of the Thirty-Seventh Congress, 1861-'62, Volume I, Report Number 2, Government Printing Office, Washington, DC, 1861, 701 [Congress, *Van Wyck Report*].
11. *OR* I, 3, 542; *Van Wyck Report*, 76, 81, 612; Goodwin, 234; United States Congress, House of Representatives, Thirty-Seventh Congress, 2nd Session, House Report No. 94, *War Claims at St. Louis*, Government Printing Office, Washington, DC, 1862, 22 [Congress, *House Report No. 94*]; Weigley, *Meigs*,196; McElroy, 218; Longacre, 16.
12. Congress, *Van Wyck Report*, 53, 114.
13. Congress, *Van Wyck Report*, 105–112; Roy Morris, Jr., "Union Quartermaster Justus McKinstry, A Handy Man with a Ledger Book, Practiced Unique Bookkeeping," *America's Civil War*, Volume 4, Number 6, March, 1992, Empire Press, Leesburg, VA, 6 [Morris]; Longacre, 17.
14. Herr, *Letters*, 326; McKinstry, *Vindication*, 196.
15. McKinstry, *Vindication*, 65; Weigley, *Meigs*, 196; *Detroit Free Press*, June 1, 1868.
16. Herr, *Frémont*, 208; McKinstry, *Vindication*, 67–68; Congress, *Van Wyck Report*, 977.
17. *Democrat*, October 4, 8, 12, 1862; Herr, *Letters*, 330; Prucha, *Sword*, 391; Congress, *Van Wyck Report*, 535; Longacre, 18.
18. Congress, *Van Wyck Report*, 534, 906–910,
19. *Democrat*, December 5, 1862.
20. *Democrat*, October 29, 1861; Congress, *Van Wyck Report*, 127.
21. Nevins, *Great Adventurer*, 534, 542–547; Johnson, *Battles and Leaders*, I, 281; Peckham, 313–317; *OR* I, 3, 545–546; Adamson, 180.
22. Johnson, *Battles and Leaders*, I, 306; Hinze, 220.
23. Jessie Benton Frémont, *The Story of the Guard, A Chronicle of the War*, Ticknor & Fields, Boston, MA, 1863, x [Frémont, *Guard*]; Missouri Historical Society, *Proclamation of Martial Law, August 14, 1861*, St. Louis, MO, [Proclamation]; Frank Moore, ed., *The Rebellion Record*, H. G. Putnam, New York, NY, 1861, 527 [Moore].
24. William Ernest Smith, The Blairs and Frémont, "*Missouri Historical Review*, Volume 23, No. 2, January, 1929, State Historical Society of Missouri, Columbia, MO, [William Smith, *Blairs*].
25. Koerner, 167; *OR* I, 3. 538.
26. Parrish, *Blair*, 120; Long, 112; Herr, *Letters*, 332; Eyre, 289.
27. *OR* I, 3, 467–469; Woodworth, *Jefferson Davis*, 38.
28. Congress, *House Report No. 94*, 32–34.
29. Congress, *House Report No. 94*, 3–4.
30. Frémont, *Guard*, 93; Heitman, 674; McKinstry, *Officer's Record*; Gerteis, 147; Congress, *Van Wyck Report*, 1044; Longacre, 19; Missouri State Historical Society, *Quartermaster's Property Receipt*, September 12, 1861, St. Louis, MO, [*Quartermaster's Receipt*].
31. Francis Hurd Stadler, *St. Louis Day by Day*, Patrice Press, Tucson, AZ, 1990, 171–172 [Stader]; Congress, *Van Wyck Report*, 729, 761; Bridgwater, 1221.
32. Eyer, 298; Nevins, *Great Adventurer*, 520.
33. Long, 118; Nevins, *Great Adventurer*, 525.
34. Frémont, *Guard*, 42; Koerner, 174.
35. Goodwin, 231; Shannon, 58; United States Congress, Reports of the Committes of the House of Representatives, Made during the Second Session of the Thirty-Seventh Congress, 1861-'62, Volume I, Report Number 2, Government Printing Office, Washington, DC, 2 [*Van Wyck Report*].
36. Long, 115; Stephen W. Sears, *The Civil War Papers of George B. McClellan, Selected Correspondence, 1860–1865*, Ticknor & Fields, New York, NY, 1989, 94 [Sears, *Papers*].
37. Long, 125.
38. McKinstry, *Vindication*, 51; Parrish, *Blair*, 129; Summers, *Era*, 16; Congress, *Van Wyck Report*, 112, 522; Longacre, 1; United States Congress, *The Congressional Globe, The Official Proceedings of Congress*, Thirty-Seventh Congress, 2nd Session, New Series, No. 150, John C. Rives, publ., Washington, DC, My 29, 1861, 2389 [Congressional Globe].
39. Congress, *House Report No. 94*, 7; Frémont, *Guard*, 76; Kenneth W. Munden and Henry Putney Beers, *Guide to Federal Archives Relating to the Civil War*, National Archives and Records Service, General Services Administration, Washington, DC, 1962, 385 [Munden].
40. Frémont, *Guard*, 76, 93, 117, 157; McKinstry, *Vindication*, 22.
41. Frémont, *Guard*, 194; Long, 131.
42. Long, 131,287; Nevins, *Frémont* I, 383; *OR* I, 53, 506; Jared C. Lobdell, ed., "The Civil War Journal and Letters of Colonel John Van Deusen Du Bois, April12, 1861, to October 16, 1862," *Missouri Historical Society Review*, State Historical Society of Missouri, Columbia, MO, [Lobdell].
43. George B. McClellan to Brig. Gen. S. R. Curtis, November 11, 1861, telegraph message in cipher, McKinstry, *Officer's Record* ; *Democrat*, December 12, 1862; McKinstry, *Vindication*, 1.

9. The Final Court

1. Hattaway, 55; Long, 138; Sears, *Papers*, 130.
2. Charles A. Dana, *Recollections of the Civil War*, D. Appleton and Company, New York, NY, 1898, 5 [Dana]; Herr, *Letters*, 351; McKinstry, *Officer's Record*.

3. McKinstry, *Vindication*, 53.
4. Parrish, *Blair*, 91, 120; National Archives, Office of the Judge Advocate General, Court-Martial Files, McKinstry, Justus, Record Group 153, Boxes 409–410, Washington, DC [Evidence File].
5. McKinstry, *Vindication*, 54–55.
6. McKinstry, *Vindication*, 56; *Democrat*, October 23, 1862.
7. McKinstry, *Vindication*, 57.
8. McKinstry, *Vindication*, 58.
9. McKinstry, *Vindication*,58; Munden, 385; *Evidence File*.
10. McKinstry, *Vindication*, 101.
11. John W. Savage, Washington, DC, to John Fiala, St. Louis, MO, February 14, 1862; original mss letter at the Missouri Historical Society, St. Louis, MO.
12. McKinstry, *Vindication*, 1; *Democrat*, September 27, 1862.
13. McKinstry, *Vindication*, 78.
14. McKinstry, *Vindication*, 1.
15. *Democrat*, December 20, 1862.
16. Long, 227.
17. *Democrat*, September 27, 1862; *Evidence File*.
18. *Evidence File*; *Democrat*, September 27, 29, 1862; Boatner, 880; 2nd Infantry, *Returns*.
19. *Democrat*, September 26, 1862.
20. *Democrat*, September 27, 1862.
21. *Democrat*, September 29, 1862.
22. The official hand-written record of McKinstry's St. Louis court-martial is at the National Archives [LL21, September, 1862, 6W4, 4:5 B, Boxes 409–411]. The author used the *Daily Missouri Democrat's* printed transcripts as sources for the testimony of this court. The transcripts are located in the newspaper collection of the State Historical Society of Wisconsin Library, Madison, Wisconsin.
23. *Democrat*, September 25, 1862.
24. *Democrat*, various dates.
25. *Democrat*, November 26, 1862.
26. *Democrat*, December 23, 1862.
27. *Democrat*, December 24, 1862.
28. *Democrat*, October 20, December 20, 23, 30, 1862.
29. *Evidence File*.
30. *Evidence File*.

10. Epitaph

1. Morris, 6, Longacre, 15.
2. *Illinois State Register*, Springfield, IL, June 19, 1863.
3. Cullum, 726; Rolle, 226; Johanna Ross, 163; Boatner, 315; Faust, 456; Hans L. Trefousse, "I Have Done My Share," *Civil War Times Illustrated*, Volume 9, Number 2, Harrisburg, PA, 1970, 22 [Trefousse]; David L. Long, *The Jewel of Liberty, Abraham Lincoln's Re-Election and the End of Slavery*, Stackpole Books, Mechanicsburg, PA, 1994, xii [David Long]; Jefferson Davis, *The Rise and Fall of the Confederate Government*, D. Appleton and Co., New York, NY, 1881, 611 [Davis].
4. Rolle, 22; William Frank Zornow, *Lincoln and the Party Divided*, University of Oklahoma Press, Norman, OK, 1954, 16 [Zornow]; Trefousse, 24; Joseph T. Glatthaar, *The March to the Sea and Beyond, Sherman's Troops in the Savannah and Carolina Campaign*, New York University, New York, NY, 1985, 44 [Glatthaar]; Effie May McKinney, *The Cleveland Convention*, A thesis submitted in partial fulfillment of the requirements of Western Reserve University for the degree of Master of Arts, March, 1928, Cleveland, OH, 13 [McKinney].
5. Zornow, 231; Elbert B. Smith, *Francis Preston Blair*, The Free Press, A Division of the Macmillan Publishing Co., Inc., New York, NY, 1980, 344 [Elbert Smith]; William S. Myers, *A Study in Personality, George Brinton McClellan*, Appleton-Century, New York, NY, 1934, 444–445 [Myers]; Rolle, 231; Everett Long, 562; Sears, *Napoleon*, 381; Sears, *Papers*, 605–606; David Long, xiv.
6. Sears, *Papers*, 605; Trefousse, 26.
7. Everett Long, 234; Johnson, *Battles & Leaders*, IV, 701.
8. Rolle, 234 ; John F. Trow, publ., *Trow's New York City Directory*, New York, NY, 1865.
9. The Goodspeed Publishing Company, *History of La Clede, Camden, Dallas, Webster, "Wright, Texas, Pulaski, Phelps, and Dent Counties, Missouri*, Chicago, IL, 1889, 659 [Goodspeed].
10. Goodwin, 240, 252; *New York Daily Tribune*, October 1, 1868; Boatner, 315; C. D. Reed, publ., *A History of the Texas Railroads and of Transportation Conditions under Spain and Mexico and the Republic and the State*, The St. Clair Publishing Co., Houston, TX, 1941, 93 [Reed].
11. Johanna Ross, 152, 159.
12. Johanna Ross, 175, 195, 199; Gould Directory Company, *Gould's St. Louis Directory for 1872*, St. Louis, MO, [Gould].
13. Johanna Ross, 199.
14. United States Congress, *Executive Documents Printed by Order of the Forty-Fourth Congress, Executive Document No. 25*, Government Printing Office, Washington, DC, 1877 [Congress, *Executive Document 24*].
15. Gould, 1878.
16. Foust, 291.
17. National Archives, Records of the Veterans Administration, Record Group 15, T-317, Washington, DC [McKinstry, *Pension File*], Gould, 1887.
18. Cora B. Kempf, Highland Cemetery Association, mss letter, September 29, 1990, Ypsilanti, MI [Kempf]; *Ypsilantian*; Charles Leitshuh, Highland Cemetery Association, mss letter, June 20, 1989, Ypsilanti, MI [Leitshuh].
19. State of Missouri, City of St. Louis, Marriage License No. 62438, Justus McKinstry and Miss Adelaide Dickinson, September 20, 1895 [*Marriage License*].
20. Kempf; City of St. Louis, Bureau of Vital Statistics, Division of Health, Certified Copy of Death No. 2992, Justus McKinstry, December 12, 1897 [*Death Certificate*]; City of St. Louis, Board of Health, Burial Certificate No. 9076, Justus McKinstry, December 22, 1897 [*Burial Certificate*]; James E. Kloos, *Graves of Union Generals in Michigan*, Classic Printing Corp., Cleveland, OH, n. d., 29 [Kloos]

Bibliography

Archival Sources

Missouri Historical Society. Proclamation of Martial Law, August 14, 1861. St. Louis, MO.
_____. Quartermaster's property receipt, September 12, 1861. St. Louis, MO.
National Archives. Office of the Adjutant General. Cadet Application Papers, 1805–1866. Application and Endorsements of Justus McKinstry. Record Group 94. Washington, DC.
_____. _____. Letters Received. Capt. J. McKinstry, After-Action Report. Record Group 182. Washington, DC.
_____. Orders Received. 2nd U. S. Infantry, *Description and Succession of Officers Book, 1825–1859*. Record Group 391. Washington, DC.
_____. Office of the Chief of Engineers. Letters Received. Justus McKinstry to Charles Gratiot, December 18, 1832. Record Group 77. Washington, DC.
_____. Office of the Judge Advocate General. Court-Martial Files. Record Group 153. Washington, DC.
_____. _____. Court-Martial Files. McKinstry, Justus. Record Group 153. Washington, DC.
_____. _____. Letters Sent. Montgomery Meigs to Justus McKinstry, June 18, 1861. Record Group 153. Washington, DC.
_____. _____. Un-indexed transcript of McKinstry court-martial. Record Group 153, LL21, September, 1862, 6W4, 4:5B, boxes 409–411. Washington, DC.
_____. Office of the Quartermaster General. Consolidated Correspondence File, 1794–1915. McKinstry, Lt. Record Group 92. Washington, DC.
_____. _____. Record of Regular Officers, Quartermaster's Department, L-P. McKinstry, Justus. Record Group 92. Washington, DC.
_____. Official Records of the Navy Department. Records of Officers. James Patterson McKinstry. Record Group 42. Washington, DC.
_____. Records of the Veterans Administration. Record Group 15. Washington, DC.
_____. *Returns from Regular Army Infantry Regiments, June, 1821–December, 1916, Second Infantry, January, 1833–December, 1848*. Record Group 391. National Archives Microfilm Publications, Washington, DC.
United States Military Academy. Cadet Index Card File. Justus McKinstry, Class of 1838. West Point, NY.
_____. *Cadets Admitted to the United States Military Academy, No. 1, 1800–1845*. West Point, NY.
_____. *Register of Delinquencies, 1834–1838*. West Point, NY.
_____. *Register of Officers and Cadets of the United States Military Academy, West Point, New York, 1835*.
_____. *Register of Officers and Cadets of the United States Military Academy, West Point, New York, 1837*.
_____. *Regulations of the U. S. Military Academy at West Point*, New York: J. and J. Harper, 1832.
_____. *Roll of Cadets Arranged According to Merit in Conduct for the Year Ending 1834*. West Point, NY.
_____. *U. S. Military Academy Staff Records, 1835 to 1842*. West Point, NY.

Newspapers

Alta California, San Diego, CA.
Daily Missouri Democrat, St. Louis, MO.
Detroit Free Press, Detroit, MI.
Hudson Bee, Hudson, NY.
Illinois State Register, Springfield, IL.
New Orleans Picayune, New Orleans, LA.
New York Daily Tribune, New York, NY.
New York Evening Post, New York, NY.
St. Louis Bulletin, St. Louis, MO.
St. Louis Republican, St. Louis, MO.
Ypsilantian, Ypsilanti, MI.

Primary Sources

Alcaraz, Ramon, et al. "The Other Side." In *Notes from the History of the War between Mexico and the United States,* translated and edited by Albert C. Ramsey. New York: John Wiley, 1850.
Austine, William A. "Letters to Cousin." Various dates, William A. Austine Papers, Southern Historical Collection, University of North Carolina Library, Chapel Hill, NC.
Chaffer, H. J. *Florida Forts Established Prior to 1860.* Typescript in the P. K. Yonge Memorial Library, University of Florida, Gainesville, FL, n. d.
Chamberlain, Samuel E. *My Confessions, Written and Illustrated by Samuel E. Chamberlain.* New York: Harper & Brothers, 1956.
Chance, Joseph E., ed. *Mexico Under Fire, Being the Diary of Samuel Ryan Curtin, 3d Ohio Volunteer Regiment, During the American Military Occupation of Northern Mexico, 1846–1847.* Fort Worth: Texas Christian University Press, 1994.
City of St. Louis. Board of Health. Burial Certificate No. 9076, Justus McKinstry. December 22, 1897.
_____. Bureau of Vital Statistics. Division of Health. Certified Copy of Death No. 2992, Justus McKinstry. December 12, 1897.
Coolidge, Richard H., M. D. *Statistical Report of the Sickness and Mortality in the American Army, Compiled from the Records of the Surgeon General's Office: Embracing a Period of Sixteen Years, from January, 1839, to January, 1855.* Washington, DC: A. O. P. Nicholson, 1856.
Croffut, W. A., ed. *Fifty Years in Camp and Field, The Diary of Major General Ethan Allen Hitchcock, U. S. A.* New York: Putnam, 1909.
Crosby, Elisha O. *Memoirs ... 1849 to 1864.* Edited by Charles Allen Barker. San Mateo, CA: Huntington Library, 1945.
Directory of the City of Hudson for the Years 1851–52. Hudson, NY: Parmenter & Van Antwerp, 1851.
Dobyns, Henry F. *Hepah, California! The Journal of Cave Johnson Couts, From Monterrey, Mexico, to Los Angeles, California, during the Years 1848–1849.* Tucson: Arizona Pioneers Society, 1962.
Donald, David, ed. *Inside Lincoln's Cabinet: The Civil War Diaries of Salmon P. Chase.* New York: Longmans, NY, 1954.
Exley, Thomas M. *A Compendium of the Pay of the Army from 1785 to 1888, Compiled under the Direction of the Paymaster General of the Army.* Washington, DC: Government Printing Office, 1888.
Frémont, Jessie Benton. *The Story of the Guard: A Chronicle of the War.* Boston: Ticknor & Fields, 1863.
History of La Clede, Camden, Dallas, Webster, Wright, Texas, Pulaski, Phelps, and Dent Counties, Missouri. Chicago, IL: Goodspeed, 1889.
Gould's St. Louis Directory for 1872. St. Louis, MO: Gould Directory Company.
Heilbrom, Carl H., ed. *History of San Diego County,* San Diego: The San Diego Press Club, 1939.
Heintzelman, Samuel P. Mss. letters to Justus McKinstry, September 3 and 17, 1853, from Fort Yuma Ceola, Arizona Territory. In National Archives, Office of the Quartermaster General, Record of

Regular Officers, Quartermaster's Department, L–P. McKinstry, Justus. Record Group 92. Washington, DC.
Heitman, Francis B. *Historical Register and Dictionary of the United States Army.* Washington, DC: Government Printing Office, 1903.
Holmes, Charles N. "The First Republican-Democratic Presidential Campaign." *Journal of American History,* Vol. VIV, no. 44, 1920.
Irwin, Ray W., ed. "Missouri in Crisis: The Journal of Captain Albert Tracy, 1861." *Missouri Historical Review,* Vol. 51, October 1956.
Johnson, Robert Underwood, and Clarence Clough Buel, eds. *Battles and Leaders of the Civil War, From Sumter to Shiloh.* Vol. 1: *In Command in Missouri, by John C. Frémont, Major General, U. S. A.,* New York: Thomas Yoseloff, 1956.
Kempf, Cora B. Highland Cemetery Association. Mss letter, September 29, 1990, Ypsilanti, MI.
Koerner, Gustav. *Memoirs of Gustav Koerner, 1809–1896, Life Sketches Written at the Suggestion of His Children.* Thomas McCormack. Cedar Rapids, IA: Torch Press, 1909.
Lant, J. H., ed. *The Hudson Directory for 1874–75, etc.* Hudson, NY: Bryan and Webb, 1874.
LeCount, Charles A. "'I Have Not Seen Niagara Falls Yet,' Dr. James H. Sargent's Visit to Fort Niagara in 1846, James Hovey Sargent to Fanny Sargent, Fort Niagara, New York, July 5, 1846." *OFN— Now and Then, A Newspaper of the Old Fort Niagara Association, Inc.,* Vol. XLIII, No. 12, 1993.
Leitshuh, Charles. Highland Cemetery Association. Mss letter, June 20, 1989, Ypsilanti, MI.
Lobdell, Jared C., ed. "The Civil War Journal and Letters of Colonel John Van Deusen Du Bois, April 12, 1861, to October 16, 1862." *Missouri Historical Society Review.* Vol. LXI (October 1966).
Mahon, John K., ed. "Joseph R. Smith, Letters from the Second Seminole War." *The Florida Historical Quarterly,* Vol. XXXVI, no. 4, April 1958.
_____. *Reminiscences of the Second Seminole War, by John Bemrose.* Gainesville: University of Florida Press, 1966.
McClellan, George B., to Brig. Gen. S. R. Curtis, November 11, 1861, telegraph message in cipher.
McGaughy, Felix P., Jr. *The Squaw Kissing War: Bartholomew M. Lynch's Journal of the Second Seminole War, 1835–1839.* Florida State University, Tallahassee, FL, April 1965.
McKinstry, Elisha Williams. *Some Reminiscences by Elisha Williams McKinstry.* Edited by Charles Hedges McKinstry. ed. No loc.: privately published, 1983.
McKinstry, Justus. *Vindication of Brig. Gen. J. McKinstry, Formerly Quarter-Master, Western Department.* St. Louis, MO: privately published, 1862.
National Archives. Department of the Treasury. Mss letter R. J. Zimmerman to Major Justus McKinstry, May 25, 1859. Washington, DC.
Nicolay, John G., and John Hay, eds. *Abraham Lincoln.* New York: Century, 1894.
Regan, James. *The Judge Advocate's Guide.* Washington, DC: Beresford, 1877.
Ross, Johanna Cecelia. *George P. McKinstry, Jr., A Manuscript Collection.* M.A. thesis, California State University, San Jose, CA, 1972.
Saffarans, George C., ed. *Historical Register of the Commissioned Officers of the Second U. S. Infantry, from its Organization, March 4, 1791, including Supplementary Tabulations of Historical Data Concerning the Regiment.* Logan, CO: Regimental, 1904.
Savage, John W. Washington, DC, to John Fiala, St. Louis, MO, February 14, 1862. Original mss letter at the Missouri Historical Society, St. Louis, MO.
State of Missouri, City of St. Louis, Marriage License No. 62438, Justus McKinstry and Miss Adelaide Dickinson, September 20, 1895.
Sunderman, James F., ed., *Journey into the Wilderness, An Army Surgeon's Account of Life in Camp and Field during the Creek and Seminole Wars, 1836–1838, by Jacob Rhett Mott,* University of Florida Press, Gainesville, FL, 1963.
Thirty-Sixth Annual Reunion of the Association of the Graduates of the United States Military Academy at West Point, New York, June 13th, 1905. Saginaw, MI: Seeman & Peters, 1905.
Trow's New York City Directory. New York: 1865.
United States Congress. *Executive Documents Printed by Order of the Forty-Fourth Congress, Executive Document No. 25.* Washington, DC: Government Printing Office, 1877.
_____. *Executive Documents Printed by Order of the House of Representatives during the Second Session of the Twenty-ninth Congress, 1847–48, Messages of the President of the United States, with Correspondence Therewith, Communicated between the Secretary of War and Other Officers of the*

Government, on the Subject of the Mexican War, House Executive Documents, Vol. 7. Washington, DC: Wendell and van Benthuysen, 1848.

_____. *Executive Documents Printed by Order of the House of Representatives during the Second Session of the Thirty-Fourth Congress, 1855–56, Executive Document 135,* "Report on the United States and Mexican Border Survey, Made under the Direction of the Secretary of the Interior, by William J. Emory, Major, First Cavalry, and United States Commissioner." Washington, DC: Cornelius Wendell, 1857.

_____. *Executive Documents Printed by Order of the House of Representatives during the Second Session of the Thirty-Seventh Congress, 1861–62, Executive Document 144.* Washington, DC: Government Printing Office, 1862.

_____. House of Representatives, Thirty-Seventh Congress, 2nd Session, House Report No. 94, *War Claims at St. Louis.* Washington, DC: Government Printing Office, 1862.

_____. Reports of Committees of the House of Representatives, made during the Second Session of the Thirty-Seventh Congress, 1861–'62, Volume I, Report Number 2. Washington, DC: Government Printing Office, 1861.

_____. *The Congressional Globe, The Official Proceedings of Congress.* Thirty-Seventh Congress, 2nd Session, New Series, No. 150. Washington, DC: John C. Rives, 1861.

United States Senate. *Executive Document No. 55,* 33rd Congress, 2nd Session, "Map of That Portion of the Boundary between the United States and Mexico, from the Pacific Coast to the Junction of the Gila and Colorado rivers, etc." New York: Ackerman Lith., 1855.

United States War Department. *Revised Regulations for the Army of the United States, with a Full Index, by Authority of the War Department.* Philadelphia: J. G. L. Brown, 1861.

_____. *The War of the Rebellion, A Compilation of the Official Records of the Union and Confederate Armies.* Four series, 129 volumes. Washington, DC: Government Printing Office, 1880–1900.

Willis, William. *Genealogy of the McKinstry Family with a Preliminary Essay on the Scotch-Irish Immigrants to America.* Boston: Henry Dalton and Son, 1852.

Ypsilanti Historical Society Museum and Archives. Mss index cards on members of the McKinstry family derived from *The Ypsilantian.* Ypsilanti, MI.

Secondary Sources

Adams, George Rollie. *General William S. Harney, Prince of Dragoons.* Lincoln: University of Nebraska Press, 2001.

Adamson, Hans Christian, *Rebellion in Missouri, 1861, Nathaniel Lyon and the Army of the West.* Philadelphia: Chilton, 1961.

Ambrose, Stephen E. *Duty, Honor, Country— The History of West Point.* Baltimore: Johns Hopkins University Press, 1966.

Archdiocese of St. Louis. "About the Archdiocese." St. Louis, MO: 2001.

Auchampaugh, Philip Gerald. *James Buchanan and His Cabinet on the Eve of Secession.* Lancaster, PA: privately printed, 1926.

Avina, Rose Hollenbaugh. *The Chicano Heritage: Spanish and Mexican Land Grants in California.* New York: Arno Press, 1976.

Bauer, K. Jack. *The Mexican War.* New York: Macmillan, 1974.

Bibb, Leland E., "William Marshall, 'The Wickedest Man in California,' A Reappraisal," *The Journal of San Diego History,* Winter, 1976, Volume 22, No. 1, San Diego Historical Society, San Diego, CA.

Bradley, Anna Rossman. *History of Columbia County, with Biographical Sketches, etc.* Hudson, NY: Record Printing Co., 1908.

Brandes, Ray. *San Diego, An Illustrated History.* Los Angeles, CA: A Rosebud Book, 1981.

Bridgwater, William, and Seymour Kurtz, eds. *The Columbia Encyclopedia.* 3rd ed. New York: Columbia University Press, 1968.

Buckmaster, Henrietta. *The Seminole Wars.* New York: Macmillan, 1966.

Burton, Clarence M., and M. Agnes Burton, eds. *The History of Wayne County and the City of Detroit, Michigan.* Detroit: S. J. Clark, 1930.

Clarke, James Mitchell. "Antonio Melendez: Nemesis of William Walker in Baja California." *California Historical Quarterly,* Vol. XII, no. 4, December 1933.

Coffman, Edward M. *The Old Army: A Portrait of the American Army in Peacetime, 1784–1898.* New York: Oxford University Press, 1986.
Colburn, Harvey C. *The Story of Ypsilanti, Written for the Centennial Celebration of the Founding of the City, in Cooperation with the Committee on History.* Ypsilanti, MI: 1923.
Columbia County at the End of the Century. Hudson, NY: published under the auspices of the *Hudson Gazette,* 1900.
Cowan, Robert C. *Ranchos of California.* Fresno: Academy Library Guild, 1961.
Coyer, Richard Joseph. "Cave Johnson Couts: On Both Sides of the Law." *La Campana de Escuela, Annual Memorial History Awards,* Vol. 1, no. 1, edited by James Robert Moriarity III. Old School House Historians, San Diego, CA: Old School House Historians, 1974.
Cullum, George W. *Biographical Register of the Officers and Graduates of the U. S. Military Academy.* Boston: Houghton Mifflin Co., 1891.
Dana, Charles A. *Recollections of the Civil War.* New York: D. Appleton, 1898.
Darby, William. *A Tour from the City of New York to Detroit, in Michigan Territory, etc., 1818.* Reprint, Chicago: Quadrangle, 1963.
Davis, Jefferson. *The Rise and Fall of the Confederate Government.* New York: D. Appleton, 1881.
Drake, Francis S., ed. *Dictionary of American Biography.* Boston: James Osgood, 1872.
Drescher, Nuala. *Engineers for the Public Good: A History of the Buffalo District, U. S. Army Corps of Engineers.* Buffalo: United States Army Corps of Engineers, n. d.
Dufour, Charles L. *The Mexican War: A Compact History, 1846–1848.* New York: Hawthorn, 1968.
Dunbar, Willis Frederick. *Michigan: A History of the Wolverine State.* Grand Rapids: William B. Erdmans, 1965.
Dunnigan, Brian Lee. *Forts within a Fort: Niagara's Redoubts.* Youngstown, NY: Old Fort Niagara Association, 1989.
_____. *Glorious Relic: The French Castle and Old Fort Niagara.* Youngstown, NY: Old Fort Niagara Association, 1987.
_____. *History and Development of Old Fort Niagara.* Youngstown, NY: Old Fort Niagara Association, 1985.
_____. *A History and Guide to Old Fort Niagara.* Youngstown, NY: Old Fort Niagara Associations, 1985.
_____. and Patricia Kay Scott. *Old Fort Niagara in Four Centuries: A History of its Development.* New York: Old Fort Niagara Association, 1991.
Dupuy, R. Ernest. *The Compact History of the United States Army.* New York: Hawthorn, 1973.
Dyer, Frederick H., *A Compendium of the War of the Rebellion.* New York: Thomas Yoseloff, 1909.
Egan, Ferol. *Frémont, Explorer for a Restless Nation.* Garden City, NY: Doubleday, 1977.
Eisenhower, John S. D., *So Far from God: The U. S. War with Mexico, 1846–1848.* New York: Random House, 1989.
Eyer, Alice. *The Famous Frémonts and Their America.* Rev. ed. Boston: Christopher, 1961.
Farmer, Silas. *History of Detroit and Wayne County and Early Michigan: A Chronological Cyclopedia of the Past and Present.* New York: Munsell, 1890.
Fenhoff, Patricia. Mss. letter. History Department, City of Hudson, NY.
Fleming, Thomas J. *West Point: The Men and the Times of the United States Military Academy.* New York: William Morrow, 1969.
Foreman, Sidney. *West Point: A History of the United States Military Academy.* New York: Columbia University Press, 1950.
Fowler, William M., Jr. *Under Two Flags: The American Navy in the Civil War.* New York: W. W. Norton, 1990.
Gerteis, Louis S. *Civil War St. Louis.* Lawrence, KS: University Press of Kansas, 2001.
Glatthaar, Joseph T. *The March to the Sea and Beyond: Sherman's Troops in the Savannah and Carolina Campaign.* New York: New York University, 1985.
Goodwin, Cardinal Leonidas. *John Charles Frémont, An Explanation of His Career.* Stanford, CA: Stanford University Press, 1930.
Gurney, Gene. *A Pictoral History of the United States Military Academy in War and Peace, From Colonial Times to Vietnam.* New York: Crown, 1977.
Hagerman, Edward. *The American Civil War and the Origins of Modern Warfare, Ideas, Organization, and Field Command.* Bloomington: Indiana University Press, 1988.
Hattaway, Herman, and Archer Jones. *How the North Won: A Military History of the Civil War.* Urbana: University of Illinois Press, 1991.

Henry, Robert Selph. *The Story of the Mexican War*. Bobbs-Merrill, New York: 1950.
Herr, Pamela. *Jessie Benton Frémont, American Woman of the 19th Century: A Biography*. New York: Franklin Watts, 1987.
_____. and Mary Lee Spence, eds. *The Letters of Jessie Benton Frémont*. Urbana: University of Illinois Press, 1993.
Hilbert, Russell Seymour. *A History of the Hilbert and McKinstry Families*. Brighton, MI: privately published, 1976.
Hinze, Donald C., and Karen Farnham. *The Battle of Carthage in Southwestern Missouri, July 5, 1861*. Campbell, CA: Savas, 1997.
History of Columbia County, New York, with Illustrations and Biographical Sketches of Some of its Prominent Men and Pioneers. Philadelphia, PA: Everts and Ensign, 1878.
Howard, Robert West. *Thundergate: The Forts of Niagara*. Englewood Cliffs, NJ: Prentice Hall, 1968.
Hulbert, Archer Butler. *The Niagara River*. New York: Putnam, 1908.
Huston, James A. *Army Historical Series: The Sinews of War: Army Logistics, 1775–1953*, Washington, DC: Office of the Chief of Military History, United States Army, 1966.
Jenks, William Lee. *St. Clair County, Michigan, Its History and Its People, A Narrative Account of Its Historical Progress and Its Principal Interests*. Chicago: Lewis, 1912.
Katcher, Philip. *The American Soldier, U. S. Armies, 1775 to the Present*. London: Osprey, 1990.
Kohn, Richard H. *Eagle and Sword: The Federalists and the Creation of Military Establishments in America, 1783–1802*. New York: The Free Press, 1975.
Kloos, James E. *Graves of Union Generals in Michigan*. Cleveland: Classic Printin, n. d.
Leech, Margaret. *Reveille in Washington, 1860–1865*. New York: Harper & Brothers, 1941.
Long, David L. *The Jewel of Liberty: Abraham Lincoln's Re-Election and the End of Slavery*. Mechanicsburg, PA: Stackpole, 1994.
Long, Everett B., with Barbara Long. *The Civil War Day by Day: An Almanac, 1861–1865*. Garden City, NY: Doubleday, 1971.
Longacre, Edward G. "A Profile of General Justus McKinstry." *Civil War Times Illustrated*, Vol. XVII, no. 4, July 1978.
Luddington, M. I. *Uniforms of the United States from 1774 to 1880, Illustrated*. New York: American Lithograph, 1890.
Lyght, Charles E., M. D., ed. *The Merck Manual of Diagnosis and Therapy*. Rahway, NJ: Merck Sharp & Dohme Research Laboratories, 1966.
Mahon, John K. *History of the Second Seminole War, 1835–1842*. Gainesville: University of Florida Press, 1991.
Mayer, Robert E., comp. and ed. *San Diego: A Chronological and Documentary History, 1535–1976*. Howard Furer, Series Editor. Dobbs Ferry, NY: Oceana, 1978.
McElroy, John. *The Struggle for Missouri*. Washington, DC: National Tribune, 1909.
McGrew, Clarence Allen. *City of San Diego and San Diego County: The Birthplace of California*. Chicago: American Historical, 1922.
McHenry, Robert, ed. *Webster's American Biographies*. New York: Dover, New York: 1978.
McKinney, Effie May. *The Cleveland Convention*. M.A. Thesis, Case Western Reserve University, Cleveland, March 1928.
McReynolds, Edwin C. *The Seminoles*. Norman: University of Oklahoma Press, 1957.
Metzer, Milton. *Hunted Like a Wolf— The Story of the Seminole War*. New York: Farrar, Straus and Giroux, 1972.
Micou, Ann McKinstry. *Patriots and Pioneers: Five Generations of McKinstrys (1712–1961)*. No loc.: privately published, 2000.
Miller, Steven Bailey. *Historical Sketches of Hudson, Embracing the Settlement of the City, Government, Business Enterprises, Churches, Press, Schools, Libraries, etc.* Hudson, NY: Bryan and Webb, 1862.
Morison, Samuel Eliot. *The Oxford History of the American People*. New York: Oxford University Press, 1965.
Morris, Roy, Jr. "Union Quartermaster Justus McKinstry, A Handy Man with a Ledger Book, Practiced Unique Bookkeeping." *America's Civil War*, Vol. IV, no. 6, March 1992.
Morrison, James L., Jr. *Best School in the World: West Point, The Pre-Civil War Years, 1833–1866*. Kent, OH: The Kent State University Press, 1986.
Moss, James E., ed. *The Journal of San Diego History*. Volume XVI, no. 2, Spring 1970.

Moyer, Cecil C. *Historic Ranches of San Diego County*. San Diego, CA: Union-Tribune, 1969.
Munden, Kenneth W., and Henry Putney Beers. *Guide to Federal Archives Relating to the Civil War*. Washington, DC: National Archives and Records Service, General Services Administration, 1962.
Musicant, Ivan. *Divided Waters: The Naval History of the Civil War*. New York: HarperCollins, 1995.
Myers, William S. *A Study in Personality: George Brinton McClellan*. New York: Appleton-Century, 1934.
Nesbitt, Robert C. *Wisconsin, A History*. Madison: University of Wisconsin Press, 1973.
Nevins, Allan. *Frémont, Pathfinder of the West*. New York: D. Appleton–Century, 1939.
_____. *Frémont: The West's Great Adventurer, etc.* New York: Harper and Brothers, 1928.
_____. *The War for the Union*. New York: Scribner, 1959.
New York Historical Resources Center, Olin Library, Cornell University. *Guide to Historical Resources in Columbia County, New York, Repositories*. Ithaca, NY: n. d
Parrish, William E., ed. *Frank Blair, Lincoln's Conservative*. Columbia: University of Missouri Press, 1998.
_____. *A History of Missouri*. Volume III: 1860 to 1875. Columbia: University of Missouri Press, 1973.
Peckham, James. *Gen. Nathaniel Lyon and Missouri in 1861*. New York: American News Company, 1866.
Peters, Virginia Bergman. *The Florida Wars*. Hamden, CT: Shoestring, 1979.
Phillips, Christopher. *Damned Yankee: The Life of General Nathaniel Lyon*. Columbia: University of Missouri Press, 1990.
Pratt, Julius W., "The War of 1812," *History of the State of New York*, Alexander C. Flick, ed., Columbia University Press, New York, NY, 1943.
Primm, James Neal. *Lion of the Valley: St. Louis, Missouri*. 2nd ed. Boulder: Pruett, 1990.
Prucha, Francis Paul. *Broadaxe and Bayonet: The Role of the United States Army in the Development of the Northwest, 1815–1860*. Madison: State Historical Society of Wisconsin, 1953.
_____. *The Sword of the Republic: The United States Army on the Frontier, 1783–1846*. Toronto: Macmillan, 1969.
Reaves, Logan U. *The Life and Military History of Gen. William Selby Harney*. St. Louis, MO: Bryan, Brand, 1878.
Reed, C. D., publ. *A History of the Texas Railroads and of Transportation Conditions under Spain and Mexico and the Republic and the State*. Houston: St. Clair, 1941.
Richardson, Albert D. *The Secret Service, the Field, the Dungeon, and the Escape*. Hartford: American Publishing Company, 1865.
Risch, Erna, *Quartermaster Support of the Army, A History of the Corps, 1775–1939*. Washington, DC: Department of the Army, Quartermaster Historian's Office, Office of the Quartermaster General, U. S. Government Printing Office, 1962.
Roberts, Robert B. *Encyclopedia of Historic Forts: The Military, Pioneer, and Trading Posts in the United States*. New York: Macmillan, n. d.
Rolle, Andrew. *John Charles Frémont, Character as Destiny*. Norman: University of Oklahoma, 1961.
Rombauer, Robert Julius. *The Union Cause in Missouri, An Historical Sketch*. St. Louis, MO: Nixon-Jones, 1909.
Rosenwaike, Ira. *Population History of New York City*. Syracuse: Syracuse University Press, 1972.
Ross, Robert B., and George B. Catlin. *Landmarks of Wayne County and Detroit*. Rev. by Clarence M. Burton. Detroit: published under the auspices of the Evening News Association, 1898.
Ryan, Gary D., and Timothy K. Nenninger. *Soldiers and Civilians: The U. S. Army and the American People*. Washington, DC: National Archives and Research Administration, 1987.
Scharf, Thomas J. *History of St. Louis City and County*. Philadelphia: Louis H. Everts, 1883.
Schlesinger, Arthur M., Jr. *The Age of Jackson*. Boston: Little, Brown, 1953.
Schuh, Miles W. Mss letter January 1, 1992, Panama City Beach, FL, to the author.
Sears, Stephen W. *The Civil War Papers of George B. McClellan: Selected Correspondence, 1860–1865*. New York: Ticknor & Fields, 1989.
_____. *George B. McClellan, The Young Napoleon*. New York: Ticknor & Fields, 1988.
Shannon, Fred Albert. *The Organization and Administration of the Union Army, 1861–1865*. Cleveland: Arthur H. Clark, 1928.
Shaw, Frederick B. *One Hundred and Forty Years Service in Peace and War: History of the Second Infantry Regiment, United States Army*. Detroit: Strathmore, 1930.

Smith, Elbert B. *Francis Preston Blair.* New York: The Free Press, 1980.
Smith, George Winston, and Charles Judah. *Chronicles of the Gringos: The U. S. Army in the Mexican War.* Las Cruces: The University of New Mexico Press, 1968.
Smith, William Ernest. "The Blairs and Frémont." *Missouri Historical Review,* Vol. XXIII, no. 2, January 1929.
_____. *The Francis Preston Blair Family in Politics.* Vol. II. New York: Macmillan, 1933.
Snead, Thomas L. *The Fight for Missouri: From the Election of Lincoln to the Death of Lyon.* New York: Scribner, 1886.
Sprague, John T. *The Origins, Progress, and Conclusion of the Florida War, etc.* Philadelphia: D. Appleton, 1848.
Stadler, Francis Hurd. *St. Louis Day by Day.* Tucson: Patrice, 1990.
Stampp, Kenneth M. *And the War Came: The North and the Secession Crisis, 1860–1861.* Baton Rouge: Louisiana State University Press, 1950.
Starr, Raymond G. *San Diego: A Pictoral History.* Norfolk: Donning, 1937.
Stevens, Walter B. "Lincoln and Missouri." *The Missouri Historical Review,* Vol. X, January 1916.
Summers, Mark W. *The Era of Good Stealings.* New York: Oxford University Press, 1993.
_____. *The Plundering Generation: Corruption and the Crisis of the Union, 1849–1861.* New York: Oxford University Press, 1987.
Tasher, Lucy Louise. *The Missouri Democrat and the Civil War.* Ph. D. diss., Department of History, University of Chicago, Chicago, IL, 1934.
Trefousse, Hans L. "I Have Done My Share." *Civil War Times Illustrated,* Vol. IX, no. 2, 1970.
Upton, Emory. *The Military Policy of the United States.* Washington, DC: Government Printing Office, 1912.
Walton, George. *Fearless and Free: The Seminole War, 1835–1842.* New York: Bobbs-Merrill, 1977.
Waugh, Elizabeth Day Jenkins. *West Point: The Story of the United States Military Academy Which, Rising from the Revolutionary Forces, Has Taught American Soldiers the Art of Victory.* New York: Macmillan, 1942.
Weigley, Russell F. *History of the United States Army.* New York: Macmillan, 1967.
_____. *Quartermaster General of the Union Army: A Biography of M. C. Meigs.* New York: Columbia University Press, 1959.
White, James T., ed. *The National Cyclopedia of American Biography.* New York: James T. White, 1893–1919.
Wilson, Peter M. *John and Jane (Dickie) McKinstry.* Spotsylvania, VA: privately published, 2000.
Woodworth, Steven E. *Jefferson Davis and His Generals: The Failure of Confederate Command in the West.* Lawrence, KS: University of Kansas Press, 1990.
_____. ed. *The American Civil War: A Handbook of Literature and Research.* Westport, CT: Greenwood, 1999.
Wynn, Dennis J. *The San Patricio Soldiers: Mexico's Foreign Legion.* Southern Studies Monograph No. 74. El Paso: Texas Western Press, TX, 1984.
Zornow, William Frank. *Lincoln and the Party Divided.* Norman: University of Oklahoma Press, 1954.

Index

Adams, John Quincy 69
Agua Caliente, California 96, 97
Albany, New York 44
Alexander, Thomas L. 174
Allen, John 148
Allen, Robert 52, 60, 72, 83, 93, 96, 98, 156, 164, 166, 170, 171
Alta California 90, 96
Ames, Francis 168
Amessari, Ignacio 65
Anderson, James W. 39
Anderson, Robert 1, 124
Andrews, Timothy P. 142, 143, 154, 155
Arnold, Ripley A. 1, 3
Asboth, Alexander 155, 163, 164
Astor House, Mexico City 67
Austine, William A. 59

Backus, Nancy 7
Baha California, Mexico 96
Bandini, Don Juan 84
Bandini, Ysidora 84, 96
Barlow, Samuel L. M. 186
Barton, Mr., partner 94
Bates, Edward 135
Baton Rouge, Louisiana 128
Beard, E. L. 142, 143, 172
Beard & Palmer 142, 143, 154, 166, 172
Beauregard, Pierre, G. T. 22, 67, 135
Benicia, California 93, 96, 98
Benton, Thomas Hart 134
Benton Barracks, Missouri 148, 175
Bell, William H. 117
Biddle, John 10
Black, Jeremiah 120
Blair, Francis Preston, Jr. 116, 117, 120, 123, 124, 126, 127, 128, 130, 131, 135, 137, 140, 145, 146, 150, 152, 154, 156, 157, 180, 186, 183, 187
Blair, Francis Preston, Sr. 116
Blair, Montgomery 22, 116, 132, 135, 137, 152, 158, 177, 180, 186
Bliss, William W. S. 1
Bonham, Milledge L. 63, 75
Bonneville, Benjamin L. E. 175
Boonville, Missouri 132, 133, 135
Botts, William B. 175
Bowen, John A. 140
Bradley, John 33
Brady, Hugh 27, 28, 31, 45, 145
Brady, Samuel P. 27, 145, 156
Bragg, Braxton 22
Brant, Sarah 142, 156
Brazos Santiago, Mexico 45, 76
Broadhead, James O. 116
Brooklyn Eagle 150
Brown, John 148
Brown, William A. 21, 59
Buchanan, James 110, 114, 118, 119, 120, 134, 162
Buckmaster, Henrietta 31
Buckmaster, Samuel 146
Buell, Don Carlos 22
Buena Vista, Mexico 83
Buffalo, New York 29
Burton, Henry S. 88, 96, 100
Butler, Benjamin 127
Butler, William O. 48

Cairo, Illinois 149
Caldwell, G. A. 68
Calhoun, John C. 25
Camargo, Mexico 45, 46, 47, 48
Cameron, J. D. 191
Cameron, Simon 122, 123, 124, 125, 127, 139, 140, 144, 158, 161, 162
Cames, Edward 39
Camp Asboth, Missouri 162
Camp Brady, Mexico 46
Camp Far West, California 87
Camp Frémont, California 96
Camp in the Mountains, California 96
Camp Jackson, Missouri 127, 128, 146
Camp on Cache Creek, California 96
Camp Upper Sacramento, California 96
Camp Washington, Mexico 51
Camp Watson, Mexico 48
Campbell, Hugh 161, 168, 169, 170, 177
Campbell, R. & Co. 161
Canby, Edward R. S. 22, 37, 40, 41, 44, 45, 83, 166
Canton, Missouri 155
Carrera, Lorenzo 61
Carrera & Garay 61, 62, 63, 64, 66
Carthage, Missouri 132
Casey, Silas 88
Cass, Lewis 8, 9, 12, 14, 45, 120
Castle San Juan de Ulua, Mexico 49
Cavender, John S. 149
Cerro Gordo, Mexico 52, 77, 93, 191
Chagres, Panama 79
Chapultepec, Mexico 59, 71
Charleston, South Carolina 31, 115, 124
Chase, Salmon P. 123, 124, 139, 186
Chicago, Illinois 186
Child, Pratt & Fox 114, 122, 143, 144, 170, 171, 182
Church, Albert E. 1
Churchill, Major 32
Churubusco, Mexico 55, 57, 58, 59, 62, 67, 80, 191
Clapp, Henry 148, 149, 179
Clarke, Henry 58
Clarke, Ransome 23
Clary, Robert E. 112, 114
Claverack Landing, New York 6
Clear Lake, California 122
Clements, H. W. G. 98, 106, 114, 159, 160, 165, 171, 174, 180

Index

Clements & Co. 144, 145
Clendennin, John M. 27, 29, 30
Cobb, Howell 120
Code, Hopper & Gratz 145
Coffey, Robert T. 147
Coghan, James P. 144
Coglin, Private, deserter 87
Colburn, Frederick M. 146
Columbia University Law School, New York City, New York 77
Commission on War Claims 160, 167, 168, 170, 174, 177
Conckling, Barnabas 41
Conroy, William 100
Contreras, Mexico 56, 57, 58, 59, 62, 67
Cooke, Philip St. G. 174, 175, 176
Corn & Auferman 188
Corpus Christi, Texas 44
Cortez, Hernando 49
Couts, Cave Johnson 76, 80, 83, 84, 85, 86, 90, 91, 94, 95, 96, 97, 99, 100, 101, 105, 107, 108, 109, 183
Couts, Cave Johnson, Jr. 109
Coyoacan, Mexico 58
Craig, Henry K. 174, 175
Crawford, George 86
Crawford, Richard H. 67
Cristy, contractor 149
Crosman, George H. 122, 123
Cross Keys, Virginia 174
Cross, Osborn 98, 101
Cummings, Alexander 28
Curley, William 91, 92
Curtis, Samuel D. 84
Curtis, Samuel R. 158, 164, 167, 169
Cutter, John 60

Dade, Francis L. 23, 37
Davidson, Delozier 39
Davis, David 161, 168, 169, 170, 177
Davis, Edward M. 142, 154, 155
Davis, Jefferson 102
Dawes, Henry L. 158, 160
Day, Hannibal 87, 88
Day Book 150
Decker, John 91
de Landa, Jose 61, 66, 67
De Russy, Rene 2, 3, 21, 23
Detroit, Michigan 8, 29, 31, 34, 44, 45, 73, 74, 77, 145
Dickey, Jane 6
Dickinson, Adelaide 192, 193
Diggs, Mr., associate 87
Donnelly, Colonel 94, 95
Dresser, Mr., McKinstry Volunteer 58
Dunbar, Willis Frederick 9
Dunn, Thomas 147
Dunn's Lake, Florida 39
Dupuy, Ernest 34
Duran, Mrs. 62

Early, Jubal 22
Eastman, Thomas W. 33
Eaton, Amos B. 102
Eddy, Asher R. 101, 105
El Paso, Texas 76
Elleard, Charles M. 114, 122, 123, 140, 146, 147, 156, 170, 171
Ellersbee, transport 48
Elzey, Arnold 22
Emory, William S. 76, 79, 80, 84, 85, 86, 98
Evans, George F. 80, 83, 85, 86, 90, 91, 95
Everett, James 146
Ewell, Richard S. 22

Falcon, steamer 79
Farrar, Benjamin 128, 140, 149
Farrar, John 140, 146
Fenton, Reuben E. 158
Ferrell, W. C. 97
Fiala, John 171
Filley, Giles R. 128, 144
Filley, Oliver D. 116, 117, 128
Finison, Private, deserter 87
Fiske, Knight & Co. 144
Fitzgerald, E. H. 88, 92
Fitzgerald. G. B. 97
Florence, river steamer 114
Floyd, John B. 120
Fort Brooke, Florida 23, 24, 32, 39, 110, 111
Fort Brooks, Florida 32
Fort Butler, Florida 30
Fort Columbus, New York 29, 31, 45
Fort Fanning, Florida 36
Fort Fowle, Florida 30
Fort Gates, Florida 32, 37
Fort Gratiot, Michigan 9, 29
Fort Hamilton, New York 75
Fort Heilman, Florida 33
Fort Holmes, Florida 36, 37
Fort King, Florida 23, 30, 40
Fort Leavenworth, Kansas 47, 76, 123
Fort Mackinac, Michigan 45, 46, 55
Fort Mellon, Florida 39
Fort Niagara, New York 40, 41, 45, 72, 83
Fort Pickens, Florida 120
Fort Putnam, New York 16
Fort Redding, California 105
Fort Riley, Kansas 106, 120, 123
Fort Scott, Kansas 118
Fort Shannon, Florida 32
Fort Smith, Arkansas 118
Fort Sumter, South Carolina 120, 124
Fort Yuma, Arizona 98, 100, 102, 107, 190
Fowle, John 2, 30
Fox, Edward L. 122, 123, 144, 156
Foy, Peter I. 116, 117
Frank, William 61, 62, 64, 64, 65

Franklin, Lewis A. 99
Freeman's Journal 150
Frémont, Jessie Benton 134, 135, 137, 150, 154, 156, 162, 164
Frémont, John Charles 114, 134, 135, 136, 137, 139, 140, 142, 143, 149, 150, 154, 157, 158, 160, 162, 164, 166, 171, 172, 174, 178, 180, 181, 182, 184, 186, 187, 191
Frost, David M. 117, 127, 128

Gambier, Ohio 77
Gamble, Hamilton R. 133
Ganoe, William Addleman 26, 36
Galt, P. H. 63
Garcia, Clement Perez 61, 62, 63, 64, 65, 66, 67, 69, 72, 73, 75, 107, 183
Garey's Ferry, Florida 31, 33
Gardner, Franklin 63, 68
Garnett, Robert 22
Garra, Antonio 97
Gatlin, Richard C. 68
Glover, Samuel T. 116, 167, 168, 177
Gorgina, Panama 79
Graham, James D. 174
Graham, Lawrence P. 174, 175
Grand Sociedad, Mexico City 67
Grandin, William S. 21
Granger, Gordon 67, 165
Gratiot, Charles 9, 13
Grayson, John Breckindge 62, 63, 67, 69
Green, Christopher A. 3, 5
Grider, Private, deserter 87
Grier, William N. 174, 175
Guadalupe Hidalgo, Mexico 71, 73
Gurnee, Walter S. 145

Hagner, Peter V. 117, 118, 122, 123, 125, 128
Hahn, William L. 114, 165, 169, 171, 174
Halleck, Henry W. 22, 166, 171, 176, 181
Halleck Tustenuggee 39, 40
Hallowell, Mr., contractor 155
Hamilton, Lieutenant 67
Hammond, William A. 120
Hancock Barracks, Maine 45
Hanley, Richard 60
Haraszthy, Augustin 97
Hardcastle, E. L. 84
Hardee, William 22
Harding, Chester 131, 132, 133, 177, 178
Harkness, James 147
Harney, William S. 48, 52, 56, 57, 58, 59, 60, 110, 114, 115, 118, 120, 123, 124, 125, 126, 129, 131, 174, 175, 179, 180
Harpers Ferry, Virginia 126

Index

Harris, Andrew 69
Haskell, Leonidas 146, 147, 182
Havens, Benny 22
Hayden, Julius 76, 80, 83, 84, 86
Heintzelman, Samuel P. 84, 88, 90, 91, 93, 96, 98, 100, 102
Hermansville, Missouri 163
Highland Cemetery, Ypsilanti, Michigan 191
Hitchcock, Ethan Allen 46, 57, 59, 60, 103, 104, 105, 158
Hoffman, William S. 158
Holt, Joseph 120, 122, 144, 162, 168, 170, 177
Hood, Thomas 125, 179
Hooker, Joseph 22
Hooper, George F. 84
Hosmer, Addison A. 174, 175, 176
How, John 116, 145
Hudson, New York 6, 28, 29, 40, 41, 43, 44, 45, 73, 79, 95, 111, 112, 114, 184, 188
Hull, William 8
Humber, L. C. 68
Hunt, Henry 22
Hunter, David 155, 162, 164, 166
Hyatt, J. B. 87, 88

Ignacio, Joseph 65, 66, 75
Illinois State Register 184
Inge, Zebulon Montgomery Pike 2
Irvine, Josephus 148
Irwin, James R. 49, 51, 50, 55, 60, 61, 62, 64, 65, 73, 93, 183
Isle of Lobos, Mexico 48
Israel, Robert D. 91, 92

Jaccard & Co., E. 156
Jackson, Andrew 31
Jackson, Claiborne E. 116, 124, 125, 127, 129, 130, 131, 132, 133
Jackson, James S. 158
Jackson, Thomas Jonathan 174
Jacksonville, Florida 31, 33
Jalapa, Mexico 52, 53
Jefferson Barracks, Missouri 75, 118, 165, 171
Jefferson City, Missouri 116, 131, 132, 133
Jenkins, Elisha 43
Jesup, Thomas S. 37, 42, 44, 47, 61, 62, 73, 75, 86, 88, 101, 102, 105, 111, 124
Johnson, Bushrod 22
Johnson, Chauncey P. 154, 155
Johnson, Edward 22
Johnston, Joseph E. 124, 130
Jones, Asa 156
Journal of Commerce 150

Kappner, Franz 143
Kearney, Stephen Watts 47, 58, 76, 134

Keene, Mr., citizen 106
Keiffer, John 32
Kellogg, James 58
Kendall, George Wilkes 50, 52
Kendrick, Henry L. 1
Kenrick, Peter R. 117
Kenyon College, Ohio 77
King, Horatio 120
King, J. N. 101
Kingsbury, Julius 33
Koerner, Gustav 142, 150, 157
Koerner, Sophie 157
Krum, John J. 156, 167, 168, 169, 170, 171, 172, 174
Kurtz, D. B. 100

La Grange, Missouri 155
Lake Xochimilico, Mexico 55
Lamb, James L. 140
Largue, Alexander 145
Las Mariposas Ranch, California 134
Lay, George 67
Lee, Elizabeth Blair 137
Lee, R. B. 88, 90
Lee, Robert E. 55
Letcher, Robert 126
Lexington, Missouri 150, 157, 164
Lincoln, Abraham 115, 116, 120, 122, 123, 124, 129, 135, 140, 152, 154, 156, 158, 164, 166, 167, 169, 181, 184
Lindsey, Lieutenant 67
Livingston, Bell & Co. 143
Loomis, Gustavus 110, 111
Los Angeles, California 80, 82, 95
Lovell, Christopher S. 88
Lynch, Bartholomew 30, 32
Lyon, Nathaniel 22, 48, 68, 83, 96, 120, 122, 123, 125, 126, 127, 128, 129, 130, 131, 132, 134, 135, 145, 149, 150, 152, 180, 146, 157

Macomb, Alexander 4, 9, 10, 14
Madison Barracks, New York 27, 28, 43, 48
Magruder, John B. 96, 100, 101
March, William 45
Marcy, Randall B. 186
Maretowsky, Francis 99, 101, 102, 103, 105, 106, 107, 108
Marshall, Bill 97
Marshall, James 77
Maryville, California 87
Matamoras, Mexico 44
McClellan, George B. 47, 136, 158, 164, 166, 184, 186
McDougal, J. D. 102
McDowell, Irvin 22, 135, 137
McKeever, Chauncy 142
McKinstry, Adelaide (Dickinson), wife 193
McKinstry, Alexander, cousin 7, 128

McKinstry, Angelica, daughter 35
McKinstry, Angelina 128, 145
McKinstry, Ann 10
McKinstry, Augustus, cousin 45, 49, 75, 77, 78, 93, 97, 108, 110, 111, 112, 188, 190
McKinstry, Augustus Tremaine, brother 7
McKinstry, Carlisle P., son 35, 111, 113, 190
McKinstry, Charles, grandfather 7
McKinstry, Charles, cousin 7
McKinstry, Charles Frederick, son 27, 35, 41, 44, 113, 148, 190
McKinstry, David Charles, father 7, 8, 9, 10, 11, 14, 72, 111
McKinstry, Elisha, brother 10, 77, 85, 87, 93, 98, 119, 190
McKinstry, George, Jr., cousin 7, 77, 78, 79, 87, 88, 93, 95, 101, 103, 108, 111, 112, 122, 184, 188, 190
McKinstry, George, Sr., uncle 7, 14, 24, 188
McKinstry, James Hamilton, son 35, 41, 113, 190
McKinstry, James Patterson, brother 7, 10, 191
McKinstry, Jane, cousin 7, 41, 45, 75, 77, 79, 108, 110, 113, 184
McKinstry, Jeannie 190
McKinstry, John, uncle 7
McKinstry, John, "Captain John," 6
McKinstry, Justus: arrest at St. Louis 165; brigadier general appointment 155; burial 193; California court of inquiry 102 et seq.; California court-martial 90 et seq.; California grand jury indictment 105; *Daily Missouri Democrat* transcript 177; death 192; Mexican War pension 191, 193; Mexico City court-martial 68 et seq.; Mexico City court of inquiry 63 et seq.; marriage, Adelaide 192; marriage, Susan 24; New York stock broker 187; orders to Florida 29; physical description 2; quartermaster, acting appointment 28; quartermaster, permanent appointment 49; Rolla land agent 187; St. Louis court-martial 174; St. Louis provost marshal 150; *Vindication* 173; West Point academics 23; West Point appointment 12; West Point cadet 13 et seq.; West Point court-martial 1 et seq.; West Point demerits 21,

22; West Point graduation 23; West Point re-appointment 14; West Point resignation 12, 14
McKinstry, Justus, uncle 7, 10, 49, 111
McKinstry, Nancy Backus, mother 7
McKinstry, Oliver 128, 145
McKinstry, Robert, uncle 7
McKinstry, Sarah, sister 7
McKinstry, Susan, daughter 35
McKinstry, Susan, wife, cousin 7, 24, 28, 29, 30, 35, 40, 41, 44, 67, 74, 75, 77, 79, 93, 95, 97, 101, 102, 106, 108, 110, 111, 113, 129, 156, 172, 182, 188, 190, 191
McKinstry Volunteers 56, 57, 59, 62, 67, 83
McMullen, Michael 33
Meigs, Montgomery C. 22, 43, 124, 130, 131, 137, 139, 140, 156, 158, 170, 171, 172, 176
Memphis, El Paso & Pacific Railroad 187, 188
Mendoza, Juan 108
Mexico City, Mexico 48, 49, 55, 58, 63, 65, 66, 71, 72, 73, 75, 86, 91, 93, 102, 120, 127, 167, 183
Michigan Garden 9
Middleburg, Florida 31
Miles, Dixon S. 68
Miller, R. S. 88
Mills, Madison 175
Minter, John 108
Minter, Seraphina 108
Mission San Luis Rey, California 84, 96
Monroe, James 25
Monroe, Michigan 34
Monroe, Thomas 41
Monterey, California 83, 84, 86
Monterrey, Mexico 46, 80, 81, 82
Montgomery, Alabama 123
Mooney, S. P 68
Morales, Juan 49, 50
Morris, Thompson 37, 40, 41, 45, 49
Mott, Jacob Rhett 31
Mullanphy family 116
Müller, Waldemar 108
Mulligan, James 157
Murray, George H. 58

Nantucket Proprietors 6
Napoleon, emperor 157
Napoleon, steamer 118
Negro allies 31, 39
Neil, James 140, 146, 147, 156
Neil, John 150, 156
New Helvetia, California 77, 87
New Orleans, Louisiana 14, 45, 73, 75
New Orleans Picayune 50, 52
New York City, New York 110, 111, 135, 145, 166, 184, 187, 191
New York Daily Tribune 187, 188
New York Evening Post 106
New York News 150
New York Stock Exchange 187
Newport Barracks, Kentucky 45
Nicolaus, California 88, 95
Nicolaus, Dr. 95
Norvell, John 37

O'Brien, Thomas 133
Ocala, Florida 30
Ocean, transport 45
Oceanside, California 109
Ogden, Alfred B. 148
Ord, Edward O. C. 22
Ortega, Jose Joaquin 97, 108, 190
Osborn, William 32
Owens, Hugh 91, 92

Padierna, Mexico 55
Palatka, Florida 40
Palmer, Joseph 142
Palmer, Thomas 9
Palo Alto, Mexico 44
Panama City, Panama 79, 80
Paris, Private, deserter 87
Patten, George W. 23, 27, 35
Patterson, Francis E. 98
Patterson, Robert 127
Pease, Joseph S. 144, 145
pedregal 55, 57
Pemberton, John 22
Pendleton, George H. 186
Penrose, James B. 33
Pensacola, Florida 34, 120
Picolata, Florida 35
Pierce, Franklin 57
Plympton, Joseph 43, 45
Polk, James 44, 48, 80
Pond, Charles H. 148, 149
Pontiac Company 9
Pope, John 149, 155, 162, 164, 174
Port Huron, Michigan 29
Portales, Mexico 56
Porter, Frank 149
Porter, G. 68
Post No. 12, Florida 39
Post No. 16, Florida 33
Post No. 18, Florida 32
Post No. 20, Florida 33
Prentiss, Benjamin 149
Price, Sterling 130, 131, 132, 149, 157, 158, 164, 180,
Prospect Hill, Hudson, New York 28, 77
Puebla, Mexico 53, 61, 63, 66, 77

Quincy, Missouri 163

Raines, James S. 150
Rancho La Punhã, California 96
Reading, California 105
Resaca de la Palma, Mexico 44

Reynolds, John F. 22
Reynolds, Thomas C. 116, 129
Richardson, Israel 22, 68
Richardson, William H. 53, 56, 58, 67, 69, 83, 87, 88, 93
Richmond, Virginia 126
Ridgeley, Samuel C. 1
Riley, Bennett 28, 31, 45, 52, 55
Robert, P. G. 192
Robinson, H. H. 84, 97
Rolla, Missouri 131, 132, 149, 150, 165, 187, 188,
Ross, R. H. 63
Royce, Josiah 137
Russell, F. S. K. 68
Rust, Richard 85
Ryan, Private, deserter 87

Sacketts Harbor, New York 27, 29, 34, 48,
Sacramento, California 77, 87, 95
Sacrificios Island, Mexico 50
St. Augustine, Florida 39
St. Louis, Missouri 75, 112, 113, 115, 116, 117, 118, 122, 123, 125, 128, 129, 133, 134, 135, 143, 146, 150, 152, 155, 156, 158, 160, 162, 164, 165, 166, 167, 168, 169, 170, 171, 172, 177, 179, 181, 182, 183, 184, 186, 188, 190, 191
St. Louis & San Francisco Railway 187
St. Louis Bulletin 131
St. Louis Daily Missouri Democrat 150, 174, 175, 177
St. Louis Evening News 150
St. Louis Republican 131
San Angel, Mexico 55
San Antonio, Mexico 55
San Augustine, Mexico 57
Sandequito, D. W. 101
Sanderson, Florida 33
San Diego, California 76, 79, 80, 83, 84, 86, 88, 90, 92, 95, 96, 97, 98, 99, 101, 103, 105, 106, 109, 112, 120, 183, 189
San Francisco, California 80, 92, 93, 96, 106
San Patricios 59
Santa Anna, Antonio Lopez de 52, 58
Santa Fe, Mexico 47, 76
Santa Ysabel Rancho 97, 98, 99, 101, 102, 103, 105, 107, 108, 182, 190
Sargent, James Hovey 41
Savage, Joseph, W. 171
Scarritt, Jeremiah 2
Schofield, John M. 150, 152
Scott, Winfield 48, 53, 55, 57, 58, 59, 60, 61, 62, 66, 68, 69, 75, 118, 126, 136, 158, 164, 167
Sedgwick, John 22
Selover, A. A. 156

Seminole Indians 31, 32, 33, 36, 39, 40, 110
Sherman, William T. 22, 187
Shields, James 52
Short Grass 39
Sibley, Ebenezer S. 130, 166, 167
Sibley, Henry 22
Sigel, Franz 131, 132, 149, 150, 155, 163, 164, 187
Silver Spring, Florida 30, 31, 32
Simonson, John 174, 175
Slaughter, James E. 84
Smith, Alfred J. 58, 62, 65, 69, 75
Smith, Bensky & Co. 87, 95
Smith, Joseph R. 27, 29, 30, 34, 35, 36
Smith, Persifor 88, 92, 122
Smithers & Wagoner 193
Snead, Thomas L. 130
Soto, Lorenzo 99
Southern Steamship Line 111
Southwester, steamer 118
Spencer, Charles L. 156
Spencer, John C. 43
Sprague, John 36, 40
Springfield, Illinois 116
Springfield, Missouri 131, 132, 134, 149, 155, 162, 164, 187
Stanton, Edwin M. 120, 171
Stearns, Able 96
Steele, William G. 158
Stendon, Captain 165
Stockton, California 96
Stockton, Robert F. 47
Stokes, Edward 97, 108, 190
Stone, Charles P. 100, 102
Stovall, Marcellus S. 1
Strebel, Charles 62
Stringer, Allen & Van Nostrand 144
Sutter, John 77,
Swan, J. C., steamer 128
Swartout, Henry 1, 2, 3

Tacubaya, Mexico 56, 59
Tampa, Florida 32, 110, 111
Tampico, Mexico 48, 49

Tarrytown, New York 187
Taylor, Joseph, P. 174, 175
Taylor, Zachary 32, 33, 38, 44, 47, 58, 110
Terry, Edward C. 113, 114
Texas, annexation 44; secession from Mexico 44
Thatcher, Daniel A. 21
Thayer, Sylvanus 4, 16, 21, 23
Thomas, Charles 126, 127
Thomas, George H. 22
Thomas, Lorenzo 135, 149, 157, 158, 161, 162, 167, 169, 177
Thomas, Philip F. 120
Thompson, Almon 156
Thompson, contractor 149
Thompson, Jacob M. 120
Thornton, Seth B. 44
Throckmorton, J. 114
Tilghman, Lloyd 22
Tilghman, Thomas 100
Tipton, Missouri 158, 160, 162, 164
Toledo, Ohio 190
Tomkins, D. D. 73
Totten, James 142, 167
Totten, Joseph 167
Toucey, Isaac 120
Trist, Nicolas 58, 59
Twiggs, David E. 47, 52

Uncas, transport 45
United States Army 24; brevet rank 58; Civil War 124 et seq.; deserters 34, 44; enlisted men 26; Mexican War 44 et seq.; officer corps 26; quartermaster department 28, 37, 46, 48, 58, 124; Second Seminole War 23, 24, 31 et seq.; Third Seminole War 31, 110 et seq.
United States Military Academy 1, 4, 10, 13, 15 et seq.
Urriguen, Philippe 61, 65, 66

Van Sank, Mary E. 193
Van Wyck, Charles 158, 160, 169

Van Wyck Committee 158, 159, 174
Vera Cruz, Mexico 48, 49, 50, 51, 53, 54, 60, 71, 73, 75, 77, 191
Verdugo, Juan 97
Victoria, Mexico 47
Vinton, David H. 83
Vogdes, Israel 22, 174, 175

Waite, Carlos A. 46, 174, 175
Walker, Henry D. 1
Walker, William 96
Ward, William S. 21
Warner, Juan Jose 96
Warner Ranch, California 97
Warsaw, Missouri 163
Washburne, Elihu, B. 158, 160
Weightman, Richard H. 2, 35, 150
Wescott, George C. 87, 88
Wessels, Henry 88, 102
Wheeler, Alfred 88, 95
Wheeling, Virginia 166, 171, 172
Whiting, Henry 79, 83
Whitzig, John J. 116
Widgery, Mr., clerk 169
Wiles, Peter 176
Williams, Alpheus 190, 191
Williams, Elisha 7
Williams, Seth 118
Williams, Thomas 52
Willson, George 10, 13
Wilson, Henry 186
Wilson's Creek, Missouri 149, 150, 152
Windrum, J. S. 96
Woodruff, Charles W. 37
Wool, John E. 105
Worth, William Jenkins 37, 39, 40, 55, 73

Yates, Richard 125, 128
Young, Charles Bedford 69
Youngstown, New York 40
Ypsilanti, Michigan 75, 93, 110, 111, 188, 190, 191, 193

Zagonyi, Charles 142, 164

www.ingramcontent.com/pod-product-compliance
Lightning Source LLC
Chambersburg PA
CBHW081554300426
44116CB00015B/2883